# TEST MATCH SPECIAL

Edited by Peter Baxter

QUEEN ANNE PRESS
MACDONALD FUTURA PUBLISHERS
LONDON

ACKNOWLEDGEMENTS

Illustrations by Griffin
Photographs by Jonathan Lincoln-Gordon
apart from the following:
BBC Hulton Picture Library: page 15
Bill Frindall: pages 93, 107 and 133
Sport and General Press Agency: pages 13, 23 and 29
Ted Walford: pages 38, 44, 48, 54 and 62

First published in 1981 by Queen Anne Press,
Macdonald Futura Publishers Limited, Paulton House,
8 Shepherdess Walk, London N1 7LW

ISBN 0362 00547 8

Reproduced from copy supplied
Printed and bound in Great Britain
by Billing and Sons Limited and Kemp Hall Bindery
Guildford, London, Oxford, Worcester

# CONTENTS

# THE ORIGINS OF 'TEST MATCH SPECIAL'

## John Arlott

*Test Match Special,* like Test matches themselves, simply happened. No one planned it; it was already itself before it was recognised and titled. Similarly, the games themselves were never envisaged as international contests. Indeed, the first cricket team to visit Australia – a strong all-professional side under H. H. Stephenson – was sent in substitution for a reading tour by Charles Dickens who had to cry off at a late juncture. The promoters – Spiers and Ponds, who were also caterers – had to find some alternative for the growing population of Australia. A series of cricket matches seemed to them a probable attraction and the guarantors at the Australian end accepted it.

So far as the English players were concerned, it was an opportunity to make some money during the winter. The games they played – against local fifteens, eighteens and twenty-twos – were intended simply as exhibition matches to amuse people starved of all but the most primitive entertainment. They became something more when the fourth touring team – of 1876-77, under James Lillywhite – was beaten by the fifteens of, first, New South Wales and, next, Victoria. To the Australians, then, as always, spoiling for a contest with the Englishmen, the obvious sequel seemed to be a match on level terms between an eleven from the two states, and the visiting team.

There was no apparent place for it in the fixture list but the touring side, only too happy to make extra money, agreed to fit it in by dint of going straight from the ship which brought them back from their mid-tour trip to New Zealand to start play at the Melbourne Cricket Ground. Their opponents, flatly called 'A Combined XI', thanks largely to Charles Bannerman, who received the first ball and scored the first century (165 in a total of

245) in the history of what had yet to be known as Test cricket, won by 45 runs. It was not described as a Test match until much later; indeed the term was not used at all before 1865. In their confident delight, they offered the tourists a return fixture 'for the benefit of the English players'. That was squeezed in at the end of the tour, and England won by four wickets.

Like Test cricket, cricket commentary, too, began in Australia. In November 1922, before there was any regular broadcasting in Australia, a certain Lionel Watt, not otherwise an historic figure, was sent to the Sydney Cricket Ground where two elevens of New South Wales cricketers were playing in a testimonial for that same Charles Bannerman who, 45 years before, had scored the first Test century. In the words of A. G. Moyes, the historian of Australian cricket, 'Watt was given a microphone and told to go on talking' – thus he became the first cricket commentator. Commentary was thus established in Australia long before it was employed in England where newsreaders donned evening dress to put out the nine o'clock bulletin.

Much of the technique and programme content of Australian broadcasting derived from American and British sources. In commentary on cricket and horse racing – the two abiding national passions – though, they were pioneers, creating their own methods which are retained in their distinctive style today. It probably is significant that one of their earlier cricket commentators, Charles Moses, went on to become, as Sir Charles Moses, General Manager of the Australian Broadcasting Commission.

The BBC did not, in general, quickly perceive the immense potential of the media it controlled. It put out the more obvious material – music, plays and talks and religious services – and soon, too, discussions and interview programmes. Commentary came appreciably later; and radio's great, unique creation, the radio feature, much later still. The broadcasters of the twenties, however, faced problems not recognised now in the 1980s. It is hard for the modern generation to understand the opposition and hostility to wireless in its early – and, in some cases, not so early – days. The press, for instance, was so fiercely opposed to the medium it foresaw robbing it of its markets that it refused to print BBC programmes. (Hence the Corporation was forced to publish the *Radio Times*, now a highly profitable ancillary operation.) Most other forms of information and entertainment, however, viewed broadcasting with suspicion. The cricketing authorities were certainly among those who believed radio would adversely affect its attendances and revenues. In the event, of course, sound radio proved a valuable shop window for the game; and, if television did reduce its gate-receipts, it put back much of the loss in the fees it paid.

Simply enough, as soon as broadcasting equipment became even remotely portable, 'the wireless' possessed the unique ability to disseminate news, in the moment it occurred, to a mass audience. That is commentary reduced to its simplest terms. Its value, and the extent of public hunger for it, were demonstrated by the coverage of the General Strike in 1926. Even then, commentary – certainly sporting commentary – hardly entered the minds of the broadcasting administrators as a practical undertaking. That occurred in the following year, spurred by three factors: the charter of 1927 gave the BBC the right to send its reporters to important events; Lance Sieveking, probably the outstanding and most creative pioneer of British broadcasting, was given a fairly free hand in programme-making; on an exploratory visit to the United States, he heard some sporting – baseball – commentary, and came home determined to experiment with the idea.

The first commentator Sieveking engaged was Captain H. B. T. (Teddy) Wakelam, a wartime soldier, by then a construction engineer who had played rugby for the Harlequins. Sieveking had never met him but, on the recommendation of a friend who described him as a good talker about rugby, after a single meeting, a brief audition and a rather sketchy practice run, he was taken to Twickenham to broadcast the England-Wales rugby international. The producer's planning included – most perceptively – a formerly sighted blind man from St Dunstan's posted in front of the box as a guinea-pig listener; a 'number two', or 'Doctor Watson' – Charles Lapworth – to prompt with reasonable questions, live; and Sieveking himself beside the box to make suggestions off-mike.

The choice was fortunate. Wakelam was a natural talker with a reasonable vocabulary, a good rugby mind, and a conscious determination to avoid journalese. On this occasion, determined to satisfy his St Dunstan's man, he galloped away until he all but lost breath. He confessed indeed – mark of a natural commentator – that the material went in through the eyes, out through the mouth and that he subsequently recollected virtually nothing of what he had described. That was the first sporting commentary in British radio. Sieveking, whose opinion was decisive, was satisfied. Wakelam not only continued to broadcast rugby but, in the same year, made the first soccer broadcast (an Arsenal match at Highbury) and, soon afterwards, the first on lawn tennis (the Wimbledon Championships of 1927). He continued with tennis commentary until the second world war.

The first cricket commentary, too, took place in 1927: on 14 May – Essex v New Zealanders at Leyton. It was made by Plum – later Sir Pelham – Warner who, in his lifetime as player, manager, selector, reporter, historian, administrator and, eventually, the elder statesman, of the English game, watched, beyond all reasonable argument, more first-class cricket than anyone else who ever lived. Authoritative as he was, his voice was subdued, almost expressionless, and he made little impact. He was followed by the Rev F. H. Gillingham, a powerful batsman for Essex whose caricature in *Vanity Fair* was titled 'Cricketing Christianity'. Normally a good and forthright talker, he had the ill-luck to be announced for his first quarter-hour when rain had prevented even the start of play. He struggled on to fill his time out of nothing, but hardly pleased his masters when, ingeniously, but ingenuously, he proceeded to read out the advertisements on the hoardings round The Oval; such blatant publicity that the BBC shuddered to its corporate spine.

So Teddy Wakelam, who had played the game at good club level for many years, became the third cricket commentator. Lord's did not even admit broadcasting equipment to the ground and Wakelam, with Alan Howland as his number two, covered a Surrey-Middlesex match at The Oval. He was unlucky in that the early Surrey batting – potentially so splendidly entertaining – collapsed, and Andrew Sandham, skilfully, valuably but unexcitingly, shored it up with a long slow innings. Wakelam laboured; as most professional broadcasters would have done in those days.

At this time Lance Sieveking moved on to the drama department and major innovations there. Gerald Cock, an alertly minded barrister, took over from him on outside broadcasts. Wakelam – justifiably recognised as the senior and most capable sporting commentator, but obviously most disappointed by his venture into cricket – convinced the new departmental head that the game was too dull to be good broadcasting material. 'That afternoon put paid to cricket as a real running commentary sport,' he wrote.

Interestingly – even sadly – Wakelam could still write, eleven years afterwards in his autobiography, *Half Time* (1938): 'When, once again, it [cricket] reappeared in the programme, in the capable hands of Howard Marshall, the method of putting it over had considerably changed and the present system of several eye-witness accounts, interspersed with very short, and very occasional, ball-by-ball commentaries, was inaugurated.'

While, no doubt, Wakelam did much for rugby, possibly soccer, and most certainly tennis, in the field of radio commentary, it must be wondered how much he set back cricket broadcasting. It seems certain that Cock accepted his sadly subjective view of it as definitive; and it may well, therefore, have coloured many subsequent planning decisions. Thus Howard Marshall, who had a most pleasing touch in commentary, was, as Wakelam accurately pointed out, given little opportunity for it in programme allocations.

There were some domestic broadcasts on the Australian series of 1930; but they did not amount to even one piece a day until the fifth Test, when there were some few minutes of commentary. Otherwise, only summaries were put out. They were done by M. K. Foster, of that famous cricketing family, and a captain of Worcestershire; Archie MacLaren, the old Lancashire and England captain; and, on the second, third and fifth Tests, Aubrey Faulkner, the former South African all-rounder, then running a highly successful cricket school in London. In the fifth – Oval – Test the BBC employed the identifying assistant, already established for rugby and soccer matches, whose duty was to place the centre of play for the listener in 'square two', 'square four', or wherever, corresponding with a plan published in the *Radio Times*. The method was adopted for the first, and last, time in cricket broadcasting at The Oval. The man responsible was John Snagge, who became an important broadcaster in several fields. The experiment was not a success in the way hoped for, but it did save a situation when Faulkner fell ill and John Snagge was left to soldier through alone.

Although commentary was now an accepted form of broadcasting, the BBC still showed no enthusiasm for cricket. Importantly, too, a school had grown up of outside broadcast engineers who were idealists, enthusiasts, masters of improvisation. Perhaps recent technical advances have rendered them unnecessary. They seem a lost breed; but their expertise and almost blinding efficiency in putting an outside broadcast on the air were memorable.

Cricket commentary was effectively thrust upon the British listening public through the series played by Douglas Jardine's England side of 1932-33 in Australia. In Australia a cricket commentary 'war' was already in progress, assisted by the fact of the vast distances. They had already resolved the issue of broadcasting affecting match attendances. Indeed, one of the first and most difficult problems of the newly formed Australian Broadcasting Commission in 1932 was to reconcile the intense competition between the private companies who competed so savagely for cricket listeners across its great distances. By historic chance, too, this was the most controversial of all Test rubbers – the Body-Line series. In Australia, players were whisked by car from ground to studio to broadcast their views on events available to the British public only later through the newspapers. Throughout Britain the special early editions of the evening papers, carrying reports on the play, constantly sold out to enthusiasts moved to immense interest by the fast bowling tactic employed to defeat the hitherto invulnerable Bradman. Yet, for the first Test, the BBC provided no more than summarised scores in the news bulletins.

By contrast, the French commercial stations broadcasting to Britain were quick to take the opportunity. Radio Paris put out two separate quarter-hour periods of detailed score with critical comment. Poste Parisien was more ambitious. It brought over Alan Fairfax, the New South Wales all-rounder who had been a member of the 1930 Australian team in England, and sat him in a studio in the Eiffel Tower. There he was fed highly detailed cables of virtually every event of play immediately after it took place. His background knowledge enabled him to put flesh on the hard facts, and his use of the present tense, and his strong Australian accent, imparted an air of authenticity. Indeed, it might well be argued that Alan Fairfax did more than anyone else to create a demand for cricket commentary in England. Moreover, his broadcasts, billed as 'At intervals from 6 a.m. Relay of the Test Match from Australia', went on almost unbroken, thus translating a day's play into two hours of highly concentrated 'synthetic' commentary. Certainly the motor firm which sponsored his broadcasts happily paid for the radio time – with advertisements, of course – directed at Britain before breakfast. Certainly, too, anyone with an interest in cricket who had access to a radio set in that winter of 1932-33 will still remember the Fairfax broadcasts as both compelling and novel. This type of composed commentary was employed by the Australians as late as the 1938 tour of England when the companies there feared they could not rely on the live service from England so set up their own cable offices on the ground.

After the first Test, the BBC characteristically exploited its highly developed technical resources, and devotion to authenticity, by using the old 'Empire' short wave service to broadcast direct from the ground a ten-minute eye witness acount by Alan Kippax who, dropped from the Australian team after the first Test of the rubber, watched the remainder as a reporter.

As the series progressed, increasingly dramatically, controversially and, most important in this country, with a series of wins for Jardine's team, a demand was created in Britain for coverage of Test cricket which could not be gainsaid. By happy historic coincidence, too, when the Australians paid their next visit – in 1934 – the BBC had discovered a highly suitable and successful cricket broadcaster. Howard Marshall was an Oxford rugby blue; he had played cricket to 'Authentic' standard and reported it for the now defunct *Westminster Gazette* until it ceased publication in 1927 when he joined the BBC. Beginning as an announcer and newsreader, he covered rugby matches and current events – such as the gathering of the hunger marchers in Hyde Park – and became a radio professional, developing that lack of fear of – and familiarity with – the microphone which is an essential for the successful ad lib broadcaster.

He was eminently suited to cricket: he had a deep, warm, unhurried voice; a respect for the hard news of event, and a friendly feeling towards the men who played the game. Unhappily for him, two factors still militated against wholehearted commitment to cricket commentary in England. The first was the attitude of the cricketing establishment. MCC, for instance, still would not allow a broadcast to take place from within Lord's. Marshall had to watch the Test match from his allotted seat in the press box and then, at each interval, make his way to a nearby point to broadcast. For some time it was the basement of a house in Grove End Road where one day, as he prepared for his tea-time summary, a small child in the flat above began her piano practice. He had barely time to race up and beg her silence before he was due on the air. Even where he was allowed to work from inside a ground, the old prejudice against cricket commentary still persisted.

In 1935, at Old Trafford, Marshall, finding that keeping an accurate score card inhibited his broadcasting, persuaded North Region of the BBC to grant him the services of a scorer. The Lancashire club recruited the ideal man in Arthur Wrigley, a member of the Lancashire ground staff (capable leg-spinner and a superb long distance spotter of the googly) who was training to be an accountant. He remained the BBC scorer for Test matches until his death in 1965.

Much of Howard Marshall's most impressive work was, in effect, reconstituted. He was a reflective broadcaster and therein lay his strength. When, however, he was given the chance of commentary in 1938, and later in wartime matches, he tended, from sheer lack of experience, to be crucial seconds behind the play. So, as he described a bowler coming in to bowl, the microphone caught the sound of the applause for the boundary struck from him. He probably is most richly remembered for his vivid account of Hedley Verity's match at Lord's in 1934 when, with seven for 61 and eight for 43, that Yorkshire slow left-arm bowler gave England their only win in a series dominated by Bradman, and given its decisive twist by the spin of Grimmett

*Top left: Howard Marshall, the man who set the style*
*Top right: Test Match Special's first scorer, the late Arthur Wrigley, in the old commentary box at Lord's*
*Above: 'What do you think, Arthur?' – A.E.R. Gilligan broadcasting from Savoy Hill*

and O'Reilly.

Marshall used to be amused to indicate to later commentators the difference between his period and theirs with an example from the first – Trent Bridge – Test of 1934. The decisive factor was the rolled leg spin and fiery googly of Bill O'Reilly, making his first visit to England and relatively unknown here. Marshall characteristically parodied the old song with:

*'As for the O'Reilly,*
*You value so highly,*
*Gorblimey, O'Reilly,*
*You are bowling well'*

He estimated the BBC received some three hundred letters of protest at his use of the 'oath' – Gorblimey.

In 1938 Wakelam made another historic debut with the first televised cricket commentary – when Lord's at last opened its gates to the cameras – on the second Test between England and Australia.

Up to the outbreak of the second world war, Marshall often worked in double harness with Michael Standing, a staff member of the BBC, a good club cricketer with an alert mind and a good turn of phrase. They were at times reinforced by E. W. (Jim) Swanton of *The Daily Telegraph* who had broadcast the 1938-39 English tour in South Africa, where in his first Test he had the commentator's gift of a hat trick – by Tom Goddard of Gloucestershire on the old Wanderers ground at Johannesburg.

By the time post-war cricket began, Marshall had gone into industry; and Standing had taken a senior executive post in the Corporation.

Once more cricket broadcasting was given a fillip by historic circumstances. For a vast number of English people the resumption of the first-class game was a nostalgic – indeed, euphoric – symbol of the post-war return to normality. That feeling was emphasised by England's Test win over India in 1946; even more by the golden 1947 summer of Compton and Edrich, with the defeat of South Africa; and finally – and finally probably is the right word – by the visit of Bradman's Australians in 1948.

The new post-war head of Outside Broadcasts was S. J. de Lotbinière (Lobby) who contributed more to the development of commentary than any other holder of that office. He had an analytical mind; and his insistence on the 'pyramid' – the shaping of information from the peak outwards and downwards to fit the time available – remains the ideal structure for commentary or summary. Although – or, perhaps, indeed, because – he had little personal interest in cricket (or any other sport), he was a most perceptive critic of style or content, able to put his finger precisely on flaws, faults or wrong tendencies. Without hurry, and never too far ahead of public or – by no means always identical – official BBC opinion, he shrewdly extended commentary, especially in the field of cricket. His first task was to build a commentary team to replace Marshall and Standing.

In the 1946 Indian series the domestic audience was given little more than

*Broadcasting county cricket in 1949 – John Arlott scans a telegram message*

two hours a day of commentary and summary, all on the Light Programme; plus a close of play score in news bulletins. The main team consisted of Rex Alston and E. W. Swanton, with Arthur Gilligan, the amiable former captain of Sussex and England, and the erudite, idiosyncratic and admirably fluent C. B. Fry helping out, largely with comments. Rex Alston, Cambridge running blue, cricketer for Bedfordshire and sometime schoolmaster who had joined the BBC in 1942 as a newsreader and announcer, had become an Outside Broadcasts assistant with responsibility for cricket, rugby and athletics. Jim Swanton carried on from pre-war days; he subsequently switched to television commentary and then – probably most effectively – to admirably authoritative summaries on both sound and vision. For Indian listeners, J. Arlott, a literary programmes producer in the Eastern Service, broadcast short commentary-cum-summary periods in English; Abdul Hamid Sheikh, a newsreader in the same department, in Hindi.

For the 1947 South African tour series, Messrs Alston and Swanton were joined again by C. B. Fry and Arthur Gilligan. Gilligan already had some years' experience as an opinions man on Australian radio, where 'What do you think, Arthur?' – which invariably heralded the mildest of comments – became a national gag. I was doing commentary to South Africa and, increasingly, on the domestic air, travelling with the touring side, as did Dana Niehaus, a senior sports reporter for an Afrikaans newspaper who gave summaries in that language.

The series against Bradman's 1948 Australians was a resounding success in every way except in terms of match results, for England. Even that fact could not blunt the immense public hunger for cricket reflected in huge crowds, not only at the Tests but at the tourists' fixtures with the counties, and in the radio listening figures. It was estimated that the number of sound-radio listeners for the last day of the fourth – Headingley – Test, when England half promised to win, was as high as seven million. It is doubtful if cricket commentary has ever attracted a larger audience. Sound radio had that story to itself for, although television of cricket had begun in 1938, its coverage was confined to the two London Tests until 1950 (Nottingham) and 1952 (Manchester and Leeds).

The sound-radio team was Rex Alston, E. W. Swanton, Alan McGilvray – the Australian commentator who had succeeded Don Bradman as pre-war captain of New South Wales – and myself; with comments and opinions from Arthur Gilligan, C. B. Fry, Herbert Sutcliffe and George Duckworth. It is worth noting that, even as late as this, the Australian Broadcasting Commission sent a senior representative to maintain a running service of cables in case reception of the short-wave broadcast was unsatisfactory, when they could provide synthetic commentary of the 1932 Fairfax type. That did not prove necessary. BBC's short-wave transmission proved satisfactory.

Apart from E. W. Swanton's move to television, the sound commentators changed little and only slowly. Now, however, wherever practicable, the

BBC chose to broadcast the voice of the visiting teams. So, on the Australian tours when Alan McGilvray was not a member of the team, Bernard Kerr, Michael Charlton and Bob Richardson joined the team. Ken Ablack – a Trinidadian who played for Northamptonshire – the amiable Roy Lawrence and, subsequently, Tony Cozier joined in for West Indian visits; Charles Fortune for South Africa; Pearson Surita and occasionally the Maharajah Kumar of Vizianagram for India; Alan Richards for New Zealand; and Omar Kureishi for Pakistan.

The immense enthusiasm led to a substantial growth in cricket broadcasting, especially of the basic county game, so essential for understanding and full appreciation of play at Test level. Confirmed by the substantial attendances at county matches, the Regions – London, West, Midlands and North – began to opt out of basic Home Service programmes to cover 'their' Championship cricket. For instance, except when a Test match was in progress, West Region would cover all matches between the teams in its area – Gloucestershire, Somerset, Hampshire and Sussex – and their fixtures with the touring side. Broadcasting periods were 12 to 12.20, 3 to 3.30, 6 to 6.35; plus a few summaries. Some five hours a match afforded a sound training and experience for the commentators fortunate enough to be working at that time. By then several others had put their names on their chairbacks. They included Peter Cranmer – rugby international and captain of Warwickshire – Alan Gibson, Robert Hudson, and Peter West.

That pattern continued until about 1969 when it became one of the casualties of 'Broadcasting in the Seventies'. Meanwhile, though, Test coverage had grown steadily from the two hours of 1946; though there proved to be a number of obstacles such as fixed programmes – especially the news bulletins – to daylong commentary. The term 'Test Match Special' was already in use before that complete coverage was first achieved (in 1957) by dint of switching between Light, Home and Third programmes.

Brian Johnston came to the sound commentary box after many years with television; and, in 1963, he became the first cricket correspondent ever appointed by the BBC. His successor was Christopher Martin-Jenkins, also, of course, a member of the commentary team. Robert Hudson, regarded as a lucky commentator because of the many exciting matches that fell to him, is a Londoner who made his way in commentary in North Region. He became an authoritative, reliable and imperturbable member of *Test Match Special* before he moved on to become head of Outside Broadcasts. Other Test commentators were the highly literate, amusing and diverting Alan Gibson, Yorkshire born, brought up in London, in his time president of the Oxford Union; and Neil Durden-Smith, who made his first appearance in Test commentary in 1969 and took part in a number of sports programmes. Don Mosey, Yorkshire by birth and persuasion, came by way of sports reporting and a staff post in North Region to cricket commentary and, in 1974, to the Test 'box'. Henry Blofeld, an opening batsman for Eton, Cambridge University and Norfolk, is one of the new generation; a fluent talker, immense enthusiast and amusing raconteur. Tony Lewis, who captained

Cambridge University, Glamorgan and England, a relative newcomer, is experienced in sound and television with a wide range of interests and a turn of unhackneyed phrase.

The number of comments men, as opposed to ball-by-ball commentators, has been extremely large. Many have been experienced Test cricketers or captains. They include, as well as Arthur Gilligan and C. B. Fry, Norman Yardley, Freddie Brown, Colin Cowdrey, Ted Dexter, W. B. Franklin, Bill Bowes, Alf Gover, and the present incumbents Trevor Bailey and Fred Trueman; from Australia, Bobby Simpson, Richie Benaud (before he became a television commentator), Bertie Oldfield and Jack Fingleton; the New Zealanders Bill Merritt and Roger Blunt; Sir Learie Constantine and Gerry Gomez with the West Indians.

The scorers are less heard, but their part is nonetheless important. After the death of Howard Marshall's invaluable aide, Arthur Wrigley, in 1965, Bill Frindall succeeded him. He has even elaborated the highly informative method evolved by Wrigley, Roy Webber (who also scored for television) and Jack Price (who handled Test matches in the Midlands). All three died within three years. He followed Messrs Wrigley and Webber, too, in compiling authoritative statistical records of the game.

From the rejection of cricket as programme material in 1927; and as subject for sustained commentary until 1938, the progress of *Test Match Special* is an unexpected story of prosperity. It has come to be accepted primarily, one hopes, for the instant service it provides of events in the match in progress. It has, though, appealed to many listeners relatively unconcerned with the course of play. Immense interest obviously has been generated by the casual chat which goes on when rain stops play and is often – in this writer's humble opinion, unpardonably – quite unconnected with cricket and irrelevant to the situation. It is an unusual formula for radio: a medley of views and ideas expressed by, often, as many as six voices – though the number and its members vary constantly as one leaves and another comes in – with no planned theme or direction, but spun at random as one idea prompts another. It is true that those taking part are all professional talkers but even that does not fully account for the apparent listener appeal of the output. It probably is an amalgam of several factors. It is, of course, extremely English, which is not a chauvinistic comment. It seems to have a considerable nostalgic impact on expatriate English people, especially in Australia – before they are conditioned to the methods there – and New Zealand. The relatively slow turnover of broadcasters means that they know one another well, can prod reactions with reasonable certainty. There is, too, especially since Peter Baxter took over as producer, an extremely friendly atmosphere in the box. To have observed only four instances of sharpness in the space of thirty-five years argues a considerable communal good humour. There has, too, always been so much leg-pulling that pomposity is impossible. One of the hardy-annual practical jokes – invariably perpetrated by Brian Johnston – is to hail a commentator coming into the box when it is off the air by saying into the microphone, 'Ah, here is so-and-so, and I know he will have strong views about this. Tell me, so-and-so, what do you feel about such and such?' Simultaneously he moves out of his seat and waves the newcomer into it. The joke lasts as long as the other occupants of the box can refrain from bursting into laughter. The joke is possible only because of the essential difference between sound radio and television commentary points. Television commentators work on lip-mikes which only gather sound when held close to the mouth. There they have, too, a 'lazy' mike through which they can talk to the producer without the listeners hearing. Sound radio, though, employs sensitive 'open' microphones which pick up virtually anything said within six or eight feet. For that reason anyone who does not know whether the mike is alive or not is in a quandary: he cannot ask the relevant question. More than one man – including the writer, more than once – has been caught out through assuming that Johnston is pulling his leg when actually the microphone is live. Then the result is staggeringly embarrassing. A television point can hum with unguarded conversation, but the sound-radio box is desperately sensitive to extraneous noises like the arrival of a waiter or messenger blithely calling for Mr So-and-so; Fred Trueman's stentorian stage whispers; Brian Johnston's and Bill Frindall's asides; Freddie Brown's snores; and, above all, the semi-stifled laughter at some horrible 'in' – and inexplicable – joke.

In 1980, Trevor Bailey and the writer were largely responsible for a fresh cricket commentary noise: the popping of champagne corks. The result was refreshing but, on the whole, uncharacteristic. The senior men and BBC representatives, Rex Alston, Robert Hudson, Brian Johnston and Christopher Martin-Jenkins, have all been temperate men; not teetotallers but, as a rule, disinclined to take wine – or any other alcoholic drink – during the course of the working day. Their attitude set the general tune. Latterly, though, Brian Johnston has been coaxed round by way of Pouilly Fumé to occasional hock and, now, fizz. The others have required little persuasion. This, probably, is the right moment to raise a valedictory glass in good wishes to that unique institution, *Test Match Special.*

# THE CAST FOR 1980

## Peter Baxter

The game of cricket has thrown up a great deal of literature, verse, and even music; perhaps most important, it has thrown up conversation. A Test match, after all, takes a week and gives plenty of time for those who take part in it, or just look on, to chew over its progress and the side issues that inevitably arise from it.

The *Test Match Special* commentators have been described as a bunch of friends going to a match and talking about it. That may be an oversimplification, but it does raise the question, Why has the programme been so successful? The answer lies partly in the fascination of the great game itself and the opportunities it affords for discussion; but also in the very different extrovert characters who make up the commentary team. Their individual differences are their collective strength. Producing such a crowd of individuals can leave one performing the duties of nursemaid, waiter, secretary, agent, chauffeur and cleaner. But above all the programme is fun and, maybe paradoxically, each member of the team is a thorough professional.

## BALL-BY-BALL COMMENTATORS

### JOHN ARLOTT

Just after twenty past two on 2 September 1980 a remarkable event occurred. Alan Curtis announced on the Lord's public address system that the end of the previous over had seen the last of John Arlott's career as a Test match commentator. The Centenary Test crowd applauded warmly and, perhaps more significantly, the players on the field looked up at the commentary box and applauded, too. It was surely a unique tribute to a member of the media.

1980 was obviously going to be John Arlott's year. He announced before the start of the season that this would be his last after thirty-four years 'in the box'. His voice, with that distinctive mellow Hampshire rumble, means cricket to listeners all over the world. Whenever schoolboys – or, it must be confessed, other commentators – imitate cricket commentary, it is the Arlott accent they strive for, with phrases like 'this of a cloudy Trent Bridge morning.' We all have our favourite bits of Arlott imagery. I always recall the Centenary Test in Melbourne and 'the seagulls like vultures for Lillee'. The Lord's Centenary Test brought Lillee into the Arlott gaze again: 'His shirt big enough for two men, if they could get into the trousers.'

John will not, I am sure, miss the climb up the pavilion stairs at Lord's. One of the essential jobs of the producer was always to have a cup of black coffee ready to aid his recovery after this feat. Then, when the enormous handkerchief had done its best for a perspiring face, came the negotiations: first for the number of doors and windows to be opened ('It's so close' – this of a distinctly chilly morning); and then over the commentators' rota. The first version of this to be pinned up in the box has only ever been regarded by John as a discussion document and by the end of a Test match it is covered by inked-in alterations.

John is a man of passion and very deep feelings. His impish sense of humour may sometimes surprise those who do not know him, but confirmation of it can be found in the merry (and often downright wicked) twinkle in his eye.

If Howard Marshall set the standard of the technique of cricket commentary, John Arlott raised it to an art form. When he was introduced to the crowd to present the man of the match award at the end of the Centenary Test and they gave him an ovation as if he had just made an undefeated double century, we all in the commentary box felt a glow of pride for a dear friend.

## BRIAN JOHNSTON

If John Arlott has an impish sense of humour, Brian Johnston's is at times nearer the music-hall. E. W. Swanton, in exasperation, has described it as 'fourth form' and any of us who have been the victim of one of his practical jokes would agree. He is the life and soul of *Test Match Special*, both because of the tremendous enjoyment he gets out of it and because of the great amount he cares about it.

Until the end of the 1972 season, Brian was the BBC's staff cricket correspondent, which, among other things, meant that the corridors of Broadcasting House reverberated to the trumpeting sound which announces his presence. His time in that job (as correspondent rather than trumpeter) is another important part of the progress of cricket broadcasting. Not only did he contribute to news bulletins on cricketing matters, but he fought hard to cover overseas tours so that we all now take for granted the early morning reports on winter mornings from distant parts.

To bend an old saying, if one were to pick a commentator to 'play for your life' it would be Brian. Breaking all the rules of commentary, he charms the airwaves with his genial personality. The prospect of a rain-affected day without him in the commentary box is a producer's nightmare.

He used to live a cricket ball's throw from Lord's, but now, reflecting perhaps his new interest, the distance is more like a sweetly struck tee-shot. ('Trouble is, when I do it it always goes over extra cover, old man!') The nicknames in the box are all his own work. Many of them need explanation, like the secretary called IMP because she used to say 'it's my pleasure'; but if you're lucky it's just Backers or Jenkers. Thus in any dressing-room around the country cricketers will greet him as Johnners. The cricketers hold Brian in real affection. During the final Test of 1976 the television commentators spent some time speculating about why Alan Knott was, for the first time, keeping wicket standing up to Bob Woolmer. In fact Brian had written an article for Knott's benefit brochure and in payment asked only that he would stand up to Woolmer for one over in a Test match. Brian was commentating when the moment came and, at the end of the over, both players looked up cheerfully at the commentary box from where they received a wave of thanks – international sportsmen in an important match making a remarkable gesture for a friend.

*Brian Johnston in his early days with the BBC, and the schoolboy who wrote to him and became his successor as cricket correspondent, Christopher Martin-Jenkins*

## CHRISTOPHER MARTIN-JENKINS

There was once a schoolboy who wrote to Brian Johnston and said that he wanted to be a cricket commentator. Not only did he succeed in that, but he became Brian's successor as BBC cricket correspondent and today Christopher Martin-Jenkins's name is associated by many with waking up on cold winter mornings to hear the news of England's progress from 'down under'. Although overseas cricket tours have given Christopher the classic conflict of interest between home and job, it is these tours that have given him the justified reputation of the master of the short report – everything you want to know crammed into the small space allowed by a busy programme without apparent hurry. This reputation has sometimes unfairly eclipsed his competence as a commentator – the role he loves best. He is also the possessor of a rare talent for mimicry and has certainly fooled me on occasions on the other end of a line.

As much as possible during the summer, Christopher preserves his Sundays to play club cricket at which he is no mean performer, having played for Surrey second eleven and, as a schoolboy, made 99 at Lord's for Marlborough against Rugby. Before joining the BBC he was, for a time, assistant editor of *The Cricketer*. After the 1980 cricket season had drawn to its close he relinquished his staff post at the BBC to return to *The Cricketer* as editor, but he will continue as an active member of the *Test Match Special* commentary team.

## DON MOSEY

Many people ask Don Mosey how he earned the Johnstonian nickname 'the Alderman'. He still looks puzzled, referring all enquiries to Brian who simply chuckles. I think it is just that B.J. saw Don one day looking aldermanic, probably in his time as the BBC North Region's senior Radio Outside Broadcasts producer, taking charge of the production side of a Test match at either Old Trafford or Headingley. Now the gamekeeper has turned poacher and Don can indulge his relish for words in descriptive commentaries. He has seemed in recent seasons to be the unlucky commentator with regard to the amount of action, or rather lack of it, in his commentary stint: if a ball goes out of shape; if a batsman needs a new glove; if there is a drinks interval, it all seems to happen when Don is at the microphone. And if a side cannot score a run for twenty minutes, they will always have waited for Don to take over before becoming becalmed.

The Alderman's fierce Yorkshire pride and meticulous delivery belie the twinkle in his eye and the fact that he is always the first to corpse at any of B.J.'s *faux pas*. He has been the victim of so many practical jokes from that direction that he regards any card that I hand him with the suspicion of a bomb disposal man. (There he may have a case: once we gave him the news that an unpronounceable – and entirely mythical – Pole had won a race in the Moscow Olympics.)

Don's arrival in the commentary box is always announced by an outbreak of 'the word game' between himself and Brian and very soon every available piece of paper has squares and letters all over it. I have found even quite important documents endorsed with these scrawlings. (The game consists of making a chart of five squares by five, then each nominating a letter of the alphabet alternately and forming words horizontally and vertically – 10 points for a five-letter word, 5 for four letters and 1 for three letters.)

Don covered the England tour to Pakistan and New Zealand in 1977-78 which started his love affair with the latter and left me still waiting for calls to be connected to the former. He is an anxious scanner of the golf scores to see how his son, Ian, is progressing and, although he does not say much about it, I know he is intensely proud of Ian's success.

*The vital telephone link at Lord's – 'Alderman' Don Mosey (left) gives orders to his office in Manchester and Henry Blofeld (right) makes his social arrangements for the evening*

## HENRY BLOFELD

Only three players have ever scored a hundred for the Public Schools against the Combined Services: Peter May, Colin Cowdrey and – Henry Blofeld. Sadly, Henry's promising career as a cricketer was cut short by a bad road accident at Eton; but first-class cricket's loss was our gain and his commentary style (described by Gillian Reynolds of *The Daily Telegraph* as 'frenetic') provides another of the delightfully individual elements of *TMS*. 1980 provided him with two great moments to describe live. First an exciting finish in the Benson and Hedges Cup final, and then, a couple of weeks later, a tie in the Gillette Cup quarter-final at Chelmsford. He rose to both occasions splendidly.

Henry is another who has covered overseas tours for the BBC with distinction and he is very proud to have cracked the Martin-Jenkins formula for one-minute reports. Stories about Blowers abound and are enjoyed in press and commentary boxes throughout the world; it says much for the man himself that not only does he enjoy them but he can usually cap them. Enjoyment is his great asset. Our programme is based on the enjoyment our commentators have in it and few manifest that as much as Henry.

Blowers' rather highly strung way of delivering his favourite stories compels people to demand them if they can find one member of the company who has not heard them before. When he does them 'off his long run', as he puts it, it's time to light your pipe and settle back – but it is always a masterpiece. Here is one of my favourites – and it's a true story!

It was in 1973. The West Indians were playing a Young England Eleven at Old Trafford and I went to Manchester to cover the last two days of the match, the Monday and Tuesday. My car was in hospital at the time and so I travelled by train, arriving on the Sunday evening. I stayed the next two nights at a high-rise instant hotel in the middle of Manchester before setting off on the Tuesday evening for Nottingham where I was going to watch Gloucestershire at Trent Bridge for the following three days.

I caught a train from Manchester to Sheffield where we arrived sometime after nine o'clock and I then found that I had missed the last connection on to Nottingham. There was nothing for it, therefore, but to stay in Sheffield and a taxi decanted me at the Hallam Towers, another modern hotel. All went extremely well and the next morning I caught a train to Nottingham where I arrived in plenty of time for the half-past eleven start.

On the way to the ground I stopped at the Bridgeford Hotel, a massive structure bordering the River Trent on one side and the cricket ground on the other. I booked a room for that night, the Wednesday, but they were full up for the following night. I asked the receptionist if she could find me a bed elsewhere in Nottingham for the Thursday night and departed for the cricket. When I returned that evening I found that I had been booked in at the Albany Hotel in the middle of Nottingham.

The next evening I did my work, had a drink with a few of the players, and then took a taxi to the Albany, an hotel which conformed precisely with the pattern of those I had stayed in for the last four nights. It rose high into the sky, glistened, and by rights should have smelt of fresh paint. I had a room on the ninth floor which had an interesting view of downtown Nottingham. After having a bath and changing I took my book downstairs to the bar and in due course to the restaurant. I had an excellent dinner, and a splendid bottle of wine, after which I staggered back to the bar to finish my book and to make sure that there was a sufficient level of alcohol in my bloodstream. At about midnight I finished the book and went up to bed.

It was now that the problems began. All my life, at least since I had left my preparatory school where pyjamas were compulsory, I have slept naked. I was soon comfortably in bed and asleep. Just before three o'clock I woke to the call of nature and slipped out of bed to answer same. At once I was confronted by the crux of the matter, although of course I did not realise it as such at the time. For the last four nights, as it happened, my bathroom door had been in the same position. Thick with sleep, I now blithely assumed the same would apply. It was not until I was standing stark naked on the ninth-floor corridor, after there had been the ominous click of the door shutting behind me, that I realised anything was wrong: naturally I did not have a key with me.

At first it was all a bit of a shock. I wandered aimlessly up and down the passage looking for an emergency exit, or something like that. There probably was one but I couldn't find it and the situation was fast becoming critical as the need for an immediate loo intensified. Then, suddenly, I spotted a tea tray outside one of the rooms. As I bent down I saw a small paper napkin folded in quarters underneath the cup. I unfolded it and hung it in front of me in the appropriate area – as fig leaves go, at three o'clock in the morning in the Albany Hotel, Nottingham, I thought it was eminently reasonable.

My plan of campaign was to summon the lift and go down to see the night porter. I didn't imagine that anyone would be around at that time of night and I hoped the porter had a philosophical nature. Well, the lift came, the doors opened and in I got. There were, I think, fourteen bedroom floors followed by an R for restaurant, a B for bar and another R for reception. With great circumspection I pressed the bottom R, the doors slowly shut, and we went down the first nine floors like a two-year-old in peak form. Then, to my horror and dismay, the thing stopped at the first R. As I cowered in the back with my paper napkin as my only travelling companion, the doors shook slightly and slowly opened to reveal six women in long dresses and six men in dinner jackets waiting to get in. It was an interesting moment. Instinctively, as the doors opened, they surged forwards. Then of course they saw me, stopped, and looked from one to the other and back at me in some disgust. For once in my life I was pretty tongue-tied. This state of suspended animation seemed to last for a long time and soon other people were coming up and having a peep. Eventually a chap in a dinner jacket came to the door of the lift.

'You seem to have a problem,' he suggested.

'How quick of you to spot it,' I replied. 'I'm looking for the night porter.'

It transpired that the night porter was also among those present and soon he had joined me in the lift. I explained in my rather flushed condition exactly what had happened. (The next day one of my friends told me I should have held the napkin up in front of my face, for then it would not have been quite so easy to recognise me in the morning.) He pressed the button marked 9, but because I had originally pushed the bottom R we went down and stopped first at B and finally at R. By then I had become a sort of late-night cabaret and people were running from one floor to the other to catch a glimpse.

Eventually we started for home and the noble night porter unlocked my door with his pass key and I fell gratefully into the bathroom. The next morning, when I fully realised what had happened, I wondered if I should apply for membership of Equity.

## TONY LEWIS

Tony Lewis's career in cricket is distinguished enough. He captained England on the India and Pakistan tour of 1972-73 and might well have done so again but for injury. Indeed his captaincy on that tour helped to make tours of the Indian sub-continent more popular with England teams. He was a double blue (cricket and rugby) at Cambridge and went on to captain Glamorgan to the County Championship title. Now he has made a name for himself in broadcasting with programmes like *Sport on Four* on the radio, and frequent appearances on television. His approach to the business of radio commentary has been of great interest to me and I have enjoyed the shared experience of making a commentator out of a man who has all the obvious ingredients for the job. It is he who makes this a shared experience, for he has great interest in the techniques of commentary and is always eager to discuss some facet of the job which may have just occurred to him. As the most recent member of our team to have played first-class cricket he can shed an interesting light, too, on the conduct of the game by players, many of whom he has played with himself.

Tony first joined our team as an expert summariser, but was soon persuaded to try his hand at the ball-by-ball description, having bridged the gap to some extent with television experience. (The latter is an entirely different business as I sometimes have to remind him!) It was while he was waiting to do his considered summary of the day's play that he earned his 'Johnstonnym'. B.J. looked at the commentary rota, saw the initials A.R.L. and said, 'and when I've read the scorecard it will be over to Arl'. And that's who he is for ever more!

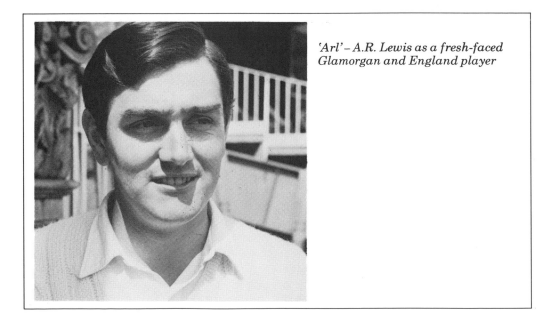

*'Arl' – A.R. Lewis as a fresh-faced Glamorgan and England player*

## SUMMARISERS

### TREVOR BAILEY

Trevor Bailey was the all-rounder who was the vital pivot of the England side of the fifties. He is no less valuable to us in the commentary box in the eighties. Blessed with a great tactical sense for the game, he is never one to flinch from sticking his neck out about the likely outcome, sometimes even enjoying being proved wrong. His definitive way of summing up an incident – 'Good ball, bad shot, nice catch' – has earned him the Dickensian nickname 'Mr Jingle'. More often, though, he is known as 'the Boil'. This nickname arose from an incident in his university days when he was playing football on the continent alongside another distinguished Essex cricketer, Doug Insole: the pair was announced to the crowd as 'Eynsole' and 'Boyley'.

Trevor gives a tremendous amount of thought to the programme. I always meet him for lunch before the season and he is usually bubbling with ideas. The first *Test Match Special* phone-in idea came from him – 'Cricket Clinic'. (This was never a popular title among those who tried to say it into a microphone; Don Mosey tried to rechristen it 'Cricket Surgery'!)

He takes ribbing about his own cricketing reputation as a stalwart defender in very good part. He enjoys the joke of living in a road called 'the Drive', complaining that he could not find a 'Forward Defensive Avenue'. Fred Trueman's main recollection of sharing the England dressing-room with Trevor is that by the end of five days there were bits of his clothing everywhere. Clothing is not normally our problem in the box, but the style is unmistakable, with notes, letters, tobacco, books etc scattered liberally.

### FRED TRUEMAN

Fred Trueman is what is known in the business as 'a natural'. He plonks himself at the microphone with a tree trunk of a pipe in his fist and his lower jaw set in a manner that makes me glad I never had to face him coming down the hill at Headingley. Good and bad cricket are seen very much as black or white by Fred. He sums up things that would not have happened in his day frequently with, 'I do not know what is going off out there!'

With 307 Test wickets behind him, the great man took his place in the commentary box as to the manner born, although I am sure he thought we were all mad. Now he knows it! Brian Johnston nicknames him 'Sir Frederick'. When sending out copies of his latest book, he inscribed it as such in the front of Fred's copy. The publishers duly addressed the envelope in the same style and Fred was surprised to find a deferential postman coming up the garden path with the package and profuse congratulations. In recounting the incident to me on the telephone, Fred ended, 'He's a right one that Johnston!'

Fred's commentary career actually began on that famous day in 1964

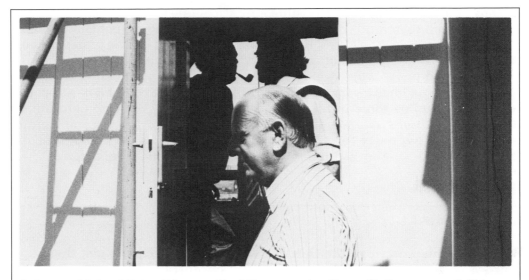

*Silhouetted behind Brian Johnston, Fred Trueman gives Trevor Bailey some useful hints on how to keep his pipe alight*

when Neil Hawke snicked a catch to Colin Cowdrey to become his three-hundredth Test victim. Later Fred was welcomed in the commentary box at The Oval and invited to try his hand at the job. I think that he worried a few of the residents then, but I wonder if they realised that he would become a permanent fixture.

## OVERSEAS GUESTS

Our overseas visitors have become very much part of the team over the years and probably no two more so than our visitors in 1980, Alan McGilvray and Tony Cozier, neither of whom are spared the practical jokes.

Alan started commentating before the second world war, which must make him comfortably the senior commentator in the business. He moved to the microphone after a distinguished Sheffield Shield career for New South Wales. His rather confidential style of delivery, talking man to man to the listener, has earned him as many fans in Britain as I am sure he has at home in Australia. Certainly the warm reception he received at Melbourne early in 1980, when the Australian Broadcasting Commission celebrated his 200th Test commentary, showed a great affection.

He is justifiably nervous of Brian Johnston since being fed a large slice of cake in the Lord's box in 1977 and then being asked a question. His digestive system has barely recovered!

Tony Cozier has a similar nervous problem brought on when B.J., during a lengthy rain stoppage, pretended to be on the air when Tony returned to the box and threw him an impossible statistical question on the averages of the West Indian team. Tony is now a very much more suspicious man.

Tony is not only a first rate commentator but a very dependable broadcaster, a journalist of high repute, and a popular man in radio, television and press boxes everywhere. He is also in great demand for club cricket teams as he is a very useful performer, although a Sunday afternoon behind the stumps sometimes yields us a very stiff-backed commentator on Monday morning! His understanding of the English cricket scene is quite remarkable. He is never thrown when I put county scores in front of him and can usually add his own comments about the players involved.

## THE SCORER

### BILL FRINDALL

Bill Frindall is known as 'the Bearded Wonder' because he is just that: very bearded and very definitely a wonder. His concentration is quite extraordinary and, like the best performers at any art, he seems to have so much time to spare. I know that when I have tried scoring for a commentator cups of coffee go cold at my elbow because I simply cannot find the time to consume them; but Bill can pour himself a cup in the back of the box without ever taking an eagle eye off the game.

The value of a scorer in the radio box was first realised because of the need to have bowling figures to hand and up-to-date. Since then the information has flowed and since 1966 Bill has trod the footsteps of Arthur Wrigley and Jack Price, delving in the record books (many of them his own work) and, most importantly, knowing what to look for.

## THE PRODUCERS

### DICK MADDOCK/PETER BAXTER

Dick Maddock and I discuss *Test Match Special* on a different plane from the others. To us it is often a series of narrowly averted crises, both in the studio and in the commentary box, most of them completely beyond the consciousness of the commentators. Problems of timing, for instance, are less important to them than whether the coffee has appeared.

Dick started his BBC career as an announcer in Bristol and in that role moved to Birmingham where he eventually became the Radio Outside Broadcasts producer. This put Test matches at Edgbaston and Trent Bridge under his control. For the Test matches in which I am the producer at the ground he has always come to London to present the programme from the depths of the Broadcasting House basement. Not the easy sinecure it may seem – especially if it is raining. He is a warm, charming man, always reluctant to say a bad word about anyone and very much part of the team. Sadly 1981 will mean farewell to him as he is retiring from the B.B.C.

# THE STATELY GROUNDS OF ENGLAND

## Don Mosey

The stately grounds of England begin, needless to say, in London NW8, where things have changed a little since Thomas Lord bequeathed his personal broad acres to the game of cricket. Mr Lord can scarcely be described as the archetypal Yorkshireman. It is not in our nature to give things away, least of all a prime building plot in an area where the ground-rent alone would make the Cornhill Insurance sponsorship look like David Steele's annual donation to charity. Yet even the philanthropic Thomas would, without any doubt, be mildly startled to return and find what has happened to his cabbage-patch in the last two hundred years.

To begin with, he would not even be allowed in since celestial garb does not – if one takes the evidence of the classical Italian School – involve wearing jacket, collar and tie. Henry Blofeld, who has no valid claim to be nearer to heaven than any of us, claims to have gained access to the pavilion at Lord's wearing a cravat in lieu of tie, but I have yet to find anyone who believes him. No, life is hard for the commentator at Headquarters. Merely to arrive there presents problems to the provincial hobbledehoy. Taxi fares are prohibitive and bus routes incomprehensible so one optimistically boards an Underground train to St John's Wood station, only to find oneself on the wrong side of the ground. Gatemen, who are the same the world over, shake their heads doubtfully when offered a pass at the Nursery end which is issued to admit the bearer to the pavilion . . . an Olympian destination unknown to those who stand guard over the portals of the North Entrances. Their role, as was that of their forefathers, is to withstand incursions by the Picts, Scots and Brigantes.

*The Victorian splendour of our perch at Headquarters – the commentary box at Lord's*

A circumnavigation of Lord's, therefore, means that after a three-mile route march (taking in the weeding of Brian Johnston's flower-beds en route) one arrives at the Sanctum (hereinafter referred to as the pavilion) in a state of high anxiety and a low state of personal hygiene. There follows the daunting procedure of being scrutinised by the stewards. Any tie other than that of an MCC member is observed with barely disguised disapproval. A Bradford League tie, one senses, would be regarded with open contempt if its identity was established. Nor is an Austin Reed tailored jacket accepted as entirely *de rigueur*. One is grudgingly admitted, and may be forgiven for thinking that fifty or a hundred pounds might have been saved by patronising Messrs Burton, Hepworth or Marks and Spencers. The effect would have been the same.

The commentators' view at Lord's is over fine leg (or fine mid-off) but its elevation counters any disadvantages involved in not being in line with the bowler. While one is not in the ideal position to comment on lbw decisions (and it is not our job to comment favourably or otherwise upon umpiring decisions in any case), it is easier to see, for instance, whether or not a slip catch has carried. All Tests at Lord's are, to some extent, historic because of the very fact that it *is* Lord's. While it is undoubtedly true that all players have the built-in ambition to play in a Test there, it is no less true that all cricket broadcasters want to commentate from that left-hand turret of the pavilion, despite – perhaps because of – the protocol and pageantry.

The Oval, to the astonishment of almost all my colleagues, is one of my favourite grounds. It has a more homely, more relaxed atmosphere altogether than Lord's. The Northern Line drops one virtually at the door and the stewards and gatemen seem glad to see one. Our commentary box gives us a down-the-wicket view from a good elevation, although on that massive ground it is possible to confuse even the massive Joel Garner with his team-mates when he is fielding in the far-flung outposts of third man or long leg at the Vauxhall end. But looking over the stands and roofs to the skyline of Westminster and St Paul's one is more acutely conscious, than at Lord's, of being in London. It was here, in 1976, that we were privileged to watch that superb exhibition of fast bowling, on a wicket so slow that it immobilised every other bowler, by Michael Holding; a magnificent double century by Vivian Richards; and a very brave, fighting double 'ton' by Dennis Amiss. Here, too, we saw that dazzling first-wicket partnership in the West Indies' second innings by Roy Fredericks and Gordon Greenidge – 182 in just 32 overs, with the field spread wider than the closing overs of a John Player League match. At the end, jubilant West Indian supporters invaded every corner of the ground, including the umpires' room. Dickie Bird, emerging from a shower as naked as a new-born babe, found his colleague (the irrepressible Bill Alley) lounging back in a chair and signing autographs on five-pound and ten-pound notes for a gathering of unscheduled Caribbean/Brixton visitors which included a fair number of nubile maidens.

Dickie, who starts each day of his life in a greater state of anxiety than the previous one, and now agonisingly conscious of his nudity, made a futile attempt to cover the family jewels with his hands and croaked, 'Gimme that towel, Alley, for God's sake.' William did not even bother to glance up from his labours. 'Don't be a four-letter word, Dickie,' he replied sadistically. 'You don't think these dollies are going to be impressed by anything *you've* got, do you?'

Edgbaston is something of an anachronism in the city of Birmingham, an oasis of green in one of the unloveliest cities in Britain. The ground is superbly appointed and rarely, if ever, filled. Warwickshire CCC's finances have been so shrewdly handled for so long that every last inch of space, down to the last brick, has been put to some practical use. One always imagines the county treasurer restlessly roaming the ground, bank statement in hand, wondering where he can fit in another restaurant, another bar, another indoor shed, another ballroom.

Our view, again, is down the wicket. It is not from such an elevated level as The Oval and one feels intimately involved with the play. Warwickshire's hospitable chairman, Cyril Goodway, appears in front of our window each morning around noon and, with mystical signs which only Bill Frindall can understand, inquires what each of us would like to drink. Watching for the first time the semaphore-order being placed, and seeing the drinks arriving, one is initiated into one of the more esoteric rituals of the *Test Match Special* summer.

It was at Edgbaston that we achieved the impossible by causing Brian Johnston to 'dry up' for the first and only time in a long and distinguished broadcasting career. The year was 1975 . . . World Cup and Australian tour year, and there was rain during the England first innings. We were indulging in one of those rain-stops-play chats, which seem to be enjoyed so by the listeners (bless 'em, because we enjoy them, too), with Brian Johnston, Trevor Bailey and myself at the microphones. We discussed the ability of the two Chappell brothers involved in that Test and I mentioned that a younger brother, Trevor, had achieved the rare distinction of a 'double' (1,000 runs and 100 wickets) in a Central Lancashire League season the previous summer.

Brian queried whether the young Chappell had played first-class cricket and seemed to think that he had had an outing with South Australia. 'I know who can tell us,' he said. 'Magillers.' And he swung round in his seat to find Alan McGilvray fast asleep in his chair. The expression on Brian's face was quite marvellous as he struggled to decide between revealing the truth of the situation or dealing with it in a politely fictitious manner. His hesitation was no more than momentary (because Johnners is *the* great professional broadcaster) but it was enough to start me shaking with suppressed laughter. We were not, in those days, quite so relaxed and informal as we are today. The talk-ins had only recently started and commentary-box disciplines were pretty rigid so that uninhibited laughter was not entirely acceptable. I found myself, therefore, like a schoolboy on one of those long, hot summer afternoons just before the holidays start when attention wanders and something amusing occurs. You know that if you laugh you are going to be in trouble but you cannot prevent yourself *from* laughing. My stifled chuckling communicated itself to Trevor and his shoulders were beginning to heave when B.J. made his decision. 'Oh,' he said airily. 'I'm afraid McGillers has just stepped out of the box. We shall have to ask him later.' And as he started to talk on another subject, McGilvray – his subconscious somehow penetrated by a mention of his name – awoke and asked, 'What's that? Somebody want me?' It was too much. I stuffed my handkerchief into my mouth, staggered out of the box and leaned against the wall of the passage linking our box with Television's, hooting with hysterical laughter. Trevor was trapped by the seating arrangements and so had to remain in his seat, positively heaving while Brian (by now caught up in the general atmosphere of hilarity) covered his microphone with one hand and struggled desperately to control himself. The silence must have seemed like a lifetime to listeners at home; it was 'logged' at 27 seconds and our engineers all the way down the line were frantically checking for faults on the circuit. B.J. had been unable to speak for the first and only time in his life.

Someone was going to suffer and Bailey, *in situ,* was the only available candidate. B.J. lured him on to disaster like a great angler playing a specimen fish. Steering the conversation back to the Chappells, Brian recalled that Mrs Chappell had spent hours practising cricket with her boys on the lawn of their home and asked Trevor, 'D'you know any bowling mums in this country?' 'Can't think of any,' replied Trevor, the crisp turn of phrase now restored. 'What about Penny Cowdrey?' continued B.J. 'Didn't you hear about her performance against her son's school at Broadstairs last week?' 'No,' answered Trevor innocently. And we waited for the specimen to be landed.

'Really,' murmured Brian. 'I'm surprised you didn't hear about it. I'm told her swingers were absolutely unplayable.' And he ducked out of his seat to the back of the box leaving the Boil alone to his fate. I mean what do you say after that? Johnston, the master of the *double-entendre,* had struck with telling effect. Trevor waffled nobly on quite irrelevant matters for a minute or two, with no one really in a state to come to his rescue, and then, to his intense relief, the umpires emerged and play was resumed. Glancing up at the commentators' batting order, Trevor told listeners, not without a certain malicious satisfaction in his voice, that commentary for the next twenty minutes would be by Don Mosey. This came as a nasty shock because by this time I was really fit only to be placed in a straight-jacket and ferried out of the ground. Somehow I managed to tread water as the field arranged itself and it was Jeff Thomson to bowl from the pavilion end. 'This burly, broad-shouldered man runs away from us, tawny hair flopping . . .' And then I made the fatal mistake of taking my eye off the ball as Fred Trueman pushed a piece of paper in front of me. Looking down, I read: 'Would Penny's swingers have got bounce on a feather-bed?' That was one ball of the first Test of 1975 which was never described to the listeners. I hope they will pardon the omission, and Mrs Cowdrey will forgive our well intentioned indelicacies. Since then B.J. has regularly described me in print as 'the worst giggler in the box'. I plead Guilty.

The other Midlands Test ground, at Trent Bridge, Nottingham, is in many ways the most pleasant of all grounds. It is well-appointed, efficiently run and has a grace and elegance and charm which is peculiarly its own. It also has a frighteningly hospitable Notts committee-room in dangerously close proximity to the commentary box!

Our view of play is very similar to that at Edgbaston – down the wicket from the pavilion and at a pleasantly elevated level. Since I once worked in Nottingham, as a newspaperman, I was able to watch historic performances like the Worrell-Weekes stand of 1950, and Alec Bedser's magnificent

*The pavilion at Trent Bridge with the open windows of its well situated commentary box*

bowling in 1953 against the Australians when I first met a handsome young all-rounder on his first tour – Richie Benaud. It was on that tour, too, that two great Australian players came over to write the Tests for English newspapers – Sir Donald Bradman and Sidney Barnes. The Australian skipper, Lindsay Hassett, had been a corporal in the Royal Australian Air Force during the war and *Daily Express* readers spent an amused and amusing summer reading Barnes, who promoted or demoted Hassett from his corporal's rank according to his estimation of his daily captaincy. A magnificent new scoreboard had been presented to Notts by the proprietor of one of the local newspapers (my rivals, as a matter of fact) and one of their reporters was instructed to get the views of the Don on the quite magnificent board, by far the most advanced in the country. 'Young man,' replied Bradman, 'my contract with the *Daily Mail* is so tight that I can't even tell you the time of day.'

At Old Trafford, as at Lord's, we look at the game from fine leg/fine mid-off and from a fairly low elevation. As the pavilion is at cover/mid-wicket we are remote from players and officials and recording interviews at the end of a day's play presents all kinds of problems. Generations of players have voted Old Trafford their favourite ground and insisted that the beautifully lush turf is less hard on the feet during a long day – even the hottest day – in the field. Equally, generations of commentators have denounced their operating quarters as the worst on the circuit . . . cramped, depressing and, on the hottest day, bordering on the insanitary. Our engineers are unable to work from the President's Pavilion (which houses our commentary position) and they have to use a large caravan parked as close to the pavilion as one of the game's great characters will allow. This is the little man in the too-long white coat who supervises the parking on the practice-ground with all the drama of Sir Donald Wolfit playing King Lear. He is one of the least favourite people of our producer, Peter Baxter. And Old Trafford is, I am bound to say, one of my least favourite grounds – perhaps because, being based in Manchester, I spend more time there than any of my *TMS* colleagues. It is not unknown for one to arrive for the first county match of a new season to find the remains of last season's sandwiches mouldering on a table; or to find a window broken, or a clock removed from the wall. Perhaps Old Trafford is a victim of its own environment which places it disturbingly close to the home of Manchester United. Where else, in that period when the cricket and football seasons overlap, would you find a cricket ground with its gates locked in late afternoon with the ground one-third full? The more liberalised drinking regulations of county cricket have a certain appeal for soccer fans which, alas, our game itself cannot induce.

At Headingley we sit in corroding splendour under the roof of the rugby league-cum-cricket stand and, enclosed as we are, one of the few pleasures there is to see the flakes of rust dropping onto Board of Control members and guests when a ball is hit on to the roof of the stand. Yorkshiremen firmly – no implicitly – believe they have a God-given right to go anywhere they like. Thus, if you are listening to commentary from Headingley you are entirely likely to hear a door flung open and a ripe West Riding voice demanding, 'Give us yer autograph, Fred.' That is characteristic old-world courtesy amongst my countrymen. The charge up the back of the rugby stand to return to duty after lunch has proved the downfall of many a less-than-fit commentator or summariser, notably Trevor Bailey who once carried out an early-afternoon stint in such a state of breathlessness that his lady wife rang up from Westcliff-on-Sea to ask, with concern, if Trevor was ill. Emerging from the box, if it is possible to wade through the massed ranks of the Fred Trueman fan club (which usually it isn't), one looks across the splendidly kept domain of Leeds Rugby League Football Club to the commentary box on the other side, the shrine of Eddie Waring, High Priest of the thirteen-a-side code.

During the 1975 World Cup it seemed that half the population of Bradford, ten miles away, had turned out to support Pakistan and one of the more orthodox followers of the Prophet spread his prayer-mat on the rugby turf to offer his evening prayer to Mecca. A slight directional maladjust-ment caused him to address himself to the rugby commentary box, *en route* to Saudi Arabia, and a cricket spectator, enjoying a leisurely pint on the seats of the rugby stand, observed the devotions with a certain detached interest. After lengthy consideration, he put down his pint and bellowed: 'Nay, lad. Tha needn't bow dahn and worship yet. Waring weeant bi back till August.'

Yorkshire gatemen, and especially the local cohort of the Corps of Commissionaires, are a race apart. I have often felt that rugby league 'gates'

are relatively small because those who man the entrances appear to feel a sacred duty to keep people *out* of the grounds. The story is told at Headingley of a winger called Terry Hollindrake who was (to Leeds eyes, at least) an unlikely selection for an international match to be played there. He presented himself at the players' entrance and identified himself, only to be told by an incredulous watchdog, 'Thar's not an international and tha's not getting in wi a tale like that.' The unfortunate Mr Hollindrake was made to pass through a turnstile and *pay* to get in before donning his first international jersey.

Reputations count for nothing at the gates of Headingley. The great Fred Trueman, presenting himself as a member of the Yorkshire committee in attendance at a Roses match, and rightly demanding a place in the VIP car park, has been asked, 'Has tha summat ter do wi Yorkshire, then?' But the finest hour of these lineal descendants of (a) the Praetorian Guard and (b) Leonidas's Spartans came during a Test match in the early seventies, before F.S. had joined the commentary team. He was scheduled to take part 'live' in a lunchtime feature on great Test occasions at Headingley. I had taken advantage of being in the area of the best fish and chips in the world (that is, a radius of ten miles from Bradford Town Hall) and had walked up to Charlie Brett's renowned establishment in North Lane. (This was later to be immortalised when John Arlott devoted the whole of his wine column in *The Guardian* to a description of a plate of Charlie's haddock, mushy peas and chips as the ideal partner to a White Bordeaux.) As I returned to the ground, a car drew up alongside and a familiar voice announced, 'Sorry I'm a bit late, sunshine. Got behind a bloody farm cart coming through Addingham.' I climbed into the car and, to my horror, heard on Fred's radio that the lunchtime feature had reached a tape by Bill Bowes which ran for two-and-a-half minutes. 'God Almighty, Fred,' I gasped. 'You're on in less than two minutes.' 'We'll be all reight, me old flower,' was the reassuring comment.

We weren't 'all reight'. On the contrary, a smooth passage into the ground and a lightning sprint up the rugby stand might just conceivably have seen a totally breathless F.S.T. in residence at the appointed hour. But the Paladins on the gate were in no mood to let the mere taker of 307 Test wickets into the committee car-park. It mattered not that Fred had bowled fast and furious on that ground for twenty colourful years. The fact that Fred was undoubtedly the most easily recognised figure on any cricket ground anywhere in the world left the Guardians of St Michael's Lane entirely unmoved. *They* didn't know him. As the Bowes tape ended and the admirable B.J. started to fill in pending the arrival of our guest, I had a flash of inspiration. 'Tell him you've brought the pies, Fred,' I muttered. Throwing personal pride to the winds, tossing his world-renown out of the window, F.S. growled at the gateman, 'Look, I've got to get in. I've brought t'bloody pies.' The transformation was immediate and complete. 'Why didn't yer say so?' demanded the commissionaire, flinging wide the gates.

They get their priorities right in Yorkshire.

# CURTAIN UP
## — Richard Maddock —

*Scene 1.* A hot, sultry June morning near the banks of the River Trent. A solitary figure, head wreathed in tobacco-smoke, contemplates the immaculately mown green sward before him. He stands in a room about twelve feet long by eight feet wide, its purpose purely functional. It is furnished only with eight straight-backed chairs, a three-bar electric fire of pre-war vintage, and a small table on which is a colour television set. The walls are bare, but for a coat of clean cream emulsion, a few metal coat-hooks attached to the back wall, and a type-written rota drawing-pinned to one of the side walls alongside a small hatch through to the room next door. On the floor is a plain cord carpet. The room is dominated by a row of hinged windows that extend its whole length, and can slide on metal runners top and bottom to leave a wide-open expanse through which the eye is drawn, as by a magnet, to the view beyond. They surmount a fixed baize-covered desk of the same length and about two feet deep, under which is a shallower shelf containing several reference books. On the desk are three microphones, four pairs of black plastic headphones attached by grey leads to a metal junction box, a couple of ash-trays and a switch connected to the red light outside, which, like those in less salubrious districts, reminds the unwary passer-by that within there are men at work.

The room may not be beautiful, it is certainly not ornate, yet, of its kind, it is generally acknowledged to be the finest in England, if not in the whole cricket-playing world. The eyes of the viewer are approximately twenty feet above ground level, in the centre of the pavilion block of Nottinghamshire's historic County Ground, and can be immediately behind any one of the principal wickets on the famous Trent Bridge square. They command a superb and totally uninterrupted view of the entire playing area, as well as of the modern and very comprehensive scoreboard at the far right-hand end of the ground.

Noises off. Heavy footsteps descend a flight of wooden stairs and approach along a linoed corridor to the accompaniment of a very passable imitation of a hunting horn. Enter, backstage, a tall sprightly man, who it is almost impossible to believe is an old-age pensioner. He looks remarkably fit, and seems hardly to have changed in the last twenty years or more. There is the usual warm smile beneath the familiar balding head and the even more famous aquiline nose. 'Morning, Madders,' he says. 'Morning, Johnners.'

It's just after 10 a.m. on 5 June, still an hour and a quarter before the curtain goes up on the first act of the 1980 summer series of *Test Match Special*, and Brian Johnston, the old pro, while at heart arguably the youngest member of the cast, is, as usual, one of the very first to make his appearance. We exchange a few pleasantries, and as we talk he gazes out of the open windows and studies the unusual sight of the entire West Indies side, in a variety of bright-coloured track suits, lying flat on their stomachs just beyond the pavilion rails, engaged in a series of exercises. As one man they move into a sitting position, their arms hugging their knees. Their physio stands behind big Joel Garner, jabs his finger-ends into the line of muscle between neck and shoulders and starts kneading. Johnners mutters to himself, but audibly, 'I didn't know you cared.' He's in training, too.

Brian is the comic of the cast; the one whose *joie de vivre* spills over to us all. His are the background chuckles and asides that punctuate the commentary even during those periods when he's supposed to be resting. And the listeners love him for it. The large proportion of all the mail that arrives that is addressed to him, and the even greater share of the cakes, sweets and other goodies, are a measure of the affection in which he's held.

I introduce him to another retired ex-member of staff, who has come into the box to say hail and farewell to John Arlott. Not surprisingly they already know each other. There are not many people who've ever met or worked with Brian in the Corporation whom he doesn't know, from top management to the lowest grades – and by their Christian names! I leave them rattling on in reminiscence and go along the corridor to a similar but slightly smaller room at the foot of the wooden staircase. It was once the television commentators' box; now it serves as the radio engineers' control point, and occasionally, in very cold or wet weather, it doubles up as the 'news position'.

There are four engineers in all, servicing two quite separate operations. One pair is responsible for the balancing and recording of the ball-by-ball material, while the other two provide the technical back-up for the regular requirements of the news editors on Radio 4 (live contributions into the one and six o'clock bulletins and most probably the *P.M.* programme, and recordings for the late evening news and *Today* programme the following morning), and also for the hourly Radio 2 sports desks, often including interviews with a player or administrator, if not, as Don Mosey often

*Johnners, always first to arrive in the box*

maintains, all and sundry including the groundsman's dog. Christopher Martin-Jenkins is doing this job at Trent Bridge, and Ian Davis, of our World Service sports unit, is performing a similar function, though neither so frequent nor so extended, for listeners overseas. They send their despatches from a small table at the top of the staircase, out in the open air.

Glyn Elledge, the senior engineer, and I go through the schedule for Day 1 for the umpteenth time to ensure that all the technical facilities that could possibly be required are readily available and that each engineer is fully aware of his own contribution to the day's output. We are fast approaching the moment of truth after a series of planning discussions that have extended over several weeks. Glyn confirms that he has spoken to the control room in Broadcasting House in London, and that the Post Office lines have been tested and found faultless. That's a relief! First mornings of first Test matches, like first nights of plays, have their nerve-racking moments, and the knowledge that the umbilical chord down which we feed our audience for the next six hours or so is in good order is remarkably comforting.

I return to the box to find that our scorer and his 1980 model female assistant have just returned from the car park with the second instalment of books from the Frindall Travelling Library. He also has his cushion under his arm, for, unlike the rest of us, by the nature of his job he is rooted to the spot for as long as there is any cricket in progress. So, in the knowledge that chairs in commentary boxes can be extremely hard, and often lumpy to boot, he comes suitably prepared. And, to the continuing astonishment of everyone, he comes equally prepared for virtually any question on the statistics of cricket and those who've ever played it at top level. He is a most meticulous man, and his impeccably inscribed score sheets are the mirrors of his nature. A bearded wonder indeed.

Trevor Bailey greets us cheerfully as he arrives to share the duties of summariser for the next five days. Were it not for a little excess baggage around the midriff he's changed little since his days as Essex captain and England all-rounder. Today he looks particularly dapper in a beautifully laundered khaki safari-suit, with a matching cravat on which is emblazoned the Essex County Cricket Club insignia. Elegant it may be, but it contravenes the one and only rule relating to the wearing of the Test Match Broadcasters' tie. This emblem was devised by the then television scorer and statistician, Roy Webber, in conjunction with radio's cricket producer in London, Michael Hastings, and its recipients are obliged to wear it on the first day of every England Test match, either at home or abroad, on pain of buying drinks all round.

'Hallo,' says a warm Northern voice behind me, and a large right arm, the scourge of batsmen the world over not so long ago, wraps itself round my shoulders. 'Hallo, Fred. How are you?' 'I'm all right, sunshine. And 'ow's my favourite producer?' This is neither a statement of concern nor of fact, but rather a thinly-veiled hint that throughout the next few days he will expect me to keep him liberally supplied with cups of tea and coffee, the odd nail file, boxes of matches and other domestic requisites. I point out to Fred the absence of the tie around Trevor's neck and remind him of the penalty. 'Aye,' says he, 'and with that lot on he looks as if he could bloody afford it and all.' He moves across the room to Trevor and they chat contentedly together. It is immediately apparent that they have the utmost regard and respect for each other.

Enter Tony Cozier, looking remarkably well for one who a few days before was in his sick-bed listening to the broadcast in which he should have been taking part, but for a bout of laryngitis. Fortunately he has now recovered, though the voice is still a little croaky. Like Fred and Chris he has not long since returned from commentating duties on the winter Test matches in Australia, and the antipodean tan, augmented by more recent Caribbean sunshine, is still much in evidence. I've not seen him since the Prudential Cup matches last year, and always find him a most engaging companion, but time for gossip is running out and anyway, at this moment, the undisputed star of the 1980 series makes his entrance.

No trumpets usher him in, but a puffing and blowing and a final gasp as, one hand clutching the door-post, the other delving in a trouser pocket for the familiar spotted handkerchief that will mop up the moisture leaking fast from his forehead, he recovers from the walk from the car park and up two flights of steep stairs. Shirt collar open, tie pulled down, jacket over his arm and braces over his shoulders, he stands there acknowledging the greetings of his colleagues. Gradually the old generous smile lights up his face; he fights off the early morning frog in his throat and manages to muster a husky 'hallo'. He wanders over to the rota on the wall, and I wait nervously for the 'No, no, no, no' which usually follows this perusal. It seems that however carefully it is concocted there's almost invariably some commentary period that conflicts with other arrangements in his busy day. This time, though, he seems satisfied and, resting his weight on a chair-back, he launches forth into the latest, quite unrepeatable, but always beautifully constructed, vulgar story. He studies the reactions of his hearers, and then, beaming from ear to ear, wheezes in time to their laughter. It's all part of the tradition of the beginning of a new Test match series. And it'll never be the same again.

I notice for the first time that Don Mosey is now with us. This is remarkable only in that he is normally among the earliest of the arrivals and leaves one in no doubt of his presence. The Alderman does not normally hide his light under a bushel, but today he is a very subdued version of his usual self. He has overslept this morning, still suffering from jet-lag after returning from a rugby tour in Florida of all places. American tours, it seems, resemble those in the more popular parts of the rugby playing world, at least in the profusion of late nights and the overindulgence, particularly of alcohol. Add to this a fair amount of excitement in connection with the race riots in Florida at the time, for which he became the BBC's temporary foreign correspondent, and it's hardly surprising that he's feeling a bit below par. But he'll revive. With this cast the producer need have no fear that any of them will fail to maintain that standard of excellence that has made *Test Match Special* so successful.

I just wish they were as tidy as they are professional. By now the desk is already littered with score cards, hot off the press; note pads with the name of the sponsors printed on every page, just as a reminder; newspapers; binoculars; cigarette packets; tobacco tins, matches and a few unopened envelopes, the first of an avalanche that will be delivered to the box in the next few days. All the bric-à-brac of busy men, who spend most of the summer months living out of suitcases.

The clock on the other side of the ground says 11 a.m. – fifteen minutes to go. I always make a point of requesting, on the afternoon before the match, that this clock should be set as near to BBC time as possible, and whatever is asked for one minute at Trent Bridge is provided the next, in this case via a walkie-talkie set in the general office to that amiable member of the Nottinghamshire staff in charge of such matters, Harry Dalling. I put on a pair of headphones and call up Peter Baxter, who should by now be in the little continuity studio in Broadcasting House which is his home throughout the Test matches played north of London, and mine for those at Lord's or The Oval. 'Pity about the rain up here,' I say. 'Hope you've got plenty of music ready.' He laughs. It's an empty joke, but we make it every year to each other. He knows exactly what the weather's like as he has a large television monitor at his side which has been showing pictures of Trent Bridge for the last ten minutes or so. And I know he knows, but it eases the tension. He sends greetings to the team, but most of them are still down-stairs enjoying a last cup of coffee before we go on the air – a mere foretaste of the incredible hospitality that has been a feature of the Nottinghamshire chairman and his committee for all the years I've known them, and which will be extended to us all over the next few days.

Bill is already at the right-hand end of the desk setting up his 'office'. He sits next to the hatch through which he can speak to and compare notes with the official scorers. He checks with Peter about the arrangements for the next match at which he's scoring, immediately after this one. Suddenly the room seems choc-a-bloc. They've all returned, and in addition a couple of the engineers have come in to check the television set that has gone on the blink. As he goes out again, one of them says, 'Can we have some level, please, Dick?' I extricate Trevor from an ardent discussion with his former England team-mate Godfrey Evans, who has just arrived in his usual chirpy fashion with the latest betting on the match, looking like something out of *Pickwick Papers* with his white mutton-chop whiskers and ample figure. I get Trevor seated at the left-hand microphone. Now, where's Johnners? Oh, blast he's out in the corridor signing a bat for Peter West. 'Arlo', go on the mike in the middle, will you, please?' He does. For easier identification by the engineers, the microphones each have a different coloured windshield – like little sponge-rubber egg cosies, to prevent the popping noise caused by 'p's and 'b's in speech – and I hear myself inadvertently echoing Reginald Perrin as I say, 'Right, it's Trevor on red, John on green and B.J.'ll come on yellow in a moment. Give us a few words, Trevor, will you? . . .' Peter speaks to each of them up the line, against the continuous bubble of background chatter. A few moments later he's starting his opening announcement. 'Coming up, everyone. Quiet please.' I switch on the red light and there is silence . . . 'Yes, thank you Backers, and welcome to you all on a lovely day here at Trent Bridge. . . .'

Once we are on the air, those not actually commentating live in semi-silence for the six hours before we're off again. Communication is by notes, whispers (though not too loud) or signs. The effect until one becomes used to it, as with a child in church, is to make the mildly humorous situation seem highly comical, and the knowledge that one cannot laugh aloud converts that to the slightly hysterical and the inevitable fit of giggles, which has caused more than one member of the team in the past to have to leave the box in order to regain his composure. There were one or two quite hilarious moments up at Nottingham, I remember.

On the first day, Don, like Trevor, had wisely decided in view of the weather to turn up in suitable summer wear. He had chosen a particularly smart pair of cream coloured slacks, and sartorially appeared far better

*On the air. Dick Maddock watches over Johnston, Trueman and Mosey*

than I knew him to be feeling physically. He had just lost the fourth word-game on the trot to Johnners, which had only added to his dejection, so, as the sponsors had kindly provided some bottles of chilled rosé, I thought that perhaps a glass might cheer the Alderman before his first commentary stint. He was sitting down at the time, I remember, and as I passed it to him our fingers became momentarily intertwined. The glass tilted and a pink stain appeared on those spotless trousers, spreading alarmingly through the material. He was not amused; but fortunately the rule of silence saved the listening millions from hearing the word that flashed, in capital letters, from his eyes.

On the Saturday, while the atmosphere was still steamy before the storm arrived to cool it, I was acting as punka-wallah for John – swinging the door from hand to hand to raise a little draught – when Trevor elected to open a bottle of bubbly in preparation for the lunch interval. Admittedly he did go out into the corridor and tried his best to open it as silently as possible, masking the neck of the bottle between his hands. Unfortunately, though, the explosion happened at the moment that the door was in the wide-open position, and also just as M.J.K. Smith, all unsuspecting, was returning along the corridor to the television box. Had he not retained the quick reactions that characterised his close fielding as Warwickshire and England captain, that cork could well have smashed his glasses. As it happened all it did was to cause the telephone to ring in the control point. It was Peter from the studio. 'What the hell's going on up there?' he asked. 'Do watch those corks. We've already had one listener suggesting that the team spend all their time drinking, as it is.'

The storm itself I shall never forget. I have seldom heard thunder like it; the makers of Hammer films would have been proud to have added it to their library of sound effects. It began, as such storms so often do, with several very large drops of rain penetrating the open windows and depositing themselves on the desk behind. Bill glanced up from his work and bestowed on these that look of horror he normally reserves only for those who suggest he might possibly have missed a no-ball, and immediately the listener was suddenly aware that something was amiss. A rumble, though not of thunder, and a series of creaks and squeaks assailed the microphones as he pulled his portion of the sliding windows across in front of him to protect his precious papers from unsightly smudges. Then the lightning, frightening in its intensity, and almost spontaneously the first clap of thunder and the downpour. The covers were on in no time to keep the wicket dry, while the ever-willing Nottinghamshire ground staff got soaked to the skin.

I imagined Peter thinking in terms of music, and wondered whether one of our regular pieces, 'The Thunder and Lightning Polka', was among the tapes he had with him. But the necessity never arose. I'd suggested to Tony Cozier earlier that, in the event of rain, he might persuade the West Indies manager to come to the box and have a chat, and right on cue in walked the tall, solid figure of Clyde Walcott. For over half an hour, accompanied initially by the rumble and crack of the elements, he reminisced, in those glorious deep Caribbean tones of his, about the great West Indian Test sides of his own period as a player, to the fascination of those present who had spent many hours describing the deeds of the three 'W's on the air. Before he was through the rain had stopped; the covers were off and the umpires had made their inspection. As they returned to the pavilion, Brian thrust his head and shoulders out of the window, cupped his hands to his mouth and yelled, 'Nymph'. The sound was lost in the general hubbub, so he shouted again even louder: 'NYMPH!' Umpire Constant, and about 300 startled spectators in front of the pavilion, peered up at us. David Constant opened one hand twice, and we knew that play would start again in ten minutes time.

So the five days passed. Brian had received a letter on the first day from a Mr Pearcey of Scunthorpe which read as follows: 'No English summer could be complete without a Test series, and no Test series could be complete without listeners to Radio 3 being able to eavesdrop on the semi-private party in the radio commentary box.' It is this very atmosphere we hope to create, and it is because of it that most of us have been doing the job for so long. But for me, the party itself and Trent Bridge can never be complete without that most admirable and stimulating companion, host and colleague, John Arlott. May he find in Alderney just a little of the kindness and the friendship that he has shown to me over more than a quarter of a century working together, and he will be a fortunate man. Bless you, John.

And now for a description of the *cricket* in the first Test match let's go over to Christopher Martin-Jenkins.

TRENT BRIDGE

# THE CORRESPONDENT'S VIEW
## —— Christopher Martin-Jenkins ——

In the English winter of 1979-80 there were twenty-five Test matches and almost as many one-day internationals. Such unprecedented and excessive activity at international level dulled the keenness even of the cricket fanatic. Yet by the time that the England and West Indies teams had assembled in Nottingham on Derby Day, 4 June, staleness had gone and one felt again the tingle of anticipation which comes before the start of any Test series.

Hopes bloom like roses each June for the cricket-followers. Few of us do not foresee an exciting series, honourably fought in glorious weather. The fact that we are often disillusioned does not quell the perennial optimism: like addicted gamblers we see a winner in every race. This time the hard-headed knew that the West Indies, captained by the somnolent Clive Lloyd, inspired by the genius of Viv Richards, powered by any four of the quintet of fast bowlers, and unified by their recent success and large financial rewards, ought to prove too strong for any combination which England could muster. But England's selectors had gambled with the youthful brilliance of Ian Botham, making him, at 24, the youngest to be officially appointed as England captain since 1882-83 when the Hon Ivo Bligh returned to England with the original Ashes. (Monty Bowden was younger still when he led England in a Test in Cape Town in 1888-89 as deputy for C. Aubrey Smith.) Botham had already rewarded the selectors by leading England to a notable victory in the second of the two Prudential internationals which preceded the Cornhill Test series itself. (Commentators these days have to be careful to identify not only the players but the correct insurance company.) Moreover, Botham had helped to choose a team for the Trent Bridge Test

which looked about as strong as possible, and the best batting side which England had produced since the return to Test cricket of the prodigal Boycott in 1977.

I travelled to Trent Bridge in my ancient Renault 4 the day before the game began. My wife had claimed the bigger car to take the children to Norfolk for the weekend. I have a special affection for Trent Bridge because on the fifth morning of the first Test against New Zealand in 1973 our first son James was born. I had driven down the motorway on the fourth evening of a memorable match (New Zealand so nearly reached an 'impossible' fourth-innings target) and with typical kindness Brian Johnston announced the birth on Radio 3 next morning.

Later that very happy year I did my first full Test match commentaries for the BBC and the only slight sadness I felt now, as I rattled up the motorway with Tony Cozier as my passenger, was that in this Test match I would not be one of the commentary team. My responsibility instead was to all the other network stations, Radios 2, 4 and (in the event of a really major story) Radio 1 as well. To be omitted from the commentary team for this first Test, having slogged around Australia the previous winter commentating for the ABC and the BBC every day of the six Tests involving Australia, England and West Indies, was a disappointment. But I am the first to recognise that John Arlott and Brian Johnston had earned almost a divine right to two of the commentators' places, and that, with a visiting commentator, the fourth spot has to be shared if others are to get experience for the future. On a tour as BBC correspondent I would be deeply involved for every minute of every day's cricket, dashing from a twenty-minute session in the commentary box to a telephone to despatch a one-minute report for whatever late-night or early-morning programme at home was due to take the latest news. At Trent Bridge this time I would feel relatively inactive, but this, of course, would have its compensations. I would actually be able to have some lunch on four of the days, and a good one too, courtesy of the brewers Ansells at the famous old Trent Bridge Inn.

This was one of many pleasant prospects as we got to the ground on a hot and sultry afternoon, soon after Henbit had won the Derby. As usual I had intended to back the winner but had not actually done so! England were just finishing their session in the nets. I found Ian Botham dressed in a towel in the dressing-room and interviewed him on my portable Uher recorder. I also recorded a brief chat with Philip Carling, a contemporary of mine at Cambridge, now Nottinghamshire's chief executive and clearly doing a fine job. I doubted whether they would use both the interviews in the *Today* programme's sports desks on the morning of the match, but I always keep hoping that one day cricket will be given prominence over soccer!

I drove Tony Cozier across from Trent Bridge to Radio Nottingham at a quarter to six. I recorded two previews of the match down the line to London, played over the interviews, then waited sympathetically for Tony's lines to the Caribbean to appear. They never did – the familiar frustration which faces all correspondents overseas to a greater or lesser extent. Tony, with a true Barbadian approach to life, seemed unconcerned. I would have dashed to a phone to get my material across but Tony clearly knew that if they wanted his stuff badly enough in the Caribbean, they would do the necessary. I got away from Nottingham at eight o' clock and visited friends in Collingham, a pleasant village with a vibrantly thriving cricket club. We had a meal in Lincoln, which I was seeing for the first time. The West Front of the great cathedral, seen by superbly effective floodlighting, was simply breath-taking. It was a balmy, even a sultry evening, the scent of honeysuckle on the air.

It was still unusually warm and close on Thursday morning. I arrived at Trent Bridge at a quarter to ten, parking in the Nottingham Forest car park. Dick Maddock, the cheery and dedicated producer of radio sport in the Midlands, was already in the commentary box in shirtsleeves. I was sweating profusely, having carried across my brief case, portable tape-recorder, binoculars, some paper and a few reference books, the essential tools of the trade. Don Mosey followed me into the box, protesting that every gateman in the ground had conspired to try to keep him out. Don would not be happy if there were nothing to protest about!

Johnners, on the other hand, finds little to ruffle him – ever. He is the true life and soul of the commentaries and there he was, bubbling and irrepressible in a summer suit, eager as usual for the fun to begin. John Arlott arrived later, looking plump, hot and world-weary. He hates the heat, so this would be a bad day for him, and a busy one for his red, white-spotted handkerchief, which would be called upon to mop the frowning brow every few minutes. But however he might look or however often he might say that he was not regretting his decision to retire at the end of the season, one knew that his commentaries would be as mellow, apt, knowledgable and evocative as ever they had been; moreover, that no one could ever directly replace him.

One of the early interests of any Test series is to meet Bill Frindall's latest girl-friend. He never fails to produce a new one each season. They all tend to be attractive, all are nutty about cricket, and all seem prepared to risk life and limb to phone through his specialist scorecards to various publications. Who is the only statistician to record a hundred girls before the end of May in ten successive seasons?

My first report was not until the one o'clock news on Radio 4, so I watched the first part of the morning's play from the smart new Trent Bridge press box. One sometimes gets a different complexion on events on the field from there than one does from the commentary box. One of the inevitable faults of *Test Match Special* is that, because every ball is described and dissected in detail, the expert analysis of Fred Trueman and Trevor Bailey sometimes becomes overcritical. They both often admit, however, that it is a much easier game to play in theory from the box than it is in practice in the middle. They were already in form when I got back to the box, Trevor looking spruce in a khaki safari-suit, cigarette burning; Fred with his huge millhouse-chimney pipe burning from his craggy jaw, unconsciously flaunt-

ing his affluence with a digital watch and a silver chain bracelet on one wrist
and a copper ring (anti rheumatism) on the other. Off-mike he was talking
at length about the much improved batting of one of the Yorkshire side, Phil
Carrick. Fred is on the committee now ('and so I should be too, sunshine')
and he espouses the cause of the white rose as loyally as he ever did. .

England made 243 for seven on the first day after Botham had won the
toss in his first Test as captain. Gooch launched the innings impressively
after his brilliant start to the season, but Roberts produced a snorter for him
and only Botham himself looked like establishing any prolonged command
of the West Indies fast bowlers thereafter. Roberts, Holding, Marshall and
Croft battered away all the sweltering day, between them delivering all but
one of the 84 overs sent down at a rate of only fourteen an hour. Boycott
played well after a torrid start; Gower briefly displayed both his genius and
his profligate use of it; Woolmer battled for three hours and twenty minutes
with what Jim Swanton would have called 'the utmost resolution'; Tavare
played soundly without quite dispelling doubts about his technique; and
Botham once hit two balls in succession for six, the second a remarkable on-
drive off Roberts – but no one played the big innings which might have led to
a major total.

By the end of the day, when I had played over interviews with Botham
and Lloyd (who had split his hand missing one of five catches put down by

*Bailey, Arlott, Cozier and Frindall enjoy the commentators' favourite view – straight
down the wicket at Trent Bridge*

the West Indies close to the bat) and delivered reports on the day of different durations for three evening sports desks and another for the late night news, the commentary box was in a rare mess. It is, I think, the best positioned commentary box anywhere in the world (another reason why I missed not seeing all the cricket from there). It is smack behind the bowler's arm and not so lofty as most other positions, so one gets a good impression of the height the ball is bouncing and also feels close to the play, making identification relatively easy. If it has a drawback it is its size – half-a-dozen people is as many as it will comfortably take and by the first evening it was ramshackle with briefcases, binoculars, half-opened letters, newspapers, empty wine bottles (it was a bit early in the match for champagne), plastic beakers and half-completed luncheon-packs, all strewn amongst the microphones, earphones and chairs. As always, the admirable engineers and I were the last to leave – that is the readily accepted lot of the cricket correspondent. Much as I like the company of professional cricketers, I still feel uneasy intruding on their dressing-room privacy at the end of the day and, in a way, shall not be sorry that it will be someone else's responsibility to get the close of play interview, which has come to be expected, in the 1981 series.

There was a dinner for John Arlott at Trent Bridge that evening, organised by the Cricketers' Association, of which he has been the honoured president, and gratefully attended also by we commentators. John was both eloquent and emotional and once interrupted the conversation with a hearty thump on the table: 'Gentlemen, the waiters are leaving soon and they want to know how many more bottles we shall need. Let's not waste good ordering time on too much conversation.'

After such indulgence it was as well that the second day was such a good one. England added only 20 more, but then discovered that the ball would move more for Willis, Hendrick, Lever and Botham than it had for the West Indies at their faster pace. Willis, glory be, was his old fast and hostile self again and but for some brilliant batting by Greenidge and Richards, who added 88 for the third wicket; a shrewd if fortunate innings by Murray; and more dropped catches; the West Indies might not have gained a first innings lead. Against my more humane judgment, but at the behest of my sports editor, I hounded a weary Bob Willis that evening and interviewed him in a kitchen!

The West Indies' advantage was 45 when England began their second innings a little before half-past twelve on the Saturday morning. Throughout the rest of the day, except when interrupted by a particularly dramatic thunderstorm, Geoffrey Boycott was planted firmly in the middle of the Trent Bridge stage. Square-cutting, or placing the ball deftly into the onside gaps, he steadily blunted the sharp edge of the attack by patient and correct defence, mainly in company with Bob Woolmer, who applied the same methods and looked equally solid, though also equally strokeless. Boycott owed his side a big innings from the moment that, at 46 for no wicket, he called Gooch for a risky single as he pushed the ball out towards mid-on. Risk became folly in the split-second that one realised that the nearest fielder was Fauod Bacchus, as quick as any in the world. He swooped *à la* Randall and his under-arm throw ended Gooch's innings, just when he seemed to be treating the West Indies bowlers with the same lofty disdain as he had mere county opponents. It was the biggest disaster which had befallen Gooch since his running-out for 99 in the Melbourne Test four months earlier. Boycott did not show his concern, although he must have felt it: he had run Randall out here in 1977 and had himself been the victim in 1973 when his partner Amiss refused to be sacrificed and went on to make a century.

England were exactly 100 ahead with eight wickets left on Saturday evening. Most commentators like to get back home for Sunday with the family, even if it means two long journeys, so there were some worried faces when the thunderstorm threatened to prevent play for more than one hour, which would have meant play continuing until 7.30, rather than 6.30, to compensate spectators for the time lost. As it was, super-efficient work by the ground staff and their part-time helpers and a perspicacious decision by the umpires to restrict the delay to 57 minutes allowed an early escape. After three days of intense concentration on a Test match, everyone needs a break. I usually try to play cricket myself on Sundays but this time went to Norfolk to join my family and had another Test match on Brancaster beach with James and Robin.

Fred Trueman had most to talk about after the weekend. He had scored 97 in a match at Newark and Brian Johnston was soon extracting details of the innings from him on the air. On the field the ultra-cautious Boycott-Woolmer stand crept past 100, then Roberts and Garner broke through and an irrevocable England rot set in. From 174 for two they declined to 252 all out, leaving West Indies 208 to win.

Ron Allsopp, a zestful and bespectacled, cheery chappy of a groundsman, had prepared a pitch with much more bounce than it used to have. This had enabled Roberts to undermine the England innings and it meant that England's six bowlers had a chance too. The rejuvenated Willis had Greenidge skilfully caught behind in his fourth over, but Viv Richards, sauntering but never swaggering, made batting look absurdly easy. Barely flexing his immense muscles to drive Lever for successive fours past mid-off and mid-on, he went on to make 48 in 65 minutes before Botham gave his colleagues renewed hope by bringing a ball back to trap him leg before. Haynes and Bacchus, however, two of the long-term hopes of West Indian cricket, played without blemish and, when the fifth day began on a misty morning after overnight rain, the West Indies required only 99 more runs, with seven wickets left.

After a tense first hour this apparently hopeless England position had altered dramatically. Bacchus chased Hendrick's wide first ball and was caught behind. This was a straightforward catch for Knott, but soon after he took another brilliant one, diving in front of first slip, to dismiss Kallicharran. When the score was 129 Lloyd shuffled across his stumps and was lbw to give Willis his third wicket of the innings. The ball was moving about a good deal, West Indies needed 79 more, and it was developing into one of those slowly drawn-out finishes which make cricket, at its best, incomparably *the* best game.

Haynes seems to thrive most when his team is struggling and he played exceptionally well. At a quarter past twelve Botham took over from Hendrick at the Pavilion end. Murray hit two long-hops for four and twelve came off a poor over. But the magnificent Willis was not giving in. He should have had Haynes caught by Hendrick when he was 49 but in his next over that most brilliant slip fielder from Derbyshire took a phenomenal airborne diving catch to get rid of Murray instead. 165 for six: 43 needed, four to fall. When lunch brought a temporary halt to the tension, only 32 more runs were needed and Haynes, 58 not out, was still in residence. Willis had taken three for 21 in his eight overs.

Lunch in a plush upper room of the Trent Bridge Inn was necessarily a hurried affair, and there was only one topic of conversation. (Well, to be honest, two because one of the waitresses had the most daring split in her dress and repeated leg-glances were unavoidable.) At twenty to two all attention returned to the climax of the match as Bob Willis drove himself in from the Radcliffe Road end again, arms and legs working like pistons. Marshall sliced a four but then cut a ball into his stumps. 180 for seven. As is so often the case when a Test match builds up to an exciting finish, the crowd on this last day was small, but the West Indians amongst them added to the feverish atmosphere, keeping properly and reverently quiet as each ball was delivered, then greeting every run with whistle-blowing and deep rhythmic drum-beats. The coming victory was being ushered in like the advance of a victorious army to a liberated town.

Roberts was Haynes's new partner and the West Indies could have wished for no better man in the crisis. He had often before shown icy cool when his side were depending upon him. Roberts it was who began to get the runs, mainly off Hendrick, whilst Haynes concentrated on a defence which looked more solid with every stroke. Botham bravely returned and there were no long-hops now. Roberts swung wildly and missed; even Haynes was beaten by a classic late outswinger. Twelve were still needed when Roberts swung at Willis and the ball skied towards Gower, that brilliant natural cricketer. He ran back and, taking his time, chose to cup the ball under his chin with his back to the wicket. He knew his recent batting form had placed his immediate Test future in doubt: did some fatal doubt in his subconsciousness tell him that he could drop that ball and thus seal his own fate, and England's? For whatever reason, he dropped it.

Tony Cozier was commentating now, conveying the excitement accurately and observantly but understandably exaggerating the possibility of England still being able to win the game. I know exactly how he felt, having often overseas broadcast simultaneously to the supporters of both competing countries. You are anxious not to offend by ruling out the chances of either side, and especially not to 'put the mouth' on your own side by saying they are home and dry when they are not. At such times it is difficult for the commentator to be entirely objective, and though you may be striving to be so, you cannot help but identify yourself to a certain extent with the side with whom you are touring.

Seven were needed when Haynes came desperately close to running himself out, Lever hitting the stumps with a perfect throw and umpire Constant giving the batsman the benefit of his doubt. But a few balls later, with only three needed, Haynes repeated his mistake and umpire Oslear, perfectly positioned, raised his finger as Willey's throw struck timber again. Haynes was in tears as he ran into the pavilion. Instead of taking his team all the way, he might just have thrown it away. But a little before half-past two Roberts opened his shoulders again and heaved a ball from Botham over mid-wicket for the winning four.

Two hours later, my reports and post-mortem interviews safely on tape in Broadcasting House, I drove out of the Nottingham Forest car-park, with much to savour on the long journey home. Tomorrow it was the Benson and Hedges quarter-final match at Northampton; next week the Lord's Test. The season was indeed in full swing and the Test series could not have had a better start.

*Christopher Martin-Jenkins, the BBC cricket correspondent from 1974 to 1980*

## ENGLAND  1st INNINGS v. WEST INDIES  1st TEST at TRENT BRIDGE, NOTTINGHAM on JUNE 5,6,7,9,10, 1980. TOSS: ENGLAND

| IN | OUT | MINS | No. | BATSMAN | HOW OUT | BOWLER | RUNS | WKT | TOTAL | 6s | 4s | BALLS | NOTES ON DISMISSAL |
|---|---|---|---|---|---|---|---|---|---|---|---|---|---|
| 11.30 | 12.00 | 30 | 1 | GOOCH | c't MURRAY | ROBERTS | 17 | 1 | 27 | · | 1 | 26 | Gloved bouncer low to wicket-keeper's left - diving catch. |
| 11.30 | 2.16 | 126 | 2 | BOYCOTT | c't MURRAY | GARNER | 36 | 3 | 74 | · | 3 | 88 | Edged ball that 'left' him off seam. |
| 12.01 | 1.17 | 76 | 3 | TAVARÉ | BOWLED | GARNER | 13 | 2 | 72 | · | 1 | 48 | Played back to late inswinger which hit off-stump. |
| 1.19 | 5.41 | 202 | 4 | WOOLMER | c't MURRAY | ROBERTS | 46 | 6 | 208 | · | 4 | 137 | Edged drive - very slight edge. |
| 2.18 | 3.18 | 60 | 5 | GOWER | c't GREENIDGE | ROBERTS | 20 | 4 | 114 | · | 2 | 43 | Edged drive to 2nd slip. ROBERTS '150th TEST WICKET |
| 3.20 | 5.34 | 114 | 6 | BOTHAM * | c't RICHARDS | GARNER | 57 | 5 | 204 | 2 | 5 | 83 | Cut hard and low to gully. |
| 5.36 | 6.19 | 43 | 7 | WILLEY | BOWLED | MARSHALL | 13 | 7 | 228 | · | 2 | 40 | Misjudged line and movement - off stump - round-the-wkt. |
| 5.43 | 11.40 | 59 | 8 | KNOTT † | LBW | ROBERTS | 6 | 8 | 246 | · | · | 40 | Beaten by ball that kept low. |
| 6.21 | 12.04 | 45 | 9 | LEVER | c't RICHARDS | HOLDING | 15 | 10 | 263 | · | 1 | 34 | Edged drive to gully. |
| 11.41 | 11.43 | 2 | 10 | WILLIS | BOWLED | ROBERTS | 8 | 9 | 254 | · | · | 3 | Yorked - attempted 'cut'. |
| 11.45 | 12.04 | 19 | 11 | HENDRICK | NOT OUT | | 7 | · | | · | · | 14 | |
| | | | | EXTRAS | b 7  lb 11  w 3  nb 4 | | 25 | | | | | | |

* CAPTAIN  † WICKET-KEEPER

TOTAL (OFF 91.5 OVERS IN 395 MIN.) 263 all out at 12.04pm

2b 22  556 balls (including 5 no balls)

13 OVERS 5 BALLS/HOUR
2.86 RUNS/OVER
47 RUNS/100 BALLS

| BOWLER | O | M | R | W | nb/w | HRS | OVERS | RUNS | | RUNS | MINS | OVERS | LAST 50 (in mins) |
|---|---|---|---|---|---|---|---|---|---|---|---|---|---|
| ROBERTS | 25 | 7 | 72 | 5 | 1/1 | 1 | 13 | 39 | | 50 | 83 | 18.3 | 83 |
| HOLDING | 23.5 | 7 | 61 | 1 | -/2 | 2 | 14 | 35 | | 100 | 165 | 37.1 | 82 |
| MARSHALL | 19 | 3 | 52 | 1 | 1/- | 3 | 13 | 37 | | 150 | 243 | 55.2 | 78 |
| RICHARDS | 1 | 0 | 9 | 0 | | 4 | 15 | 37 | | 200 | 294 | 66.4 | 51 |
| GARNER | 23 | 9 | 44 | 3 | 3/- | 5 | 13 | 55 | | 250 | 374 | 86.3 | 80 |
| | | | 25 Bat | | | 6 | 15 | 36 | | | | | |
| | 91.5 | 26 | 263 | 10 | | | | | | | | | |

2ND NEW BALL taken at 11.35am 2nd DAY - ENGLAND 245-7 after 85 overs

**LUNCH: 74-2** BOYCOTT 36* (120 min) WOOLMER 0* (11 min)
OFF 27 OVERS IN 120 MINUTES

**TEA: 148-4** WOOLMER 30* (132 min) BOTHAM 16* (111 min)
OFF 55 OVERS IN 241 MINUTES

**STUMPS: 243-7** KNOTT 6* (49 min) LEVER 14* (11 min)
(1ST DAY) OFF 84 OVERS IN 362 MINUTES

2ND DAY: ENGLAND'S LAST 3 WICKETS ADDED 20 RUNS OFF 7.5 OVERS IN 34 MIN.

ROBERTS TOOK 5 WKTS IN A TEST INNINGS FOR 10th TIME

| WKT | PARTNERSHIP | | RUNS | MINS |
|---|---|---|---|---|
| 1st | Gooch | Boycott | 27 | 30 |
| 2nd | Boycott | Tavaré | 45 | 76 |
| 3rd | Boycott | Woolmer | 2 | 17 |
| 4th | Woolmer | Gower | 40 | 60 |
| 5th | Woolmer | Botham | 90 | 114 |
| 6th | Woolmer | Willey | 4 | 5 |
| 7th | Willey | Knott | 20 | 36 |
| 8th | Knott | Lever | 18 | 21 |
| 9th | Lever | Willis | 8 | 2 |
| 10th | Lever | Hendrick | 9 | 19 |

## WEST INDIES 1st INNINGS   In reply to ENGLAND'S 263 all out

| IN | OUT | MINS | No. | BATSMAN | HOW OUT | BOWLER | RUNS | WKT | TOTAL | 6s | 4s | BALLS | NOTES ON DISMISSAL |
|---|---|---|---|---|---|---|---|---|---|---|---|---|---|
| 12.15 | 2.57 | 123 | 1 | GREENIDGE | c't KNOTT | HENDRICK | 53 | 2 | 107 | · | 9 | 91 | Edged away-seamer to 'keeper. |
| 12.15 | 12.47 | 32 | 2 | HAYNES | c't GOWER | WILLIS | 12 | 1 | 19 | · | 1 | 29 | Drove to cover - not at pitch of ball. |
| 12.49 | 4.02 | 154 | 3 | RICHARDS | c't KNOTT | WILLIS | 64 | 4 | 165 | · | 10 | 110 | Edged off-drive to 'keeper. 5th successive Test fifty |
| 2.58 | 3.44 | 46 | 4 | BACCHUS | c't BOTHAM | WILLIS | 30 | 3 | 151 | · | 5 | 42 | Edged defensive push to 1st slip. |
| 3.46 | 4.54 | 48 | 5 | KALLICHARRAN | BOWLED | BOTHAM | 17 | 5 | 208 | · | 2 | 36 | Played on aiming drive at inswinger. |
| 4.03 | 12.20 | 178 | 6 | MURRAY † | BOWLED | WILLIS | 64 | 10 | 308 | · | 8 | 121 | Middle stump - withdrew to leg and missed 'slog'. this HS v. ENG |
| 4.56 | 5.24 | 28 | 7 | LLOYD * | c't KNOTT | LEVER | 9 | 6 | 227 | · | · | 24 | Failed to withdraw bat from off side ball. Batted with stitched hand |
| 5.26 | 6.22 | 56 | 8 | MARSHALL | c't TAVARÉ | GOOCH | 20 | 7 | 265 | · | 1 | 42 | Edged outswinger to 1st slip. |
| 6.24 | 12.15 | 52 | 9 | ROBERTS | LBW | BOTHAM | 21 | 8 | 306 | · | 2 | 54 | Beaten by ball that kept low - played back |
| 12.17 | 12.18 | 1 | 10 | GARNER | c't LEVER | BOTHAM | 2 | 9 | 308 | · | · | 3 | Ballooned simple catch to mid-off. |
| 12.19 | (12.20) | 1 | 11 | HOLDING | NOT OUT | | 0 | · | | · | · | 0 | Did not receive a ball. |
| | | | | EXTRAS | b 1  lb 9  w 2  nb 4 | | 16 | | | | | | |

* CAPTAIN  † WICKET-KEEPER

TOTAL (OFF 91.1 OVERS IN 367 MIN) 308 all out

σ 38  552 balls (including 5 no balls)

WEST INDIES LEAD: 45

14 OVERS 5 BALLS/HOUR
3.38 RUNS/OVER
56 RUNS/100 BALLS

| BOWLER | O | M | R | W | nb/w | HRS | OVERS | RUNS | | RUNS | MINS | OVERS | LAST 50 (in mins) |
|---|---|---|---|---|---|---|---|---|---|---|---|---|---|
| WILLIS | 20.1 | 5 | 82 | 4 | 5/- | 1 | 15 | 50 | | 50 | 56 | 13.5 | 56 |
| LEVER | 20 | 2 | 76 | 1 | | 2 | 15 | 55 | | 100 | 113 | 28.3 | 57 |
| HENDRICK | 19 | 4 | 69 | 1 | | 3 | 16 | 54 | | 150 | 169 | 43.1 | 56 |
| WILLEY | 5 | 3 | 4 | 0 | | 4 | 13 | 64 | | 200 | 213 | 53.1 | 44 |
| BOTHAM | 20 | 6 | 50 | 3 | -/2 | 5 | 14 | 42 | | 250 | 279 | 67.3 | 66 |
| GOOCH | 7 | 2 | 11 | 1 | | 6 | 17 | 40 | | 300 | 356 | 88.5 | 77 |
| | | | 16 | | | | | | | | | | |
| | 91.1 | 22 | 308 | 10 | | | | | | | | | |

2ND NEW BALL taken at 11.51am 3RD DAY - WEST INDIES 278-7 after 85 overs

**LUNCH: 63-1** GREENIDGE 22* (76 min) RICHARDS 29* (42 min)
OFF 19 OVERS IN 76 MINUTES

**TEA: 177-4** KALLICHARRAN 2* (24 min) MURRAY 10* (7 min)
OFF 49 OVERS IN 196 MINUTES

**STUMPS: 270-7** MURRAY 49* (128 min) ROBERTS 3* (7 min)
(2ND DAY) OFF 79 OVERS IN 317 MINUTES

WEST INDIES added 38 runs in 50 mins off 12.1 overs before losing their last 3 wickets in 5 balls.

| WKT | PARTNERSHIP | | RUNS | MINS |
|---|---|---|---|---|
| 1st | Greenidge | Haynes | 19 | 32 |
| 2nd | Greenidge | Richards | 88 | 89 |
| 3rd | Richards | Bacchus | 44 | 46 |
| 4th | Richards | Kallicharran | 14 | 16 |
| 5th | Kallicharran | Murray | 43 | 31 |
| 6th | Murray | Lloyd | 19 | 28 |
| 7th | Murray | Marshall | 38 | 56 |
| 8th | Murray | Roberts | 41 | 52 |
| 9th | Murray | Garner | 2 | 1 |
| 10th | Murray | Holding | 0 | 1 |

## ENGLAND 2ND INNINGS — 45 RUNS BEHIND ON FIRST INNINGS

| IN | OUT | MINS | No. | BATSMAN | HOW OUT | BOWLER | RUNS | WKT | TOTAL | 6s | 4s | BALLS | NOTES ON DISMISSAL |
|---|---|---|---|---|---|---|---|---|---|---|---|---|---|
| 12.31 | 2.18 | 67 | 1 | GOOCH | RUN OUT (BACCHUS) | | 27 | 1 | 46 | · | 3 | 44 | Called by Boycott for quick single to mid-wicket who threw down wkt. |
| 12.31 | 1.09 | 345 | 2 | BOYCOTT | BOWLED | ROBERTS | 75 | 6 | 183 | · | 3 | 263 | Played on – fended bouncer off edge. |
| 2.20 | 2.55 | 35 | 3 | TAVARÉ | C' RICHARDS | GARNER | 4 | 2 | 68 | · | · | 27 | Edged lifting outswinger to 3rd slip. |
| 2.57 | 12.34 | 203 | 4 | WOOLMER | C' MURRAY | ROBERTS | 29 | 3 | 174 | · | 4 | 145 | Legside bouncer touched gloves. |
| 12.36 | 12.48 | 12 | 5 | GOWER | LBW | GARNER | 1 | 4 | 175 | · | · | 12 | Played back – beaten by breakback. |
| 12.50 | 1.00 | 10 | 6 | BOTHAM * | C' RICHARDS | ROBERTS | 4 | 5 | 180 | · | 1 | 7 | Bouncer hit splice and skied to gully. |
| 1.02 | 3.21 | 100 | 7 | WILLEY | BOWLED | MARSHALL | 38 | 8 | 237 | · | 6 | 84 | Played on – edged cut. |
| 1.11 | 3.03 | 73 | 8 | KNOTT † | LBW | MARSHALL | 7 | 7 | 218 | · | · | 49 | Misjudged bounce of short ball- ducked- hit on left arm. |
| 3.05 | 3.48 | 43 | 9 | LEVER | C' MURRAY | GARNER | 4 | 10 | 252 | · | · | 27 | Edged firm-footed drive. |
| 3.23 | 3.34 | 11 | 10 | WILLIS | BOWLED | GARNER | 9 | 9 | 248 | · | 2 | 7 | Yorked leg-stump. |
| 3.36 | (3.48) | 12 | 11 | HENDRICK | NOT OUT | | 2 | · | · | · | · | 12 | – |
| | | | | EXTRAS | | | 52 | | | | | | b 19  lb 13  w 10  nb 10 |

*CAPTAIN  †WICKET-KEEPER

0s 19 4s 677 balls (including 10 no balls)

TOTAL (OFF 111·1 OVERS IN 463 MINUTES) 252 all out at 3·48 pm 4th DAY.

14 OVERS 2 BALLS/HOUR
2·27 RUNS/OVER
37 RUNS/100 BALLS

| BOWLER | O | M | R | W | nb/w | HRS | OVERS | RUNS |
|---|---|---|---|---|---|---|---|---|
| ROBERTS | 24 | 6 | 57 | 3 | 7/5 | 1 | 13 | 43 |
| HOLDING | 26 | 5 | 65 | 0 | | 2 | 13 | 31 |
| MARSHALL | 24 | 8 | 44 | 2 | 7/5 | 3 | 16 | 35 |
| GARNER | 34·1 | 20 | 30 | 4 | 3/1 | 4 | 15 | 34 |
| GREENIDGE | 3 | 2 | 4 | 0 | 1/5 | 5 | 15 | 26 |
| | | | 52 | 1 | | 6 | 15 | 22 |
| | | | | | | 7 | 14 | 27 |
| | 111·1 | 41 | 252 | 10 | | | | |

2ND NEW BALL TAKEN AT 2·11pm ON 4th DAY
– ENGLAND 196-6 after 89 overs.

| RUNS | MINS | OVERS | LAST 50 (in mins) |
|---|---|---|---|
| 50 | 72 | 15·1 | 72 |
| 100 | 163 | 38·4 | 91 |
| 150 | 255 | 60·2 | 92 |
| 200 | 381 | 91·4 | 126 |
| 250 | 456 | 109·1 | 75 |

LUNCH : 43-0  GOOCH 27*  BOYCOTT 13*
OFF 13 OVERS IN 59 MINUTES
BAD LIGHT STOPPED PLAY at 3·33 p.m. (56 min LOST)
TEA : 83-2  BOYCOTT 27* (142 min)  WOOLMER 4* (36 min)
LEAD 38  OFF 32 OVERS IN 142 MINUTES
STUMPS : 145-2  BOYCOTT 61* (245 min)
(3RD DAY) LEAD 100 OFF 58 OVERS IN 245 MINUTES  WOOLMER 20* (139 min)
LUNCH : 196-6  WILLEY 11* (30 min)  KNOTT 0* (21 min)
(151 AHEAD)  OFF 89 OVERS IN 367 MINUTES

WEST INDIES NEED 208 TO WIN
IN A MINIMUM OF 502 MINUTES.

| WKT | PARTNERSHIP | | RUNS | MINS |
|---|---|---|---|---|
| 1st | Gooch | Boycott | 46 | 67 |
| 2nd | Boycott | Tavaré | 22 | 35 |
| 3rd | Boycott | Woolmer | 106 | 203 |
| 4th | Boycott | Gower | 1 | 12 |
| 5th | Boycott | Botham | 5 | 10 |
| 6th | Boycott | Willey | 3 | 7 |
| 7th | Willey | Knott | 35 | 73 |
| 8th | Willey | Lever | 19 | 16 |
| 9th | Lever | Willis | 11 | 11 |
| 10th | Lever | Hendrick | 4 | 12 |
| | | | 252 | |

## WEST INDIES 2ND INNINGS — REQUIRING 208 RUNS TO WIN IN A MINIMUM OF 502 MINUTES.

| IN | OUT | MINS | No. | BATSMAN | HOW OUT | BOWLER | RUNS | WKT | TOTAL | 6s | 4s | BALLS | NOTES ON DISMISSAL |
|---|---|---|---|---|---|---|---|---|---|---|---|---|---|
| 4.08 | 4.37 | 29 | 1 | GREENIDGE | C' KNOTT | WILLIS | 6 | 1 | 11 | · | · | 21 | Edged very low to keeper's right - superb catch. |
| 4.08 | 2.24 | 309 | 2 | HAYNES | RUN OUT (WILLEY) | | 62 | 8 | 205 | · | 3 | 184 | Backed up - sent back - beaten by point's direct return. |
| 4.39 | 5.44 | 65 | 3 | RICHARDS | LBW | BOTHAM | 48 | 2 | 69 | · | 8 | 59 | Played across inswinger. Ended run of five fifties in Tests. |
| 5.46 | 11.01 | 47 | 4 | BACCHUS | C' KNOTT | HENDRICK | 19 | 3 | 109 | · | 2 | 41 | Edged off-drive at wide half-volley - FIRST BALL 5TH DAY. |
| 11.03 | 11.33 | 30 | 5 | KALLICHARRAN | C' KNOTT | WILLIS | 9 | 4 | 125 | · | · | 23 | Edged ball angled across him low to keeper's left. |
| 11.35 | 11.42 | 7 | 6 | LLOYD * | LBW | WILLIS | 3 | 5 | 129 | · | · | 8 | Played back and across - beaten by pace. |
| 11.44 | 12.30 | 46 | 7 | MURRAY † | C' HENDRICK | WILLIS | 16 | 6 | 165 | · | 2 | 33 | Edged wide of 3rd slip's right- brilliant diving catch. |
| 12.32 | 1.42 | 31 | 8 | MARSHALL | BOWLED | WILLIS | 7 | 7 | 180 | · | 1 | 20 | Played on - attempted cut. |
| 1.44 | (2.26) | 42 | 9 | ROBERTS | NOT OUT | | 22 | · | · | · | 3 | 35 | Made winning hit. |
| 2.25 | (2.26) | 1 | 10 | HOLDING | NOT OUT | | 0 | · | · | · | · | – | |
| | | | 11 | GARNER | | | | | | | | | |
| | | | | EXTRAS | | | 17 | | | | | | b-  lb 8  w-  nb 9 |

*CAPTAIN  †WICKET-KEEPER

0s 19 4s 424 balls (including 12 no balls)

TOTAL (OFF 68·4 OVERS IN 311 MIN.) 209-8

13 OVERS 1 BALLS/HOUR
3·04 RUNS/OVER
49 RUNS/100 BALLS

| BOWLER | O | M | R | W | nb | HRS | OVERS | RUNS |
|---|---|---|---|---|---|---|---|---|
| WILLIS | 26 | 4 | 65 | 5 | 12 | 1 | 13 | 37 |
| LEVER | 8 | 2 | 25 | 0 | | 2 | 14 | 55 |
| HENDRICK | 14 | 5 | 40 | 1 | | 3 | 13 | 33 |
| BOTHAM | 16·4 | 6 | 48 | 1 | | 4 | 13 | 42 |
| GOOCH | 2 | 1 | 2 | 0 | | 5 | 13 | 34 |
| WILLEY | 2 | 0 | 12 | 0 | | | | |
| | | | 17 | 1 | | | | |
| | 68·4 | 18 | 209 | 8 | | | | |

| RUNS | MINS | OVERS | LAST 50 (in mins) |
|---|---|---|---|
| 50 | 82 | 18·1 | 72 |
| 100 | 138 | 31 | 56 |
| 150 | 221 | 48·4 | 83 |
| 200 | 298 | 65·5 | 77 |

STUMPS : 109-2  HAYNES 29* (144 min)  BACCHUS 19* (46 min)
(4TH DAY)  OFF 33 OVERS IN 144 MINUTES
REQUIRING 99 RUNS TO WIN
LUNCH : 176-6  HAYNES 58* (265 min)  MARSHALL 3* (29 min)
OFF 59 OVERS IN 265 MIN.
REQUIRING 32 RUNS TO WIN

WEST INDIES WON BY 2 WICKETS
at 2·26pm on 5th DAY - narrowest margin
of victory in England v West Indies Tests
TOTAL TIME LOST : 56 MINUTES
MAN OF THE MATCH : A.M.E. ROBERTS

| WKT | PARTNERSHIP | | RUNS | MINS |
|---|---|---|---|---|
| 1st | Greenidge | Haynes | 11 | 29 |
| 2nd | Haynes | Richards | 58 | 65 |
| 3rd | Haynes | Bacchus | 40 | 47 |
| 4th | Haynes | Kallicharran | 16 | 30 |
| 5th | Haynes | Lloyd | 4 | 7 |
| 6th | Haynes | Murray | 36 | 46 |
| 7th | Haynes | Marshall | 15 | 31 |
| 8th | Haynes | Roberts | 25 | 40 |
| 9th | Roberts | Holding | 4* | 1 |
| | | | 209 | |

# THE FRINDALL SCORING METHOD

## Bill Frindall

My scoring method is based on a system which most probably originated in Australia. When continuous ball-by-ball radio commentaries were introduced, my BBC predecessors found the orthodox scoring system totally inadequate for the commentators' needs and adapted the 'Australian' method. On becoming the BBC's Test match scorer in 1966, I revised the method and redesigned the sheets, which are now used by all BBC radio and television scorers.

The method follows the basic conventions of the standard system as described in *Cricket Umpiring and Scoring*, a textbook for umpires and scorers compiled by R. S. Rait Kerr (secretary of the MCC 1936–1952). During BBC commentaries it involves the use of three types of scoresheet: ball-by-ball record of play *(Sheet 1);* innings scorecard *(Sheet 2);* cumulative record of bowling analyses and extras *(Sheet 3).* If we study a completed sample of each of the three sheets the method is easy to follow. It accommodates more facts during play than the more conventional system.

*Sheet 1*, the ball-by-ball record of play, forms the basis of the scoring method and, unlike the other two sheets, it is not used by the commentators. It contains three sections: one for the bowlers, one for the batsmen, and one for recording the totals at the end of each over (or at the fall of a wicket, interval or stoppage of play for rain). Each line across these columns records one over, the time at which the bowler commences it being entered in the first column. The sample *Sheet 1* shows part of England's second innings of

*Bill Frindall preparing for action at Trent Bridge*

the Centenary Test at Melbourne. You will see that there are two bowling columns (one for each end of the ground) and two batting columns which list the batsmen in the positions (left or right) in which their scores are shown on the scoreboard. The elaborate Melbourne scoreboard gives the complete batting order of the innings in progress and lists the two not out batsmen one above the other. My sheets were designed for use in England where only the Trent Bridge board follows the Australian style. In this match the left-right separation serves only to identify the batsmen in the END-OF-OVER TOTALS columns.

My sheet starts shortly after tea on the fourth day with England, needing 463 to win, 122 for two after 34 overs. Derek Randall has scored 53 off 90 balls with six fours, and Dennis Amiss has made six off 11 balls with one four. There have been eight extras or sundries. M5 NB/7 in the NOTES column shows that five of the 34 eight-ball overs have been maidens and that seven no balls have been called. As Dennis Lillee starts a new over we note the time (4.14) in the first column. He is bowling from the Pavilion end, so we

| 4TH DAY TIME | BOWLERS Pavilion End BOWLER | O. | Southern End BOWLER | O. | BATSMEN Scoreboard Left SCORING | BALLS | 6s/4s | Scoreboard Right SCORING | BALLS | 6s/4s | ENGLAND 2ND INNINGS NOTES | O. | RUNS | W. | L BAT | R BAT | EXTRAS |
|---|---|---|---|---|---|---|---|---|---|---|---|---|---|---|---|---|---|
| | | | | | RANDALL | 90 | 6 | AMISS | 11 | 1 | M5 NB/7 | 34 | 122 | 2 | 53 | 6 | 8 |
| 4.14 | LILLEE | 11 | | | ⌐·······  | 98 | | | | | M6 | 35 | | | | | |
| 19 | | | O'KEEFFE | 11 | ·2······ | 19 | | | | | | 36 | 124 | | | | 8 |
| 23 | " | 12 | | | L P 6 ···.1 | 103 | | 2B 1· .4· | 22 | 2 | • Dropped 3rd slip (HOOKES) (2B) | 37 | 131 | | 54 | 12 | 10 |
| 30 | | | " | 12 | ·····Q· | 112 | | | | | (NB) NB/8 M7 | 38 | 132 | | | | 11 |
| 33½ | " | 13 | | | ·8 ·1 | 114 | | ···6·· | 28 | | Gulls. | 39 | 134 | | 55 | 13 | |
| 39 | | | " | 13 | 4.1 ····· | 119 | | ··3 | 31 | | | 40 | 138 | | 56 | 16 | |
| 43 | " | 14 | | | | | | ········ | 39 | | M8 | 41 | | | | | |
| 48 | | | " | 14 | 2.1 | 120 | | ·······2 | 46 | | • Edge nr sh.leg (COSIER) | 42 | 139 | | 57 | | |
| 52 | WALKER | 11 | | | 6 3 43 ··41 | 125 | 7 | ··7 | 49 | | | 43 | 148 | | 65 | 17 | |
| 57 | | | " | 15 | 7+x 4·...1 ·2 | 131 | 8 | ·1 7 | 51 | | † all-run | 44 | 154 | | 70 | 18 | |
| 5·01 05 DRINKS | " | 12 | | | | | | ·2···2·· | 59 | | | 45 | 158 | | | 22 | |
| 09 | | | " | 16 | 3 3 | 132 | | ········ | 66 | | 4HR → | 46 | 161 | | 73 | | |
| 13 | " | 13 | | | 92 ·21 | 135 | | ··2·3 | 71 | | 50 p'ship in 69 min | 47 | 169 | | 76 | 27 | |
| 18 | | | " | 17 | | | | ·······2 | 79 | | • Bat/pad catch to short sq.leg (COSIER) | 48 | 171 | | | 29 | |
| 22 | " | 14 | | | ·····(B)+ | 141 | | ·.2 | 81 | | (W) | 49 | 174 | | | 31 | 12 |
| 27 | | | " | 18 | 3B 6 ·.·.1 | 147 | | 7 8 1 1 | 83 | | (3B) | 50 | 180 | | 77 | 33 | 15 |
| 32 | LILLEE | 15 | | | 8 184 3 222·1 | 152 | | 7s 1 ·· | 86 | | | 51 | 188 | | 84 | 34 | |
| 38 | | | CHAPPELL | 1 | ·····1 3 | 158 | | ·· | 88 | | 1 + 2 overthrows | 52 | 191 | | 87 | | |
| 42 | " | 16 | | | † | 158 | 8 | ·· | 88 | 2 | † light consultation | 52 | 191 | 2 | 87 | 34 | 15 |
| 5·43 | BAD LIGHT | STOPPED | PLAY | | | | | | | | M8 NB/8 | | | S T U M P S | | | |
| 5TH DAY 11·02 | LILLEE (of shorter run) | 16 | | | ·····2• | 165 | | · | 89 | | • nr. O'keeffe (gully) | 53 | 192 | | 88 | | |
| 07 | | | O'KEEFFE | 19 | 9 x 2 ··4·.:3 | 171 | 9 | ·· | 91 | | • Appeal ct sh.leg (Gilmour) bat/pad. | 54 | 199 | | 95 | | |
| 11 | " | 17 | | | 49 ·41 ·.·. | 177 | 10 | 7s ·1 | 93 | | RANDALL'S 100 in 233 (ON DEBUT v. AUSTRALIA) | 55 | 205 | | 100 | 35 | |
| 17 | | | " | 20 | | | | ········ | 101 | | • Hit on head -2mins lost. M9 | 56 | | | | | |
| 21 | CHAPPELL | 2 | | | ·E····· | 185 | | | | | M10 | 57 | | | | | |

put his name in that column. It is his eleventh over of the innings, so we mark '11' in his Over column. Now we are ready to record the first ball. It hits Randall on the pad and there is an appeal for lbw which umpire O'Connell turns down. We put a dot at the left-hand end of Randall's first column to show that no runs have been scored off that ball. As this column is required to record eight balls in Australia (more if no balls or wides are called), we must mentally sub-divide it to hold the entire over. Above the dot I add a small L to denote the lbw appeal. If a ball hits the pad and there is no appeal I put P above the dot except when leg byes result (LB). Randall plays out the next seven balls without scoring. At the end of the over I rule a line under the eight dots to denote a maiden and put M6 in the NOTES section to show that it is the sixth of the innings. The only totals which require amending are the number of balls received by Randall (90+8) and the number of overs bowled in the innings (35).

Now we are ready to score the next over. We note the time (4.19), and enter the bowler's name (O'Keeffe) and the number of his overs (11) in the columns for the Southern End. He is bowling to Amiss who scores two runs off the second ball. We enter '2' in Amiss's column and that one figure is all that is required to record that scoring stroke. Less recording is necessary while the over is in progress than with the standard scoring method. Instead of marking each run in the batting, bowling and tally sections of the normal scorebook, my method requires just the one entry. It is also immediately possible to tell exactly what has happened to each ball: who bowled it to whom, from which end, at what time, and how the batsmen reacted. Unless a wicket falls, all totalling is done at the end of the over when the fielders are changing positions and there is no action to record.

For Test match broadcasts I need to elaborate upon the basic method of scoring to record many other·details which are essential to the commentators. The little number '2' above the two runs just scored by Amiss is a cryptic way of showing in which part of the field those runs were scored. It is based on the following key, which is reversed for left-handed batsmen:

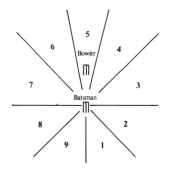

This method is only approximate but it does show if a batsman has a favourite scoring area and if a bowler is prone to conceding runs to a particular stroke. It is also possible to construct a scoring chart of a batsman's innings from the little numerals. After Viv Richards had scored 232 against England at Nottingham in 1976, the England captain asked me for a set of charts showing the batsman's scoring strokes against each of the six bowlers used against him. I was able to construct these from my sheets and also to separate the 313 balls received by Richards in that innings to show his scoring rate against each bowler.

O'Keeffe did not concede any more runs during his over to Amiss. Between overs we amend the totals which have changed: Amiss has now scored eight off 19 balls and England have reached 124 off 36 overs. We record the time at which Lillee starts his twelfth over but, as he bowled the previous over from that end, it is not necessary to write his name – ditto marks (") will suffice. His first ball produces an unsuccessful lbw appeal (L), his third is taken on the pad without an appeal (P), and his fifth is hit by Randall to mid-on and the batsmen take a single (1 with a '6' above it). Now Amiss is facing and we continue the over in his column. The sixth ball produces two byes and we enter a dot with 2B above it. We must also record the same symbol in the NOTES section to enable us to check the breakdown of the extras. Lillee's next ball is edged by Amiss to third slip where Hookes drops the catch and allows the ball to go to the boundary. Above the '4' we put a little 'l' and a red dot. A similar dot in the NOTES section links that ball with the note of the dropped catch. Amiss survives the last ball.

While the field is changing for O'Keeffe to begin his next over, we must complete the totals which have changed: Randall 103 balls, Amiss 22 balls, two fours, 37 overs, total 131, Randall 54, Amiss 12, extras 10.

The fifth delivery of the next over produces a 'no ball' call. Randall did not score off it and it is recorded as $\odot$. No balls are also itemised in the notes column (NB) and a tally is kept of them (NB/8 as this is the eighth call of 'no ball' in the innings) to facilitate a check of the number of balls received by each batsman. I usually do this during the drinks interval and at the end of each session of play. The total number of overs is multiplied by six and the no balls are added to that total. This is then compared with the total number of balls received by the dismissed and not out batsmen. At the end of O'Keeffe's twelfth over, 38 overs have been bowled, including eight no balls: $38 \times 8 + 8$ no balls = 312; 36 (Woolmer) + 142 (Brearley) + 112 (Randall) + 22 (Amiss) = 312.

If the no ball had been hit for four runs, it would have been shown as 4 in the batsman's column. A no ball counts as a ball received because the batsman can score off it. Even though O'Keeffe's twelfth over contained a no ball, it counts as a maiden because no runs were scored off any of the nine balls. The dots must be underlined and M7 added to the NOTES section.

After Lillee and O'Keeffe have each bowled two more overs, Greg Chappell replaces Lillee with Max Walker at the Pavilion End and we must enter the new bowler's name in the appropriate column. By referring to *Sheet 3* we find that this will be Walker's eleventh over of the innings and we put 11 in his Overs column. The first ball of O'Keeffe's fifteenth over produces an all-run four which I record in the NOTES section. This column also records the end of the fourth hour of the England innings (46 overs, 161 runs), the fifty partnership between Randall and Amiss in 69 minutes, overthrows, and an umpires' consultation over light. Randall played and missed the second ball of O'Keeffe's fifteenth over and I denote this by putting a small X above that dot.

I record the time at which drinks were taken (5.01) and also the time when the next over started (5.05). By tradition this counts as playing time and those four barren minutes have to be included in the individual batting times. It is far more logical to measure the duration of an innings by the number of balls faced and my system makes such calculations extremely simple.

The seventh ball of Walker's fourteenth over is called a 'wide' and this is recorded as $+$. Four wides would be shown as $+$. It is also marked as W in the NOTES column. It is not included in the number of balls faced by Randall because the batsman cannot score off a wide.

At 5.43 play is stopped by bad light when Lillee is about to begin his sixteenth over. As the players leave the field I stop my three stop watches – one for each batsman and one for the England innings as a whole – and enter up the totals of every column even though they have not changed. I take similar action when a wicket falls, but only the dismissed batsman's watch is stopped unless it happens also to be the end of the team's innings. I also rule off the outgoing batsman's columns in red.

The fall of a wicket produces a pressure point in any scoring system but practice will soon help you evolve the best action sequence and you will normally have two minutes before the new batsman starts his innings.

Here is a list of symbols I use in the batsmen's columns:

| | | | |
|---|---|---|---|
| B | Bye | P | Hit on pad – no appeal |
| E | Edged stroke | S | Sharp (quick) single |
| EP | Edged ball into pads | x | Played and missed |
| F | Full toss | Y | Yorker |
| G | Hit on glove | ↑ | Bouncer |
| L | Hit on pad – lbw appeal | ↓ | Shooter |
| LB | Leg bye | | |

*Sheet 2*, the innings scorecard, is the commentator's main source of reference. It records the starting and finishing times of each batsman's innings, the length of his innings, his score, his method of dismissal, the total at which his wicket fell, details of his boundaries and number of balls faced, and a note of his dismissal. The lower part of the sheet shows the final bowling analyses (taken from *Sheet 3* at the completion of the innings), the hourly run and over rates, the time taken for each fifty runs scored by the team, the full details of each wicket partnership, and the total and individual scores at the end of each session of play. Coloured inks (not shown in the scoresheets reproduced in this book) highlight the more important entries and make it easier for the commentator to select the main items of interest from a sheet containing so much data. Names and run totals are shown in blue – as is the close of play score. Red is used for hundred partnerships, exceptionally fast run and over rates, and lunch and tea totals. Exceptionally slow over and run rates appear in blue.

*Sheet 3*, the cumulative record of bowling analyses and extras, is also for commentator reference. Entries are made only at the end of each over or at the completion of a session of play. A red line is ruled under a bowler's figures when he is taken off. Intervals, close of play and interruptions for rain and bad light are also noted, thus enabling the commentator to deduce easily the length of a bowler's current spell. The number of boundaries conceded by each bowler is also shown cumulatively. Extras are recorded in separate columns on the right hand side of the page. No balls and wides are also recorded against the name of each bowler. This sheet also enables a number of cross-checks to be carried out. The total of the overs bowled by each bowler should equal the number bowled at that stage of the innings (15+14+4+18+1=52 at stumps on the fourth day). The total maidens, runs, wickets and boundaries can be checked in the same way.

ENGLAND 2ND INNINGS — REQUIRING **463** RUNS TO WIN IN **650** MINUTES

| IN | OUT | MINS | No. | BATSMAN | HOW OUT | BOWLER | RUNS | WKT | TOTAL | 6s | 4s | BALLS | NOTES ON DISMISSAL |
|---|---|---|---|---|---|---|---|---|---|---|---|---|---|
| 12.11 | 12.58 | 47 | 1 | WOOLMER | LBW | WALKER | 12 | 1 | 28 | · | 1 | 36 | Beaten by big inswinger – played well forward. |
| 12.11 | 4.03 | 170 | 2 | BREARLEY | LBW | LILLEE | 43 | 2 | 113 | · | 2 | 142 | Late on near-yorker that came back off pitch. |
| 1.40 | 3.27 | 446 | 3 | RANDALL | Ct COSIER | O'KEEFFE | 174 | 5 | 346 | · | 21 | 353 | Edged googly via pad to short square leg. 100 ON DEBUT v. AUSTRALIA (14th ENGLAND PLAYER) |
| 4.05 | 1.53 | 227 | 4 | AMISS | BOWLED | CHAPPELL | 64 | 3 | 279 | · | 3 | 185 | Beaten by sharp off cutter which kept low. |
| 1.55 | 2.07 | 12 | 5 | FLETCHER | Ct MARSH | LILLEE | 1 | 4 | 290 | · | · | 8 | Edged ball which lifted and left him off the pitch. |
| 2.09 | 4.10 | 100 | 6 | GREIG * | Ct COSIER | O'KEEFFE | 41 | 6 | 369 | · | 7 | 82 | Edged googly via pad to short square leg (caught at 2nd attempt) |
| 3.30 | 5.12 | 81 | 7 | KNOTT † | LBW | LILLEE | 42 | 10 | 417 | · | 5 | 51 | Missed hit to leg. |
| 4.13 | 4.18 | 5 | 8 | OLD | Ct CHAPPELL | LILLEE | 2 | 7 | 380 | · | · | 4 | Edged cut to 1st slip. |
| 4.20 | 4.35 | 15 | 9 | LEVER | LBW | O'KEEFFE | 4 | 8 | 385 | · | · | 25 | Played back – beaten by faster ball. |
| 4.37 | 4.58 | 21 | 10 | UNDERWOOD | BOWLED | LILLEE | 7 | 9 | 410 | · | · | 19 | Swung across yorker. |
| 5.02 | (5.12) | 10 | 11 | WILLIS | NOT OUT | | 5 | · | · | · | 1 | 5 | – |
| | | | | EXTRAS | b 8 lb 4 w 3 nb 7 | | 22 | | | 0 | 40 | 910 balls (Inc. 10 no balls) | |

* CAPTAIN † WICKET-KEEPER

TOTAL (OFF 112.4 OVERS IN 575 MINUTES) **417** all out at 5.12 pm on 5th day

11 OVERS 6 BALLS/HOUR
3.71 RUNS/OVER
46 RUNS/100 BALLS

| BOWLER | O | M | R | W | w/nb |
|---|---|---|---|---|---|
| LILLEE | 34.4 | 7 | 139 | 5 | –/1 |
| WALKER | 22 | 4 | 83 | 1 | 2/– |
| GILMOUR | 4 | 0 | 29 | 0 | 1/6 |
| O'KEEFFE | 33 | 6 | 108 | 3 | –/1 |
| CHAPPELL | 16 | 7 | 29 | 1 | –/2 |
| WALTERS | 3 | 2 | 7 | 0 | –/– |
| | | | 22 | Ext | |
| | 112.4 | 26 | 417 | 10 | |

2ND NEW BALL taken at 12.03 pm 5th day
ENGLAND 237-2 after 66 overs

| HRS | OVERS | RUNS |
|---|---|---|
| 1 | 10 | 38 |
| 2 | 12 | 43 |
| 3 | 12 | 41 |
| 4 | 12 | 39 |
| 5 | 13 | 51 |
| 6 | 13 | 52 |
| 7 | 11 | 35 |
| 8 | 12 | 34 |
| 9 | 11 | 52 |

| RUNS | MINS | OVERS | LAST 50 (in mins) |
|---|---|---|---|
| 50 | 70 | 12.1 | 70 |
| 100 | 152 | 29 | 82 |
| 150 | 224 | 43.1 | 72 |
| 200 | 278 | 54.2 | 54 |
| 250 | 349 | 69.1 | 71 |
| 300 | 423 | 84 | 74 |
| 350 | 505 | 99.6 | 82 |
| 400 | 552 | 108.4 | 47 |

LUNCH : 28-1 — BREARLEY 14* — OFF 8.2 OVERS IN 47 MINUTES

TEA : 113-1 — BREARLEY 43* (167 min), RANDALL 50* (120 min) — OFF 32 OVERS IN 167 MINUTES

STUMPS : 191-2 — 4TH DAY (NEEDING 272 IN 360 MINS) — RANDALL 87* (222 min), AMISS 34* (97 min) — OFF 52 OVERS IN 268 MINUTES

LUNCH : 267-2 (NEEDING 196 IN 240 MINS) — RANDALL 129* (340 min), AMISS 63* (215 min) — OFF 77 OVERS IN 386 MINUTES

TEA : 354-5 (NEEDING 109 IN 120 MINS) — GREIG 32* (92 min), KNOTT 6* (11 min) — OFF 100 OVERS IN 506 MINUTES

| WKT | PARTNERSHIP | | RUNS | MINS |
|---|---|---|---|---|
| 1st | Woolmer | Brearley | 28 | 47 |
| 2nd | Brearley | Randall | 85 | 123 |
| 3rd | Randall | Amiss | 166 | 227 |
| 4th | Randall | Fletcher | 11 | 12 |
| 5th | Randall | Greig | 56 | 78 |
| 6th | Greig | Knott | 23 | 19 |
| 7th | Knott | Old | 11 | 5 |
| 8th | Knott | Lever | 5 | 15 |
| 9th | Knott | Underwood | 25 | 21 |
| 10th | Knott | Willis | 7 | 10 |
| | | | 417 | |

AUSTRALIA BOWLING — ENGLAND 2ND INNINGS

LILLEE (NB 1, WIDES)

| O | M | R | W | 6s | 4s |
|---|---|---|---|---|---|
| 1 | 0 | 5 | 0 | | |
| 2 | 0 | 6 | 0 | | |
| 3 | 0 | 8 | 0 | | – |
| 4 | 0 | 12 | 0 | | – |
| LUNCH | | | | | |
| 5 | 1 | 12 | 0 | | |
| 6 | 1 | 16 | 0 | | |
| 7 | 1 | 17 | 0 | | – |
| 8 | 1 | 29 | 0 | | 2 |
| 9 | 1 | 33 | 0 | | 2 |
| TEA | | | | | |
| 10 | 1 | 35 | 1 | | |
| 11 | 2 | 35 | 1 | | |
| 12 | 2 | 40 | 1 | | 3 |
| 13 | 2 | 42 | 1 | | |
| 14 | 3 | 42 | 1 | | 3 |
| 15 | 3 | 50 | 1 | | 3 |
| STUMPS | | | | | |
| 16 | 3 | 51 | 1 | | |
| 17 | 3 | 57 | 1 | | 4 |
| 18 | 4 | 57 | 1 | | |
| 19 | 5 | 57 | 1 | | |
| 20 | 5 | 60 | 1 | | |
| 21 | 6 | 60 | 1 | | |
| 22 | 6 | 62 | 1 | | |
| 23 | 7 | 62 | 1 | | 4 |
| LUNCH | | | | | |
| 24 | 7 | 72 | 1 | | 6 |
| 25 | 7 | 79 | 1 | | 7 |
| 26 | 7 | 89 | 2 | | 9 |
| 27 | 7 | 103 | 2 | | 10 |
| 28 | 7 | 104 | 2 | | 10 |
| TEA | | | | | |
| 29 | 7 | 111 | 2 | | 11 |
| 30 | 7 | 120 | 3 | | 13 |
| 31 | 7 | 123 | 3 | | |
| 32 | 7 | 128 | 3 | | |
| 33 | 7 | 137 | 3 | | |
| 34 | 7 | 139 | 4 | | |
| 34.4 | 7 | 139 | 5 | | 13 |

WALKER (NB, WIDES II)

| O | M | R | W | 6s | 4s |
|---|---|---|---|---|---|
| 1 | 0 | 2 | 0 | | |
| 2 | 0 | 5 | 0 | | – |
| 3 | 0 | 8 | 0 | | |
| 3.2 | 0 | 8 | 1 | | – |
| LUNCH | | | | | |
| 4 | 1 | 8 | 1 | | |
| 5 | 1 | 11 | 1 | | |
| 6 | 1 | 18 | 1 | | 1 |
| 7 | 2 | 18 | 1 | | |
| 8 | 2 | 19 | 1 | | |
| 9 | 2 | 20 | 1 | | |
| 10 | 2 | 22 | 1 | | 1 |
| TEA | | | | | |
| 11 | 2 | 31 | 1 | | 2 |
| 12 | 2 | 35 | 1 | | |
| 13 | 2 | 43 | 1 | | |
| 14 | 2 | 45 | 1 | | 2 |
| STUMPS | | | | | |
| 15 | 2 | 54 | 1 | | 3 |
| 16 | 2 | 60 | 1 | | 4 |
| LUNCH | | | | | |
| 17 | 3 | 60 | 1 | | |
| 18 | 3 | 65 | 1 | | 5 |
| 19 | 3 | 69 | 1 | | 6 |
| 20 | 4 | 69 | 1 | | |
| 21 | 4 | 72 | 1 | | |
| 22 | 4 | 83 | 1 | | 8 |
| TEA | | | | | |

GILMOUR (NB ~~||||~~ 1, WIDES 1)

| O | M | R | W | 6s | 4s |
|---|---|---|---|---|---|
| 1 | 0 | 6 | 0 | | 1 |
| LUNCH | | | | | |
| 2 | 0 | 13 | 0 | | |
| 3 | 0 | 17 | 0 | | 2 |
| 4 | 0 | 29 | 0 | | 4 |
| TEA | | | | | |
| STUMPS | | | | | |
| LUNCH | | | | | |
| TEA | | | | | |

O'KEEFFE (NB 1, WIDES)

| O | M | R | W | 6s | 4s |
|---|---|---|---|---|---|
| 1 | 0 | 2 | 0 | | |
| 2 | 0 | 7 | 0 | | 1 |
| 3 | 1 | 7 | 0 | | |
| 4 | 1 | 9 | 0 | | |
| 5 | 2 | 9 | 0 | | |
| 6 | 2 | 12 | 0 | | |
| 7 | 2 | 14 | 0 | | |
| 8 | 2 | 15 | 0 | | |
| 9 | 2 | 21 | 0 | | 2 |
| TEA | | | | | |
| 10 | 2 | 28 | 0 | | 3 |
| 11 | 2 | 30 | 0 | | |
| 12 | 3 | 30 | 0 | | |
| 13 | 3 | 34 | 0 | | |
| 14 | 3 | 35 | 0 | | |
| 15 | 3 | 41 | 0 | | 4 |
| 16 | 3 | 44 | 0 | | |
| 17 | 3 | 46 | 0 | | |
| 18 | 3 | 49 | 0 | | 4 |
| STUMPS | | | | | |
| 19 | 3 | 56 | 0 | | 5 |
| 20 | 4 | 56 | 0 | | |
| 21 | 4 | 59 | 0 | | |
| 22 | 4 | 63 | 0 | | 6 |
| 23 | 4 | 64 | 0 | | |
| 24 | 4 | 65 | 0 | | |
| 25 | 4 | 73 | 0 | | 7 |
| LUNCH | | | | | |
| 26 | 5 | 73 | 1 | | |
| 27 | 5 | 80 | 1 | | 8 |
| TEA | | | | | |
| 28 | 5 | 90 | 2 | | 10 |
| 29 | 5 | 92 | 2 | | |
| 30 | 6 | 92 | 3 | | |
| 31 | 6 | 97 | 3 | | |
| 32 | 6 | 103 | 3 | | 11 |
| 33 | 6 | 108 | 3 | | 12 |

CHAPPELL (NB 11, WIDES)

| O | M | R | W | 6s | 4s |
|---|---|---|---|---|---|
| 1 | 0 | 3 | 0 | | – |
| STUMPS | | | | | |
| 2 | 1 | 3 | 0 | | |
| 3 | 1 | 6 | 0 | | |
| 4 | 1 | 8 | 0 | | |
| 5 | 1 | 11 | 0 | | |
| 6 | 1 | 16 | 0 | | 1 |
| LUNCH | | | | | |
| 7 | 2 | 16 | 0 | | |
| 8 | 2 | 18 | 1 | | |
| 9 | 2 | 21 | 1 | | |
| 10 | 2 | 23 | 1 | | |
| 11 | 3 | 23 | 1 | | |
| 12 | 4 | 23 | 1 | | |
| 13 | 5 | 23 | 1 | | |
| 14 | 6 | 23 | 1 | | |
| 15 | 6 | 29 | 1 | | 2 |
| 16 | 7 | 29 | 1 | | 2 |
| TEA | | | | | |

WALTERS (NB, WIDES)

| O | M | R | W | 6s | 4s |
|---|---|---|---|---|---|
| 1 | 0 | 7 | 0 | | 1 |
| 2 | 1 | 7 | 0 | | |
| 3 | 2 | 7 | 0 | | 1 |
| LUNCH | | | | | |
| TEA | | | | | |

EXTRAS

| B | LB | W | NB | TOTAL |
|---|---|---|---|---|
| | | | 1 | 1 |
| | | 1 | | 2 |
| 2 | | | 2 | 5 |
| | | | 3 | 6 |
| | | 2 | | 7 |
| | | | 4 | 8 |
| 4 | | | | 10 |
| | | | 5 | 11 |
| | | 3 | | 12 |
| 7 | | | | 15 |
| | | | 6 | 16 |
| | | | 7 | 17 |
| | 2 | | | 19 |
| | 3 | | | 20 |
| 8 | 4 | | | 22 |

# CRICKET MASTERMIND

*Or 'Never mind the answer, we can't understand the question'.* The Scene: The commentary box at Trent Bridge on the first day of the first Test. Brian Johnston has just taken over from John Arlott.

| | |
|---|---|
| BJ | I'll give you the details of the innings in a minute but I think probably that Fred's coming to the end of his spell so I want to leave you with this thought. Fred, I want from you, the next time we're on together, the names of six Somerset players who've captained their countries at cricket. <br><br> Right, now for the scoreboard *(reads scorecard)*. Fred's lighting his pipe so he can give that question a bit of thought. |
| FST | Well I can give you three. |
| BJ | Well, give three to go on with and come back with the other three. |
| FST | Close, Botham and Chappell. |
| BJ | Very good, you've got the three easiest ones. |
| FST & DM | Richards and Gavaskar. |
| FST | That's five. |
| BJ | All right, let's have number six before the play resumes. |
| DM | J. C. White. |
| BJ | No – er – J. C. White? We're going to have seven then. |
| FST | Oh, you've got the question wrong again Johnston. |
| BJ | There's another one you haven't got – he used to wear a Homburg hat when he kept wicket. I'll go on *(reads bowling analysis)*. John Woodcock started this in *The Times* the other day. He missed out one and I added an extra one for him which made six and now you've added one which made seven – and you still haven't got it. |
| WF | Richards hasn't captained in a Test match. |
| BJ | No, that's right; I think Richards is wrong in fact. Captain in a Test match was the question, so it is still six and you've still got the mystery man – I wonder if anyone at home can get it before Fred. |
| FST | The one with the big hat. |
| BJ | He wore a big Homburg hat behind the timbers. |
| FST | That's going back to your time. |
| BJ | It is indeed. He and Mr. J. Daniel, he wore a hat too like that. |

J. C. W. McBryan, S. G. U. Considine and who was that other chap with a long name – Critchley Salmonson. Those were the days! Right! (*laughing*) We're going to see Marshall now coming into Gower – and that's outside his leg stump. Fred's gone away absolutely flummoxed – he can't think of this sixth name and we'll wonder after tea if he comes back with it. 111 for three – the Boil has resumed the seat here.

|     |     |
| --- | --- |
|     | I don't know if you can get it. What are you laughing at? |
| TB  | I didn't get the question. |
| BJ  | Well, I'll give it to you – after this ball. Marshall coming in from the Radcliffe Road end to bowl to the left-handed Gower. He drives this one away square on the leg side and Haynes goes to field. He picks up and they don't come for a second. Just the one run. Gower goes up to 20 – 112 for three, England. Yes Fred? |
| FST | Richards captained the West Indies at Lord's last Friday. |
| WF  | Not in a Test match. |
| BJ  | Will those who didn't listen to the question please come again. I said captained their country in a Test match. It's really too bad when people can't listen. It's a very difficult one – he wore a floppy hat when he kept wicket. There is a lot of discussion going on in the back of the box. I'll reveal to you who it was in a few minutes. In comes Marshall now to bowl to Woolmer. And that one he turns round the corner, but once again Haynes is there and there is no run. You keep on leaning over, Fred, with fresh ideas – what is this one? |
| FST | Well, I still say Viv Richards has captained his country in a Test match. He's captain now! |
| BJ  | Oh dear – they were each appointed captain before a match started. |
| DM  | Jeremy Thorpe – a West Country man in a Homburg? |
| BJ  | Up comes Marshall now, to bowl to Woolmer – back to the cricket. And he pushes this one up towards mid-on and there's a slight misfield there by the substitute for Clive Lloyd, Parry, and that's one more run to Woolmer. He goes up now to 16, England 113 for three. Yes Fred? |
| FST | Your sixth man – delving into my memory bank. |
| BJ  | Called *Wisden*. |
| FST | Captained New Zealand and his name was Tom Lowry. |
| BJ  | T. C. Lowry – you're dead right, that's the mystery man. Well done, Fred. |
| JA  | He didn't say that I told him did he? (*from the back*) |
| BJ  | His memory bank was John Arlott. Anyway it is not a bad question. Thanks to John Woodcock, who unearthed it and got it wrong himself. How nice to get back to the cricket after all that – isn't it Trevor? |

# THE NEWCOMER
## ─── Tony Lewis ───

In the days when I was playing first-class cricket, I was aware that an elite band of ball-by-ball commentators was at large but, like most practising players, rarely had the chance to hear them work. Occasionally, at matches, the transistor radios in the crowd sent their commentaries booming across the field. Spectators were plugged in by one ear to those most popular personalities of the commentary box, and by one ear and two eyes to us. I remember having to retrieve a ball from the boundary three times in the same over. On the last time a red faced man, surrounded by icebox, binoculars, score-book, *Wisden*, umbrella, and radio to which he was attached by an earpiece, shouted at me: 'Hey. Tony, mate. D'y know what Alan Gibson just called your captaincy? He called it eso . . . something . . . . What was it Fred?'

Fred, his colleague, was similarly connected to the ball-by-ballers, and because his volume level was well turned up he shouted his reply so loudly that everyone stopped and listened. 'He called 'im eso-bloody-teric mate. That's what he called 'im: eso-bloody-teric.'

The first man turned back to me. 'Yes, Tony, mate: esoteric you are. Mind you, you don't look esoteric to me; y'look knackered.'

I record that with affection for Alan Gibson, a kindly commentator, who brought the delicious gift of language and style to the game of cricket. I got to know him better in the rugby season when we sidled up to each other in freezing press boxes to write up match reports, or shared a railway carriage to one of his favourite far western fields, Redruth, Truro or perhaps

Penzance. It was only when I learned that he was part of the team which commentated ball-by-ball on cricket that I decided, for the first time, to squeeze in a little listening to Test matches in the summer.

So, oddly enough I arrived at Arlott through Gibson. I had known John probably longer than Alan but he was always perched distantly on his scaffold throne for television, or on the roof-top of the Cardiff Athletic Club, savouring delicious prawn sandwiches with a glass of wine, and broadcasting of course.

I spent many hours with John Arlott roaming antique shops around the cricket circuit, picking up pieces of Sunderland lustre or glassware, or Stevengraphs or furniture. John supervised my first antique purchase, an oak chair from the Bown family of Pontypridd. There was time, too, to taste a little Veuvray at Turnbulls of Brighton, or a rich Rioja with Vintage Wines of Nottingham.

As soon as I heard John Arlott the commentator I knew that I would stay with the masses of listeners to the ball-by-ball men. His cricket knowledge, and his poet's art of condensing the actions and impulses of the cricketers into a few rich words of description, trapped me. Indeed, I have never escaped the web of exquisite language which Gibson and Arlott spun around me. With respect to others, they got me listening to *Test Match Special*.

I finished playing cricket in 1974 and continued my freelance work in writing, radio and televison. There was plenty to do, most varied work too – presenting a Saturday morning sports programme on radio, *Sport on Four*; presenting and interviewing a light entertainment show from Birmingham, *Saturday Night at The Mill*; presenting HTV's *Sports Arena* programme from Cardiff; and writing as rugby and cricket correspondent for the *Sunday Telegraph*. I mention all these to make the point that when Peter Baxter asked me in 1979 if I would like to try some commentary on cricket, I was not simply a raw recruit straight out of cricket. Even so, the idea of commentary brought on an almost nightmare fear of failure. Most of my broadcasting had been done from scripts. I had never been left alone with my mind, which I recognised as an extremely slow moving, get-there-in-the-end sort of mind. In fact I had made two stumbling attempts at commentary before, which had put me off.

Once I had been flown in a helicopter up above the bustle and excitement of the British Open Golf Championships at Turnberry. In five minutes, all I spluttered in a microphone was: 'Ahead of me is the famous lighthouse and there is the sea and the green grass . . . and now I'm going over the green grass over the sea and the famous white lighthouse is underneath me . . . and now I'm coming back in from over the sea to the green grass and behind is the famous white lighthouse.' Back on the ground my producer was shaking his head.

Another optimistic producer asked me to commentate on part of the Arts Festival which accompanied the Commonwealth Games in Edmonton in 1978. In one of the city's squares an African dancer was to climb a sixty-foot wooden pole and dance at the top. How? Well, I was poised with my microphone ready to tell everyone that. Yet, by the time I had come out with 'writhing muscles, his black silk skin, marble thighs entwined around the pole, and now he is performing all sorts of gyrations with his buttocks at the top,' this producer shook his head too, suggesting that radio in the seventies was not yet ready for my particular brand of eroticism.

However, on a sunny day in June I took my place behind the microphone at Edgbaston; West Indies were bowling to India in the Prudential World Cup competition, and I proceeded to speak twice as quickly as Andy Roberts was bowling. Every so often there was a message from Peter Baxter, master controlling from London: 'Would A. R. Lewis mind telling us the score occasionally?'

On this debut day, fate, or clever selection, had placed me alongside John Arlott. I hardly noticed him. I had put on blinkers and I clung to the game's technicalities which I understood best. Was it sunny, or cold, or cloudy? Was it Sunday, or Monday, or Tuesday? Oh! and what was the score? Of all these facts the nation went uninformed. They were tuned into a ranting Welshman, or was it an Indian, and all the time the persevering Baxter was calling out, 'Would Lewis have the kindness to let us know the score?'

Later in the day I ventured the question to John Arlott: 'How did it go?' He dropped the corners of his mouth in the familiar scowl, the thick eyebrows were raised in thought and the eyes twinkled out the answer: 'You weren't good. In the first twenty minutes you used two words which you would never have used to me in conversation. You never call the bat the willow, and the verb you used was so long I can't even remember it. Look, don't broadcast to them; talk to them. Talk to the blind man at home, who, once upon a time, could see.'

Suitably chastened I moved on and in August came the proper debut, a Test match at Leeds. What a narrow commentary box! How wide Fred Trueman was! How splendidly Brian Johnston kept the pot boiling and stopped everyone taking themselves too seriously! How natural it all was!

As umpire Dickie Bird was undergoing his usual trauma of whether play should start in blistering sunshine or not, I meant to say on the air, 'What the spectators need now is a quick, clear decision.' What I actually said was, 'What the spectators need now is a queer. . . .' In leapt Brian Johnston with, 'Oh, no, ARL! It's not going to be "welcome to another gay day at Headingley is it?"'

By the Tuesday Peter Baxter was screaming uncontrollably down the line from London. 'Do tell that so-and-so Lewis to give us the so-and-so score.'

Relaxed as commentary should be there is a lot of learning to be done. Alan McGilvray issued me the stern complaint that I used the word 'we' when describing England, and that bias was not part of a commentator's art. I accepted the criticism but am still only at the half-way stage, referring instead to W'England.

If those were lessons, there is also experience to gather. Doing ball-by-ball commentaries from Bombay during the Jubilee Test match in 1980 was a rare experience. Henry Blofeld and I sat in a large glass box, beautifully air conditioned. The glass was so thick that it was impossible to hear a single crowd reaction through it. Henry began his commentary and I suddenly realised that I could not hear him. He was in some discomfort too and it turned out that he could not hear himself either. The earphones were just like ear muffs. 'We can't hear a thing,' pleaded Henry to our two women engineers. 'Ah! But you have no need to hear,' one gleamed so charmingly. 'Sound is coming out OK.'

'Yes,' insisted Henry, 'but I must hear what I am saying.'

'You wanna hear what you are saying? Oh dear! Indian commentators never want to hear what they are saying.'

Her eyes gleamed with misunderstanding but next day she fixed the head sets and we were aware at last that there was a cricket match going on.

A lot of my friends say to me, 'What's it like in the commentary box?' I guess the short answer is that, architecturally, the boxes all differ slightly and have their special characteristics. What you find inside the box then depends on the listeners' habit of sending in presents. But, if you are looking for the spirit of the box, then I believe it is the same everywhere, no matter which commentators are involved. The Penates, the household gods, are itinerant.

Let's talk architecture. The boxes are not works of Christopher Wren, nor are they based on the original drawings of Michelangelo. They are constructed on a primeval building conception – the wooden hut! Sometimes they take the form of two or three wooden huts joined together.

Old Trafford has a box of simple but practical accommodation, with a hole in the wall leading through the windings of the scorebox to box number two. The hole is about two feet off the ground and it requires an athletic doubling-up of the trunk to thread a way through. Whereas Chris Martin-Jenkins can throw up a hurdler's leg, lower his nose to his toe, and leap through like David Hemery (or is it John Cleese?), Fred Trueman is a larger lad altogether. He can be heard wrestling through the darkness of the middle area and then be seen edging backwards through the hole like a miner working a two-foot seam in reverse! Don Mosey, unruffled and aldermanic, is wise enough never to attempt the exercise.

Trent Bridge is what Arlott calls 'cool and civilised', which probably means that all the windows will open! Edgbaston puts us just a partition away from the television commentators. It is a tip-toeing job at the back of the box, worried floor managers saying 'Shhhh! Jim's on', or 'Westy's doing an interview', or 'Richie's doing his highlights' – which does not mean that he is touching up his old grey fox hair-do.

Headingley is the box with the restricted vision. The roof-top of the grandstand in which we are positioned blocks out the sky like a visor and the limit of the commentator's descriptions is a row of trees (whose variety still remains unknown despite many a personal speculation from Henry Blofeld) and the red-slated roofs of the houses which curl around the ground in many streets. Once you have called them Edwardian red brick, what do you say next? Because of the roof cover, the commentary game at Leeds is always a five-day floodlit event inside the box: electric light is on all the time. The box is a narrow corridor which seats six or seven bodies side by side. A perambulation along the back of the seats is unwise, unless you enjoy putting your foot in a Cornhill packed lunch, ramming the chicken into the gateaux and treating your shoes to a coating of mayonnaise.

At Lord's and The Oval the boxes are positioned on the flat roof towers of the pavilions. That gives commentators of all varieties the opportunity to chat on the concourse behind the boxes, especially at The Oval where again we share with the television boys. It can be quite a social occasion, especially in pleasant sunshine, and one of the arts, no better performed than by Brian Johnston, is of lunching in an upright position, hacking through the packed lunch with plastic knife and fork and yet still keeping a steady glass available for that phantom pourer of highly considered trifles, T.E. Bailey.

*Trevor Bailey, pourer of 'highly considered trifles', at The Oval with Brian Johnston*

It was at Lord's in the Gillette Cup of 1980 that the least comfortable of commentary jobs befell me. I was asked to perform the duty of informing listeners to Radio 2 all day how the game was going. There is a small box, locked away all on its own, where you are imprisoned throughout the day. Every so often a voice perks up from Broadcasting House, 'Could you give us forty seconds for the next sports desk,' or perhaps 'a minute for the news'. This is a chore brilliantly accomplished by Chris Martin-Jenkins and Henry Blofeld in particular. They are wizards of the forty-second summary; they have raised it to an art form. All I did was to visit the nation with a great deal of confusion. It was now, not only a question of 'Give 'em the score Lewis,' but also 'Who the hell is playing? Try telling them that.'

Statistics, to me, are the greatest single irrelevance in the game of cricket. The height of obscenity are the John Player Sunday League averages, a worthless bunch of figures if ever there was one. But, I concede, the names of the combatants and the score are fairly important. W. Frindall persists in his uphill task with me.

Being shut in that tiny box on a roasting afternoon, away from the others, was like being Alec Guiness shut in that tin shed in the film *Bridge over the River Kwai*. When I was let out after eight inserts into the Pete Murray show, a hundred into *Sport on Two*, and many sawn-off minute pieces into the News, I staggered across the flat roof, blinked my eyes and gulped in outside air before wobbling off to Paddington to catch the train home to Wales. I proceeded to talk in frantic forty second bursts to my travelling companion who left the train slightly bemused at Newport.

The gifts addressed to the ball-by-ball team usually come via Brian Johnston. Brian acts as postmaster-general, chief sorter, taster of toffees and acknowledger of all goodies. Thousands write for autographs but I suppose what surprised the Newcomer most was the honest thanks for the commentaries which come in from all parts of the world. This can take the form of a seed cake, cream buns, chocolates or tins of toffees, or cases of champagne, the last of which I noticed early on is the one serious weakness shared by the whole team – and how rude of me if I had not joined in.

I have been amazed by the reaction of people from all over the world to Test match commentaries. I was once telephoned at the Lord's commentary box from Saudi Arabia: 'This is Chris Syer, remember we first met when you came with MCC to play Singapore. Well look, Tony, we have all been waiting all day for our commentary spell, and we only get ten minutes. Now it has the devil to rain. We have four minutes left of our allocation. Can't you do something to get them out there, or just say hello to us: we are sitting out in roasting sunshine around the radio.' I passed the message on to Brian Johnston who was talking on the air at the time, and he sent good wishes out East, speculating as he did on the nature of playing conditions in the desert areas of the world. To the next Test came a parcel containing a photograph of the golf course where Chris Syer and his friends play. It was rough dried-up earth with odd flags stuck in it. His last line was: 'Brian Johnston asked what the cricket conditions are like. Well . . . just take up the flags and then you'll know.' Not a blade of grass to be seen.

Lastly, to the spirit of the box. I can see that everyone who sits behind a microphone high above a Test match feels the privilege of being the eyes for so many who cannot be there. Every commentator loves the game. I am sure that that comes over. Everyone admires the players, and the two summarisers, Fred Trueman and Trevor Bailey, respect the highest standards of the game, and will know very quickly if we are being treated to the authentic Test match piece or a bad imitation, and they will say so.

I have played the role of all-rounder on the team. I have done close-of-play summaries, those short Radio 2 reports, ball-by-ball commentary proper, and have also stood in for Fred or Trevor when they have been unable to be there: a sort of have-voice-will-travel role. Indeed it was at Manchester that Chris Martin-Jenkins rang through to say that he would be late arriving at the ground. He had unluckily been involved in a road accident. John Helm was producer that day and he whisked me straight out of the press tent to fill in for Jenko for twenty minutes. As I prepared to sit in, Trevor Bailey informed the listeners of the late substitution and asked that they should be patient for a few seconds while he made a note of my number and inspected the studs of my boots.

Now, as one Newcomer begins, the master retires. 1980 was John Arlott's last summer of commentary. We had dinner at Leeds when he was moved to advise me, 'Don't want too much and don't try too hard in this commentary game, just talk to them.'

He stepped out of the commentary box for the last time at Lord's in the Gillette Cup final. Why had he decided to make his departure so final? Surely he could come back; there must be more Arlott for us. Surely, there was too much romance left in cricket, I said to him, just to leave it like that?

He made the pause, set the scowl beneath the kindly eyes, sipped his claret, swilled a little around his palate and replied, 'What's more romantic than the clean break?'

How do we follow that?

# A MATCH AT HEADQUARTERS
## Brian Johnston

**Thurs**

The first day of a Lord's Test always starts early at our house in St John's Wood. John Woodcock – *The Times'* cricket correspondent and now editor of *Wisden* – stays with us and brings up the papers and a cup of tea at some unearthly hour. We then discuss the prospects for the match with a special eye on the weather. Our best guide as to whether it has rained overnight is the state of our Yorkie's (Mini) paws after she has had her morning trip round the garden. On Thursday the weather was blustery and cloudy, and unusually on a first day there was not the steady stream of people passing our house with their lunch bags, cushions and rugs. So the indications were that there might be interruptions of play and a non-capacity crowd.

I always aim to be at the ground by 10 o'clock in order to savour the unique atmosphere of a first morning at Lord's. This year the crowds outside Grace's Gate were smaller than usual, but inside on the forecourt behind the 'Q' and Tavern stands there were hundreds of members and ticket holders waiting to greet friends or spot the celebrities. Many people make an annual pilgrimage to Lord's especially for this, and it is amazing how many people you 'haven't met for years' turn up – plus of course the many old Test and county players who get invited by MCC. Very noticeable these days are the number of red and yellow MCC ties that are worn by members. Up to 1954 this was considered *de rigueur*. But as president of MCC in that year Charles Cobham started to wear *his* tie, others soon followed suit.

After reserving a seat in the Tavern stand for my wife I spotted my first celebrity, Gerry – the greatest all-rounder in the world – Gomez. He had

*B.J. and 'Sir' Frederick in the box at Lord's*

flown over with his wife from Trinidad especially for the occasion – proof of the pull of a Lord's Test, even for overseas players. Gerry has the unique record of having been a selector, umpire and broadcaster in one and the same Test match – West Indies v Australia at Georgetown in 1965.

It was soon time to make my way up to our commentary box on the left of the top balcony of the pavilion. It's quite a climb – five flights up and two floors directly above the visitors' dressing-room. We have hinted to MCC for years that a lift might be a good idea, but so far without success – much to John Arlott's disgust! The box is spacious and comfortable with a magnificent view looking down over mid-off at the batsman at the Nursery end. Our producer Peter Baxter, the engineers and the bearded wonder Bill Frindall were already there. The box can sit five of us in a row, so the engineers had already placed five microphones in position. Peter was pinning up the day's duty roster for the commentators, and Bill was unloading books, pens, pencils, rubbers, watches and a Thermos out of his many brief-cases. On the baize-covered desks were piles of letters and one or two parcels obviously containing sweets. I quickly sorted out my letters in case any needed to be answered over the air and noted the names of the sweet senders so that we could acknowledge and thank them. One of my letters was from the Ministry of Defence and for one ghastly moment I thought it must be my call-up papers. But it was from someone who worked there saying that during the Old Trafford Test two submarines would be visiting Manchester! Could one or two members of their crews visit us in the commentary box? A leg pull, surely? Or do submarines go up the Manchester Canal?

Our first visitor was Bill Alley, happily back on the Test match panel. He always adds gaiety to the rather serious Test atmosphere. He had climbed up to apologise to Backers for unintentionally cutting him dead earlier in the morning. A nice gesture from a busy man on such an important occasion. Soon the box was full of all the other commentators and as we sipped our morning coffee I once again reflected on how lucky I am to work in such a happy atmosphere with so many nice people.

Ian Botham is obviously a lucky spinner and when England won the toss and batted we had a thrilling morning's play to describe with Gooch playing some magnificent strokes. As Trevor (Mr Jingle) Bailey said of him: 'Fine player – beautiful strokes – top class – he's grown up.' Two of our early prophecies came true: play was held up for fifteen minutes due to bad light and Lord's surprisingly was only about two-thirds full. It did fill up a bit later – 18,000 was the official crowd figure. But it is a strange thing: many people cannot believe there are ever any tickets available at Lord's and so don't bother to find out – hence empty seats when, for instance, 6,000 *unreserved* seats are available each day through the gates.

During the morning the tantalising smell of cooking invaded the box from the committee dining-room and kitchen immediately below us. Here the fabulous Nancy and her gallant band of helpers provide the lunches for players, officials etc., and it is universally considered to be the finest table on the first-class circuit. The morning commentary was also interrupted by a series of clicks from a photographer from *The Sunday Times*. They were doing a special feature on John Arlott. He is certainly going out in style with countless dinners, presentations and articles about him. It is as well that it is all being recorded. There will never be another like him.

The commentators lunch in a number of ways. Some go off to private boxes, others eat the excellent fare sent up by the sponsors, Cornhill. Personally I always try to join my family for a picnic on the grass lawn behind the Warner stand. Here on a fine day are lots of similar picnics, people sitting on the grass or on the brick wall alongside the lawn. This is one of the pleasantest features of a Lord's Test and it is remarkable the number of friends one sees lurking behind a ham sandwich or a glass of cold white wine. Very civilised. One regular visitor to the lawn is the Rév – Hugh Pickles, captain and demon bowler of the Oxford clergy. This year he was accompanied by a Preb, and a Canon – a distinguished trinity. He had had to cancel his early morning Communion that day in order to get to the match and had pinned up a notice in the church porch announcing that he would be going on his annual pilgrimage to LOuRDeS!

The afternoon and evening brought triumph to Gooch with his really great first Test hundred, a massive display of defence from Tavare, and the inevitable England collapse from 165 for one to 232 for seven. Botham was out to the first ball of the last over and could perhaps be considered unlucky. At the end of the previous over the clock had nearly reached 6.30 p.m. As decreed by the law, Bill Alley from square leg walked 'at his normal pace' to the stumps before checking whether there was time to start another over.

But being Bill Alley, even in a Test match he could not resist a bit of a leg-pull. Although he walked at his normal pace he put on an exaggerated limp as if he was never going to reach the stumps. Having done so he then pretended to take off the bails. Seeing this, Botham turned to go back to the pavilion. 'Sorry, skipper,' shouted Bill. 'There's time for one more over.' No wonder Botham played across and missed the next ball to be given out lbw by Bill!

In our summing up of the day's play the outstanding features were Gooch's innings, fine fast bowling by Holding, and the excellence of the pitch provided by groundsman Jim Fairbrother. We interviewed Gooch in the box after his innings and I was most struck by his humility and his pride in playing for England: 'I don't mind where I bat in the order so long as I am in the team.'

## Friday

I was at the ground again early as before play started we had to record a session of answering overseas listeners' questions. Chris Martin-Jenkins was in the chair reading out the questions and it was lucky for us that it *was* a recording. One of the questions was from someone with rather a rude sounding name. As Chris read it out someone (not me of course) started to giggle – Chris dried up and we all burst out laughing. In theatrical language we 'corpsed' and, try as he could, every time Chris read out the name we all burst out again. Had it been live I don't know what would have happened. Chris finally solved the problem by only giving the first name of the questioner and we were able to give our answer. The engineers subsequently put the laughter on to a separate tape. So next time play gets boring in a Test, we can always play it as a background to the commentary.

The weather was fine if still rather cool and there was a full house. And a splendid day we had, with a comic last-wicket partnership of 24 by Willis and Hendrick in England's final total of 269. The day then belonged to Richards and Haynes, Richards playing one of the best Test innings I have ever seen. The power, the timing and variety of his strokes were breathtaking. As a commentator I longed to have my *Roget's Thesaurus* alongside me as I quickly began to run out of superlatives. What a difference it makes to a commentary when batsmen are playing strokes and not maiden overs. As someone wrote to me in a letter, people don't come to watch great *Tests* – they come to watch great *innings*. The way in which Viv Richards placed the ball wide of the fielders reminded us all of Don Bradman.

In the commentary box some of us missed our lunch as we were answering telephone calls in 'Call the Commentators' during the interval. Most of the questions were about the number of overseas players in county cricket, the pros and cons of the 100-over limit in the Schweppes Championship, and what has happened to England's batting. We also talked to band leader, impresario and cricket lover Vic Lewis. Last year he collected over 2,000 cricket ties which he was going to have photographed for a book to be called *The Result is a Tie*. Each tie was labelled with the name of its owner, and the club or society. Unfortunately Vic was burgled recently and the ties were flung all over the place. The labels were separated from their ties, so now poor Vic has to start all over again.

During the day I met Denis Compton, Tom Graveney and Charlie Barnett, all highly complimentary about Gooch's positive stroke play but predictably critical of the prodders and pushers. I couldn't resist asking Charlie why he failed to make his hundred before lunch against the Australians at Trent Bridge in 1938. You may remember that with one over to go he was 98 not out. He went up to Len Hutton, his young partner who was due to take strike, and said: 'Look. I have taken off my batting gloves. We have put on 169 for nought – enough to give them indigestion during lunch. Don't try to give me the bowling so that I can get my hundred.' So Len played a maiden over, and Charlie reached his hundred with the first ball after lunch.

It is more or less impossible to be at Lord's and not run into Gubby Allen –

*The view for commentators off the air at Lord's, in the shadow of the box*

he always seems to be there. Not surprising really. As a past president and treasurer of MCC and now a trustee, he has an honorary key to the back door of his garden which opens on to Lord's! He was in good form from having just recently done a round of golf in one under his age (77).

## Saturday

Lord's was once again full and the gates closed for the second day running. The weather, except for a five-minute shower, was kind; and the cricket was full of incident – an ideal day for commentary. First of all there was Willis, who, as at Trent Bridge, bowled with renewed life and vigour at a very fast pace. He was in fact the only English bowler to get any life out of the placid pitch. He started the day with a personal vendetta against the nightwatch-man Croft, who had bowled one or two bouncers when Willis was batting. So Willis retaliated with two unpleasant short balls to Croft. He was spoken to by Barry Meyer, who then went over and said something to Ian Botham. This looked like a warning but at the time it seemed as if Barry had forgotten the new law whereby the umpire must *first* call no-ball and *then* warn the bowler, captain and other umpire. Over the weekend it was announced that Willis had *not* been warned. I wonder then what they were talking about? The hero of the day was Desmond Haynes who, like Richards, made a hundred in his first Test at Lord's – 184 to be exact, out of the final score of 518. What a fine marathon of an innings – a mixture of concentration and patience and the ability to score off the bad ball. It was nice to see Lloyd at his best in spite of his bad right hand. How beautifully he picked up that six to mid-wicket off Underwood. And how sad, as he walked back, to think that this must be his last Test innings at Lord's.

I have said and seen many strange things during a Test match, but none stranger than when Geoff Boycott came on to bowl. Just before he ran up he reversed his cap so that the peak was down his neck, just like the old-fashioned motor-cyclists used to do. He did it at least three times. Why he did it I just don't know. Anyway, it made his many supporters in the crowd roar with laughter and possibly affected the batsmen's concentration. There was also the strange occurrence of the second new ball going out of shape after only four deliveries which surely must be a record. Something else I won't forget was the weary look on Derek Underwood's face as he bowled Andy Roberts to take his only wicket for 108 runs. I couldn't help wondering if he felt that he had bowled his last ball for England. We shall see. Incidentally, quite a percentage of our post contained complaints about the reinstatement of the Kent Packer players. Some even said it was one of the reasons for the disappointing gates at Trent Bridge, and the first day at Lord's. Both Bob Taylor and David Bairstow may well have been harshly treated. But my goodness Alan Knott kept wicket well, though he seemed to have lost his old powers of improvisation in his batting. We all agreed in the box that England are no longer the great fielding side that they have been over the last two years or so. They are now much slower and heavy footed and sadly missed the dash and skill of Randall and Gower. But could even they have stemmed Richards's strokes?

During the lunch interval we had one of our celebrity spots. In this we talk to a famous personality who loves cricket but has achieved his fame in some other field. We were lucky that our choice for this Saturday was the 94-year-old playwright and author Ben Travers, who sadly died at the end of the year. Without turning a hair he climbed up to the top of the pavilion and entertained us and the listeners to 25 minutes of pure magic. He reminisced about players and matches he had seen. Without a note he quoted detailed scores – in 1896 when he saw W. G. Grace make 24 in the Oval Test, or in 1902 at The Oval when he watched the famous innings of 104 by G. L. Jessop when England won by one wicket. It was a fantastic performance by Ben and except for an occasional question to prompt him it was a superb monologue – funny, nostalgic, and memorable in every sense. I had a letter from him afterwards saying how much he enjoyed it, apologising for not letting any of us get a word in edgeways. I could assure him that we were too spellbound to speak – and as for enjoyment, the reactions from listeners has been wildly enthusiastic, clamouring for more.

**Monday**

We had left the ground on Saturday encouraged by a bright start by Gooch and Boycott and for another 35 minutes they continued to bat confidently. But at 51 for nought, at 12.05 p.m., down came the rain and there was no more play for the day. So it was 'chat-show' time. In addition to answering listeners' letters throughout the lunch interval we kept talking for 3 hours 54 minutes, reading letters, telling stories and interviewing various celebrities. The first was Bertie Clarke, the old West Indies leg-spinner who used to bowl so effectively for the BBC; Tom Graveney came up to get two score-cards signed and was immediately kidnapped and interviewed for half an hour; and Ian Botham kindly came up to talk to us. He confirmed that he was thoroughly enjoying being captain of England and did not feel it would affect his play. He turned down our entreaties not to risk injury by playing soccer for Scunthorpe and revealed that he would keep his beard since his wife had now grown to like it. The chairman of selectors, Alec Bedser, also paid us a visit and was with us until, stuck for any more questions, I asked him: 'What would you like me to ask you *now?'* – something I don't think I have ever asked anyone in all my 35 years of interviewing. The afternoon was lightened and honoured by the traditional Monday visit of Her Majesty The Queen. In recent years she has not had much luck with the weather at Lord's. Not, I suspect, that she minds too much, as the Royal Family are not great cricket watchers, though Prince Philip used to bowl useful off-breaks and The Prince of Wales once rode to the wicket on a horse. The Queen's two longest conversations were with the tall Joel Garner and Bill Alley. With the latter the conversation appeared to be rather one-sided! The game was then soon called off for the day and it was also announced that Ian Botham would captain England in the next three Tests. In celebration the door of the box suddenly opened and Trevor Bailey, in his role of butler, made an opportune entrance with a tray containing glasses and two bottles of champagne. What perfect timing! Typical of his batting.

It had certainly been a marathon day for us all in the box and I only hope that we lived up to our dubious reputation of being at our best when it's raining! The many letters we quoted ranged on a number of subjects, the 100-over limit as usual looming large. A writer also corrected me having credited Flanagan and Allen with the joke about the difference between a stoat and a weasel (one is stoately different – the other weasely distinguished). He claimed the originators were that splendid double act of Murray and Mooney. He was probably right, but I definitely heard it once when seeing the Crazy Gang. A lady writer also sent me a splendid story about a titled lady who enquired of a small hotel where she was going to stay in Germany whether her room was close to the W.C. The hotelier, not understanding, checked with the local schoolmaster who told him that W.C. stood for Wesleyan Chapel. So the hotelier wrote back, as follows:

The W.C. is situated about seven miles from your lodgings in the centre of the forest, amid lovely surroundings and is open on Sundays, Thursdays and Fridays.

This is unfortunate if you are in the habit of going regularly but you will no doubt be glad to know that a number of people take their lunch with them and make a day of it; others who cannot spare the time go by car and arrive just in time, as they are in a great hurry and cannot wait. As there are many visitors I advise you to go early. The accommodation is very good and there are 20 seats, but should you be last, there is plenty of standing room also. I would advise your ladyship to pay a visit on Thursday as there is an organ accompaniment. The acoustics are excellent on the premises, even the most delicate sounds are quite audible. I shall be delighted to reserve the best seats for your ladyship and have the pleasure of escorting you around.

P.S. My wife and I have not been able to get there for eight months and it pains us very much, but it is a long way from home. Hymn sheets are provided at the door.

And so to the end of yet another disappointing day's play, England still needing 198 to make West Indies bat again. The skies were threatening as I left Lord's and by 7.30 there was an absolute deluge with hailstones whitening our garden lawn – as I gather they also did the ground at Lord's.

I must say that when we were *not* talking during the rain I missed my word games with the Alderman – especially as I was in the lead after Trent Bridge. On the other hand, during our chats on the air Fred and I had our usual mini-quiz contest. He stumped me with, 'What two England captains were born in the West Indies?' I got Sir Pelham Warner straightaway but never realised that Lord Harris had been born in Trinidad. However, I clean bowled Fred with, 'In what Test were two England players over 50 years of age?' Like me he answered one easily enough – Wilfred Rhodes. But only some prompting from John Arlott gave him the second – George Gunn. They both played at Kingston in 1930 when Wilfred was $52\frac{1}{2}$ and George nearly 51.

**Tuesday**

Thanks to Jim Fairbrother and his young team of helpers, play started on time. They deserve nothing but praise for their work throughout the match. Gooch again impressed, once hitting a short ball from Holding for six. He was out for 47 and Tavare for six after another completely defensive innings. Boycott and Woolmer were beginning to look as if they and England might be able to save the day. But soon after lunch another thunderstorm shook Lord's – the lightning was terrifying and reverberated round our box. Lord's was soon awash and the match was called off, as a draw, with Tom Graveney making Viv Richards the man of the match. It was a disappointment for the West Indies but a relief for England, though they might well have made a draw of it without the help of the rain. What has gone wrong with the Lord's and Wimbledon weather? A writer from the north suggests that Lord's has now a worse record than Old Trafford. He could well be right. It was certainly sad for all the spectators. Only the seagulls nesting once again in the grandstand roof appeared unaffected by the weather. For us it was frustrating but nevertheless enjoyable, thanks to the happy atmosphere in the box and the encouragement from so many kind listeners who either write to us or send us so much welcome refreshment. One of these brought round an enormous tin of toffees to my house before play. We gratefully consumed a fair proportion of them but sent the remainder round to a children's home in Abercorn Place. But the gift enabled me to trap Trevor Bailey by asking him a question just after he had inserted a very sticky toffee into his mouth. For once his defence had been penetrated! I left Lord's a happy man.

## ENGLAND   1ST INNINGS • WEST INDIES 2ND TEST at LORD'S, LONDON, on 19, 20, 21, 23, 24 JUNE, 1980.   Toss: ENGLAND

| IN | OUT | MINS | No. | BATSMAN | HOW OUT | BOWLER | RUNS | WKT | TOTAL | 6s | 4s | BALLS | NOTES ON DISMISSAL |
|---|---|---|---|---|---|---|---|---|---|---|---|---|---|
| 11.30 | 3.56 | 211 | 1 | GOOCH | LBW | HOLDING | 123 | 2 | 165 | 1 | 17 | 162 | FIRST TO 1000 RUNS. (1st in TESTS. Misjudged line. |
| 11.30 | 12.11 | 26 | 2 | BOYCOTT | Ct MURRAY | HOLDING | 8 | 1 | 20 | · | 1 | 15 | Late on stroke – edged defensive jab to 'keeper. |
| 12.13 | 6.06 | 294 | 3 | TAVARÉ | Ct GREENIDGE | HOLDING | 42 | 5 | 220 | · | 2 | 202 | Edged offside push to 2nd slip. |
| 3.58 | 5.09 | 51 | 4 | WOOLMER | Ct KALLICHARRAN | GARNER | 15 | 3 | 190 | · | 2 | 37 | Misjudged bounce – edged to 1st slip. Aimed square drive. |
| 5.11 | 5.55 | 44 | 5 | GATTING | BOWLED | HOLDING | 18 | 4 | 219 | · | 2 | 47 | Missed drive at fast, straight ball. Aimed across line. |
| 5.58 | 6.29 | 31 | 6 | BOTHAM * | LBW | GARNER | 8 | 7 | 232 | · | 2 | 19 | Missed on-drive – first ball of final over of 1st day. |
| 6.08 | 6.21 | 13 | 7 | UNDERWOOD | LBW | GARNER | 3 | 6 | 231 | · | · | 9 | Missed forward defensive stroke – front leg. |
| 6.23 | 12.18 | 54 | 8 | WILLEY | BOWLED | HOLDING | 4 | 9 | 245 | · | · | 33 | Beaten by pace – off stump out. |
| 11.30 | 12.10 | 40 | 9 | KNOTT † | Ct GARNER | HOLDING | 9 | 8 | 244 | · | 1 | 36 | Edged lifting ball low to gully's left – superb catch. |
| 12.12 | 12.36 | 24 | 10 | WILLIS | BOWLED | GARNER | 14 | 10 | 269 | 1 | 1 | 13 | Yorked behind legs. |
| 12.20 | (12.36) | 16 | 11 | HENDRICK | NOT OUT | | 10 | | | · | 2 | 12 | |
| | | | | * CAPTAIN  † WICKET-KEEPER | | EXTRAS | b 4  lb 1  w 4  nb 6 | | 15 | 1 6  5  30 | | 585 balls (including 12 no balls) | |

TOTAL  (OFF 95.3 OVERS IN 410 MIN.)  269 all out at 12.36pm 2nd DAY

13 OVERS 5 BALLS/HOUR
2.82 RUNS/OVER
46 RUNS/100 BALLS

| BOWLER | O | M | R | W | |nb/w| HRS | OVERS | RUNS |
|---|---|---|---|---|---|---|---|---|
| ROBERTS | 18 | 3 | 50 | 0 | 1/- | 1 | 14 | 38 |
| HOLDING | 28 | 11 | 67 | 6‡ | 1/- | 2 | 12 | 47 |
| GARNER | 24.3 | 8 | 36 | 4 | 3/- | 3 | 17 | 50 |
| CROFT | 20 | 3 | 77 | 0 | 8/- | 4 | 12 | 37 |
| RICHARDS | 5 | 1 | 24 | 0 | | 5 | 16 | 40 |
| | | | | | 15 | 6 | 14 | 23 |
| | 95.3 | 26 | 269 | 10 | | | | |

2ND NEW BALL taken at 11.46am 2ND DAY
– ENGLAND 235-7 after 85 overs.

| RUNS | MINS | OVERS | LAST 50 (in mins) |
|---|---|---|---|
| 50 | 78 | 18.1 | 78 |
| 100 | 143 | 32.4 | 65 |
| 150 | 207 | 48.2 | 64 |
| 200 | 291 | 68.4 | 84 |
| 250 | 397 | 92.5 | 106 |

BLSP at 11.45am – 15 minutes lost.
LUNCH: 77-1  GOOCH 48* (105 min)  TAVARÉ 15* (77 min)
OFF 23 OVERS IN 105 MINUTES

TEA: 167-2  TAVARÉ 27* (197 min)  WOOLMER 1* (12 min)
OFF 52 OVERS IN 225 MINUTES

STUMPS: 232-7  WILLEY 1* (6 min)
(1ST DAY)  OFF 81-1 OVERS IN 344 MINUTES

‡ WEST INDIES RECORD ANALYSIS AT LORD'S

| WKT | PARTNERSHIP | | RUNS | MINS |
|---|---|---|---|---|
| 1st | Gooch | Boycott | 20 | 26 |
| 2nd | Gooch | Tavaré | 145 | 184 |
| 3rd | Tavaré | Woolmer | 25 | 51 |
| 4th | Tavaré | Gatting | 29 | 44 |
| 5th | Tavaré | Botham | 1 | 8 |
| 6th | Botham | Underwood | 11 | 13 |
| 7th | Botham | Willey | 1 | 6 |
| 8th | Willey | Knott | 12 | 40 |
| 9th | Willey | Willis | 1 | 6 |
| 10th | Willis | Hendrick | 24 | 16 |
| | | | 269 | |

## WEST INDIES   1ST INNINGS   In reply to ENGLAND's 269 all out

| IN | OUT | MINS | No. | BATSMAN | HOW OUT | BOWLER | RUNS | WKT | TOTAL | 6s | 4s | BALLS | NOTES ON DISMISSAL |
|---|---|---|---|---|---|---|---|---|---|---|---|---|---|
| 12.48 | 2.14 | 48 | 1 | GREENIDGE | LBW | BOTHAM | 25 | 1 | 37 | · | 5 | 37 | Aimed vast drive – misread swing. |
| 12.48 | 4.32 | 490 | 2 | HAYNES | LBW | BOTHAM | 184‡ | 7 | 469 | 1 | 27 | 395 | Missed pull at short ball that kept low. ⟩ HUNDREDS ON FIRST |
| 2.17 | 6.04 | 196 | 3 | RICHARDS | Ct SUB (G.R. DILLEY) | WILLEY | 145 | 2 | 260 | 1 | 25 | 159 | Mistimed semi-sweep to short square-leg. ⟩ APPEARANCE AT LORD'S |
| 6.06 | 11.39 | 18 | 4 | CROFT | RUN OUT (GATTING) | | 0 | 3 | 275 | · | · | 12 | Backed up to Haynes' straight drive off a no ball. |
| 11.41 | 12.56 | 77 | 5 | KALLICHARRAN | Ct KNOTT | WILLIS | 15 | 4 | 326 | · | 2 | 64 | Faint off-side edge to outswinger (2nd ball with changed ball). |
| 12.58 | 1.14 | 7 | 6 | BACCHUS | Ct GOOCH | WILLIS | 0 | 5 | 330 | · | · | 6 | Edged defensive back stroke (3rd slip). |
| 1.16 | 3.40 | 104 | 7 | LLOYD * | BOWLED | WILLEY | 56 | 6 | 437 | 1 | 7 | 85 | Missed cut – misjudged length. Top-spinner. |
| 3.42 | 4.54 | 52 | 8 | MURRAY † | Ct TAVARÉ | BOTHAM | 34 | 8 | 486 | · | 5 | 52 | Edged cut to 1st slip. |
| 4.34 | 5.39 | 65 | 9 | ROBERTS | BOWLED | UNDERWOOD | 24 | 10 | 518 | · | 4 | 51 | Beaten by 'arm' ball – middle stump. |
| 4.56 | 5.33 | 37 | 10 | GARNER | Ct GOOCH | WILLIS | 15 | 9 | 518 | · | 2 | 28 | Edged lifting ball to 1st slip. |
| 5.35 | (5.39) | 4 | 11 | HOLDING | NOT OUT | | 0 | - | - | · | · | 5 | |
| | | | | * CAPTAIN  † WICKET-KEEPER | | EXTRAS | b 1  lb 9  w 1  nb 9 | | 20 | 3 7 | 894 balls (inc. 10 no balls) | |

TOTAL  (OFF 147.2 OVERS IN 557 MIN)  518 all out at 5.39pm on 3RD DAY (LEAD: 249)

15 OVERS 5 BALLS/HOUR
3.52 RUNS/OVER
58 RUNS/100 BALLS

| BOWLER | O | M | R | W | |nb/w| HRS | OVERS | RUNS |
|---|---|---|---|---|---|---|---|---|
| WILLIS | 31 | 12 | 103 | 3 | 4/1 | 1 | 16 | 54 |
| BOTHAM | 37 | 7 | 145 | 3 | | 2 | 15 | 54 |
| UNDERWOOD | 29.2 | 7 | 108 | 1 | 4/- | 3 | 16 | 68 |
| HENDRICK | 11 | 2 | 32 | 0 | | 4 | 17 | 81 |
| GOOCH | 7 | 1 | 26 | 0 | -/1 | 5 | 15 | 36 |
| WILLEY | 25 | 5 | 81 | 2 | | 6 | 16 | 41 |
| BOYCOTT | 7 | 2 | 11 | 0 | | 7 | 15 | 64 |
| | 147.2 | 35 | 20 518 | 9 1 | | 8 | 17 | 60 |
| | | | | | | 9 | 17 | 49 |

2ND NEW BALL taken at 12.49pm 3RD DAY
– WEST INDIES 325-3 after 90 overs.

| RUNS | MINS | OVERS | LAST 50 (in mins) |
|---|---|---|---|
| 50 | 59 | 15.3 | 59 |
| 100 | 110 | 29 | 51 |
| 150 | 148 | 38.3 | 38 |
| 200 | 206 | 53.5 | 58 |
| 250 | 235 | 62.2 | 29 |
| 300 | 318 | 84.4 | 83 |
| 350 | 376 | 99.3 | 58 |
| 400 | 422 | 110.4 | 46 |
| 450 | 475 | 125.3 | 53 |
| 500 | 526 | 140 | 51 |

LUNCH: 37-0  GREENIDGE 25* / HAYNES 12*
OFF 12 OVERS IN 44 MINUTES
BLSP at 3.30pm – TEA taken at 3.40pm. (10' lost)
TEA: 124-1  HAYNES 26* (124 min)  RICHARDS 71* (73 min)
OFF 32 OVERS IN 124 MINUTES
BLSP at 6.14pm  RAIN CAUSED 6.20pm ABANDONMENT
STUMPS: 265-2  HAYNES 92* (257')  CROFT 0* (8')
(2ND DAY)  OFF 68 OVERS IN 257 MIN.
LUNCH: 335-5  HAYNES 136* / LLOYD 1* (14')
RSP&P at 11.50am (9 min lost)  OFF 97 OVERS IN 368 MINUTES
TEA: 469-6  HAYNES 184* / MURRAY 26* (28')
OFF 130 OVERS IN 488 MINUTES
‡ RECORD WEST INDIES SCORE AT LORD'S.

| WKT | PARTNERSHIP | | RUNS | MINS |
|---|---|---|---|---|
| 1st | Greenidge | Haynes | 37 | 48 |
| 2nd | Haynes | Richards | 223 | 196 |
| 3rd | Haynes | Croft | 15 | 18 |
| 4th | Haynes | Kallicharran | 51 | 77 |
| 5th | Haynes | Bacchus | 4 | 7 |
| 6th | Haynes | Lloyd | 107 | 104 |
| 7th | Haynes | Murray | 32 | 30 |
| 8th | Murray | Roberts | 17 | 20 |
| 9th | Roberts | Garner | 32 | 37 |
| 10th | Roberts | Holding | 0 | 4 |
| | | | 518 | |

**ENGLAND** 2ND INNINGS  249 RUNS BEHIND ON FIRST INNINGS

| IN | OUT | MINS | No. | BATSMAN | HOW OUT | BOWLER | RUNS | WKT | TOTAL | 6s | 4s | BALLS | NOTES ON DISMISSAL |
|---|---|---|---|---|---|---|---|---|---|---|---|---|---|
| 5.50 | 11.33 | 109 | 1 | GOOCH | BOWLED | GARNER | 47 | 1 | 71 | 1 | 5 | 78 | Beaten by breakback that kept low & hit off stump. |
| 5.50 | (2.05) | 216 | 2 | BOYCOTT | NOT OUT | | 49 | | | . | 1 | 161 | - |
| 11.35 | 12.28 | 50 | 3 | TAVARÉ | LBW | GARNER | 6 | 2 | 96 | . | . | 40 | Misjudged line – ball kept low. |
| 12.30 | (2.05) | 53 | 4 | WOOLMER | NOT OUT | | 19 | | | . | 3 | 46 | - |
| | | | 5 | GATTING | ⎱ | | | | | | | | |
| | | | 6 | BOTHAM * | | | | | | | | | |
| | | | 7 | WILLEY | ⎬ DID NOT BAT | | | | | | | | |
| | | | 8 | KNOTT † | | | | | | | | | |
| | | | 9 | UNDERWOOD | | | | | | | | | |
| | | | 10 | WILLIS | | | | | | | | | |
| | | | 11 | HENDRICK | ⎰ | | | | | | | | |
| * CAPTAIN  † WICKET-KEEPER | | | | EXTRAS | b 1  lb –  w –  nb 11 | | 12 | | | 1⁶ | 9⁴ | 325 | (including 13 no balls) |

TOTAL  (OFF 52 OVERS IN 216 MIN.)  **133-2**

14 OVERS 2 BALLS/HOUR
2.56 RUNS/OVER
41 RUNS/100 BALLS

| BOWLER | O | M | R | W | nb | HRS | OVERS | RUNS |
|---|---|---|---|---|---|---|---|---|
| ROBERTS | 13 | 3 | 24 | 0 | - | 1 | 14 | 35 |
| HOLDING | 15 | 5 | 51 | 0 | 1 | 2 | 12 | 41 |
| GARNER | 15 | 6 | 21 | 2 | 7 | 3 | 17 | 26 |
| CROFT | 8 | 2 | 24 | 0 | 5 | | | |
| RICHARDS | 1 | 0 | 1 | 0 | - | | | |
| | | | | | 12 | | | |
| | 52 | 16 | 133 | 2 | | | | |

| RUNS | MINS | OVERS | LAST 50 (in mins) |
|---|---|---|---|
| 50 | 74 | 16.5 | 74 |
| 100 | 173 | 41.2 | 99 |

STUMPS: 33-0   GOOCH 21*
(3RD DAY)           BOYCOTT 10*
OFF 10 OVERS IN 40 MINUTES
BL&R STOPPED PLAY at 12.06 pm (324 MIN. LOST)
LUNCH: 51-0   GOOCH 32*
                      BOYCOTT 13*
(STUMPS – 4TH DAY) OFF 17 OVERS IN 76 MINUTES
LUNCH: 111-2   BOYCOTT 41* (193')
                        WOOLMER 6* (30')
OFF 47 OVERS IN 193 MINUTES
BL & RAIN STOPPED PLAY at 2.05 pm (215 MIN LOST)
MATCH ABANDONED (DRAWN) at 3.35pm.
MAN OF THE MATCH : I.V.A. RICHARDS
TOTAL TIME LOST : 9 HOURS 52 MINUTES

| WKT | PARTNERSHIP | | RUNS | MINS |
|---|---|---|---|---|
| 1st | Gooch | Boycott | 71 | 109 |
| 2nd | Boycott | Tavaré | 25 | 50 |
| 3rd | Boycott | Woolmer | 37* | 53 |
| | | | 133 | |

# LETTER FROM BARBADOS
## —— Tony Cozier ——

People, I have learned over the years, enjoy listening to their cricket in some of the oddest circumstances.

Last summer, someone I met at one of the interminable sponsors' parties said she found it most relaxing to lie in a warm bath while the attendant radio relayed the Thoughts of Trueman Now, the latest Johnston witticism, or whatever the fertile (idle?) minds in the commentary box happened to be concocting at the time. Mostly, she said, she tried to coincide her bath with periods when it was raining, when there was no play and, as she put it, when the chatter was not interrupted by the cricket. Apart from anything else, she must have ended the season spotlessly clean.

My own favourite spot for keeping abreast of what is happening – or not happening, as the case may be – at Lord's or Old Trafford or Headingley is on a Barbadian beach, rum punch nearby and a pair of sunglasses, both to shield the glare and to render the eyes roving in the direction of the passing bikinis less obvious. Arlott, somehow, always seems more lucid in such a repose than he does when actually sitting next to him in some spartan commentary box on a cold, damp English day.

Like many West Indians, my early recollections of Arlott's dulcet tones, and, in those days, of Rex Alston, Robert Hudson, Jim Swanton and Ken Ablack, go back to schooldays, a little (but not much) before the Japanese were to have their profound effect on the game of cricket by providing us with little radios which needed no electrical outlet and which we could take anywhere.

Although local cricket broadcasting had been going (if that is the appropriate word) from just before the war, it was the West Indies tour to

England in 1950 which popularised it throughout the Caribbean. It was the first time listeners back home could actually hear, with an immediacy which made it compelling radio fare, how the West Indies were getting on on tour. They were, of course, getting on wonderfully as the three Ws demonstrated their batting power and Ramadhin and Valentine mesmerised England's batsmen with their spin. For the first time, arguments could rage in the bars long into the night about the ball that dismissed Hutton, or the catch that accounted for Simpson, or the drive that brought yet another Weekes century. Usually, 'Arlott said so, man' or 'I heard it with my own two ears' was a retort telling enough to win a point.

In every series since then, both at home and overseas, West Indians have demanded and received ball-by-ball commentaries on their team's Tests. They have come not only from England, but from Australia, India, Pakistan and New Zealand in the middle of the night and in the small hours of the morning, excuses enough for all-night parties. With communications revolutionised by the introduction of the transistor, the voices of the cricket commentators have been carried further than could have been imagined by those who had to wait on the cabled reports for news of George Headley's latest accomplishments during his heyday in the 1930s. Now we intrude into listeners' lives in their cars, in their offices and, as the lady in the bath previously alluded to confirmed, even in their boudoirs.

It has meant, inevitably, that the commentator has become almost as famous – or is it infamous – as the leading players. Certainly, in my own experience, John Arlott is as revered the world over as any cricketer I can think of. As boys, the make-believe commentator at the make-believe Test match taking place on the beach, or on someone's lawn, or in a back yard would always be John Arlott. Somehow, his lovely, deliberate Hampshire accent describing Worrell's late cut or Weekes's hook was magic to our ears and was easy to copy. Or so we thought. I don't know what John himself would make of a Barbadian struggling at an imitation of his style, but it used to give us no end of fun – and, I am sure, still does to those of the modern generation.

Somehow, the Arlott phraseology stuck more easily in our young and imaginative minds than the verses of Homer or the problems of Pythagoras. 'Fielders scattering like missionaries to far places' was one favourite I particularly remember. And his descriptive references to the trains pulling into the Warwick Road Station, with the Pennines shrouded in cloud and rain imminent, provided us all with a graphic mental picture of an Old Trafford which we had never seen.

Sadly, John has never been to the Caribbean for an official series and now never will, confining himself to a brief trip to Jamaica with a Cavaliers side in 1970. The heat, he complains, does not agree with him – although I am sure he would have appreciated the warmth of the welcome which would have greeted him.

This is not to say that those who have been to the West Indies on official BBC duty have not attracted a legion of admirers. Christopher Martin-

*Miles from a Barbadian beach but feeling at home – Tony Cozier at The Oval*

Jenkins's reading of the game has made him widely popular, while Brian Johnston and Henry Blofeld both have a sense of *joie de vivre* with which West Indians can easily identify. If not all his colleagues appreciated his rather bizarre liking for a practical joke, Brian enjoyed himself immensely on tour – even during the riot in the Jamaica Test of 1968 when, amidst all the tear gas and confusion, his wife, Pauline, kept her cool and snapped some excellent photographs.

Johnners takes a malicious delight in practical jokes and I happen to have been the butt of them on one or two occasions. He has taken such delight in a particular stunt that he has reproduced it in one of his several auto-biographies, but, although Peter Baxter has already made a passing reference to it, I will relate it here nevertheless.

It was at the Queen's Park Oval in Port-of-Spain and play had been halted by rain. Having completed some work in the press box on the opposite side of the ground, I was making my way across the empty outfield to the broadcast position when the evil Johnston eye spotted me. By the time I arrived, he was ready to perpetrate his devious act. I found him talking earnestly into the microphone, with red warning light illuminated.

As soon as I entered, puffing from a climb up the stairs, he glanced around and told his supposed listeners: 'Ah, here's Tony Cozier, so I'll hand over to him as I know he has all the latest averages for the series which he'll pass on to you.' None the wiser, I stepped in, with nothing resembling a statistic near me, and attempted to cover up by waffling on about the weather, the state of the games and whatever would come into my panic-stricken mind.

'No,' Brian interrupted, 'we've promised the listeners the averages and we know you can provide them.' More panic and signalling for old scoresheets until Johnston could not keep his delighted laughter to himself any longer. We had, he announced, never been on the air at all. Everyone else seemed to think it was great fun but, to this day, I have never quite been able to appreciate what amused them so!

It was one of the few occasions, in fact, that we were off the air in that series – or any other. Nowadays, so the producers and the lady in the bath tell us, listeners want us to carry on even when there is no cricket to describe. Certainly this would appear to be the case in the Caribbean where, during a Test series at home or away, the dreaded radios are everywhere. Pedestrians scurry about their business, one hand holding the transistor tightly to an ear. Bicyclists pay more attention to the commentary emanating from the box on their handlebars than they do the oncoming bus, whose driver is probably tuned into the same wavelength. Company executives and parliamentarians couldn't care less how silly they look at their desks with an earphone securely plugged in, so long as they can follow Viv Richards's latest escapade stroke by stroke.

Nowhere, however, is there such a concentration of radios as at the matches themselves. It may turn out to be of some promotional advantage for one of the Japanese manufacturers to take a survey of, let us say, Kensington Oval in Bridgetown or Queen's Park Oval during the Saturday of a Test to determine just how many of their products are in use. It has now reached such a state of affairs that the size, value and volume of the transistor brought into the ground have become very much status symbols. The spectator with the pocket model (and they seem to be fewer and fewer) will conceal it shame-facedly in deference to the owner of the twin-speaker, four-band radio cassette recorder resembling some satellite earth station.

Constantly during a day's play, the producer will stick a card in front of his commentator who will go through the ritual of asking spectators to 'kindly turn your radios down as the quality of the broadcast is being affected by feedback'. It makes not one iota of difference, mind you. Only when a batsman, who can no longer stand the comments on his strokeplay or lack thereof clearly audible in the middle, pulls away and begs for quiet does the noise temporarily abate.

It is, at one and the same time, a flattering and dangerous situation for the commentator. On the one hand, it is pleasing to know that even crowds as knowledgeable as they are in the West Indies feel that their understanding of the game can be embellished by the radio broadcasts. On the other, it is worrying that they are waiting for every mistake and every comment which does not meet their favour to let you know all about it. A leg-bye inadvertently called a run, or a dropped catch given when the ball may have bounced, or any one of the hundred and one little traps designed to ensnare the commentator, is guaranteed to bring whistles and cat-calls from spectators who are listening. I have actually heard a Guyana crowd boo a certain, perfectly reputable broadcaster whenever it was his turn to take over the microphone, but I believe there was a political motive for that.

Politics, of course, is never far from the surface in the Caribbean and neither are fierce inter-island rivalries. Naturally, any commentator needs to be above these and relate the cricket as he sees it. Yet the pressure can be great as a couple of instances may illustrate.

When the West Indies were winning their first Test for ages at the Oval against England in 1973, the large West Indian section gathered in the south-western bleachers were understandably ecstatic. I made the comment that I felt their spirit had been helped in no small measure by the consumption of large volumes of a Jamaican beer and a Barbadian rum, both of which I identified by brand. Within a few days, two letters arrived from competing bottlers in the Caribbean angered that I had not included their products in my observation!

Some years later, when Colin Croft was first making an impression, I recalled how he had played club cricket for two seasons in Trinidad while studying there but had not been included in that island's Shield side. (Croft, by the way, is from Guyana.) At the time, there was a controversy raging in Trinidad over an Antiguan, rejoicing in the name of Lord Short Shirt, who had been banned from their annual calypso competition, which they wanted to retain as purely local. Perhaps the same thing applied to Croft, I suggested. It was a flippant, perhaps ill-advised aside and it brought the wrath of Trinidad down on my head. Apologise, you Barbadian, demanded one newspaper – which I did. In addition, I got a rather indignant letter on the matter from no less a person than the president of the West Indies Cricket Board of Control, himself a Trinidadian!

So you should complain, I can hear it said. To tell the truth, I am not. I am the first to admit that we cricket commentators are a privileged species, travelling the world over, watching the best players in action, meeting interesting people, making new friends. What bother is it, then, if we have to put up with the occasional complaint and with fellow commentators who pull awful practical jokes?

# THE TEAM GOES NORTH
## Henry Blofeld

Every Test match I have broadcast with the *Test Match Special* team has been a separate and highly entertaining adventure. This has been particularly true when the match has been played out of London and it has meant the best part of a week together in the same hotel. As I had been allotted only one Test match in 1980, the third at Old Trafford, I looked forward to it with even greater anticipation than usual.

I suppose that the match really began for me some time in the spring when a telephone call from Peter Baxter told me that I was on the panel for this particular match. My next move was to write to the manager of the Swan Hotel at Bucklow Hill, about fifteen miles south of Manchester, which has become the annual and extremely comfortable watering hole for most of the commentators and a good many writers for matches at Old Trafford.

By the time I let in my clutch to start the journey north after an early lunch on Wednesday 9 July, I was extremely excited at the prospect of the next few days. I knew I would see John Arlott, Brian Johnston and Chris Martin-Jenkins that evening at the Swan, together with other old habitués such as Johnny Woodcock of *The Times,* Michael Melford of *The Daily Telegraph,* Peter Laker of the *Daily Mirror* and Basil Easterbrook from Thompson's newspapers. There would be much laughter, a fund of good stories and any amount of wine, to say nothing of the petty dramas which always seem to form a part of every away match. Gossip spreads like wildfire.

I arrived at the Swan soon after five o'clock and found to my dismay that I had been allotted a room overlooking the main road to Manchester. Even allowing for the double-glazing there never seemed to be less than two lorries about to enter my room at any one time. Fortunately the staff were able to find me another overlooking the inner courtyard.

Having lugged my cases upstairs and unpacked I went down to the reception desk for an evening paper and ran into Brian Johnston who was talking to Johnny Woodcock. It took Johnners about 45 seconds to make his first punning contribution to this Test match. Woodcock was talking about an acquaintance whom he went on to describe as a nutter, to which Johnners responded instantly, 'A.E. of Lancashire and Northamptonshire'. It was reassuring to know so soon that nothing had changed.

When I returned to my room the telephone rang revealing Claud Brownlow on the other end. He had driven up from Essex with his lovely wife Morag, who is one of *Test Match Special*'s greatest supporters, and they were also staying at the Swan. It had been Morag who had written to Tony Lewis for his Saturday morning sports programme on Radio 4 suggesting that the *TMS* team should be cast in the roles of characters from Dallas and went on to show how it could be done. I am not prepared to reveal who was given the role of 'J.R.', and will only go so far as to say that a suit for libel and defamation is pending, although strictly *sub judice.*

They asked me to go down to their room where Claud was busily engaged in removing the first cork of the Test match. We had hardly settled down when their telephone rang and the caller was none other than 'Sir' Frederick Trueman, a great friend of the Brownlows. For some reason he had not been able to get back to Yorkshire that night and so he had booked himself into the Swan. He burst through the door soon afterwards in his usual cheerful and ebullient manner and was in great form. Vigorously, he discussed Yorkshire's cricketing fortunes and then the merits of a gold chess set he had won in some pro-am golf tournament, and he told us a couple of his latest jokes.

By now John Arlott had clocked in and as soon as Fred and I left the Brownlows' room we were being poured another glass by John. Before dinner I ran into Chris Martin-Jenkins in the courtyard and when we all sat down to dinner it was like a beginning of term party. Anyone would have thought that we had not seen each other for months when in fact the Lord's Test match had ended barely two weeks before and we had met several times since.

The next morning arrived and mercifully it was fine. The car park tickets we had originally been given were for the Warwick Road end of Old Trafford, the opposite end to the commentary box. When I got up I found some replacements had been shoved under my door by, as it turned out, Chris Martin-Jenkins. I set off early to Old Trafford, turning right on to the motorway, past the turning to Manchester Airport, into the speed limit, left at the cemetery, then a long curving right-hander, left just after the undertakers, over the railway bridge and into Old Trafford. The new car park tickets survived a detailed scrutiny by an overzealous attendant and I parked just alongside the nets where both sides were practising.

Johnners, who always likes to arrive early on the first morning of a Test match to watch the sides practising, was already there resplendent in his co-respondent shoes. He always wears them for Test matches and they are a hangover from an earlier age, probably the days of the British Raj in India. They are highly polished and are brown and white in about equal measure and are as much a part of Johnners as his punning and his hunting-horn imitation.

The commentary box at Old Trafford is a musty heirloom from the past. It is at the southern end, or Stretford end, of the ground and to reach it is a complicated business for the uninitiated. First one has to go through a green wooden door at the back of the Committee stand which is smartly opened as one approaches by an ever-alert attendant. Then it is up the first winding flight of stairs, a sharp right turn and up another, this time narrower and steeper, giving one the impression that one is heading for a seldom used attic. The commentary box itself is small: there is just about room for four people to sit in front of the table with the microphones, although the one on the outside is always in everyone's way. An uncomfortably unyielding slatted bench, which leaves one's behind feeling like a passable piece of corrugated iron, runs along the back wall and it is almost impossible to sit down on it without bumping into a commentator in front. In the far corner at the back of the box a television set is perched so that we can watch the replays.

Johnners had beaten me up there and the Bearded Wonder, who has his own hotel hideaway on these occasions, had already arranged his papers and books and stopwatches meticulously at the far end of the table and was giving instructions to his assistant, who would help him through the match by telephoning his copy to various newspapers. The only other chap present was John Helm, our producer who had only recently moved back to the north and was producing his first Test match.

His first duty was to pin the commentators' rota on the wall at the back of the box where we studied it carefully and swopped around with our colleagues when some timing was working in direct opposition to our lunch plans. Helm also had to make sure that the number-two position was set up. During a Test match there always has to be a number-two position from which Ian Davis can do his reports for World Service at Bush House. Also, C.M.J. and myself would be taking it in turns to do the inserts into the sports desks and news bulletins through the day.

Getting to the number-two position presents considerable problems and requires the agility of a mountain goat. On the left-hand side of the main box there is a small door which looks as if it might belong to a rabbit hutch. In fact, it is a trap door on its side for it does not reach down to the floor. It opens onto the top tier of the scoreboard at the Stretford end which is presided over by two or three small boys with reasonable skill but considerable noise. There is a trellis-work gangway on which they sit and work which leads across to the number-two point. During the day those who have to do these extra pieces are endlessly appearing and disappearing out of and into this hole in the wall with its green door. It seems to be almost automatic to fall over on one journey or other, making a fearful noise in the process and sending the producer's hair grey.

There probably seems to be an awful lot of extraneous noise going on all around when *TMS* is on the air, quite apart from Bill Frindall's famous off-mike snorts. In a cramped area such as Old Trafford (The Oval is no better, with six or seven people constantly changing positions), I think it is a wonder it is as quiet as it is. Then, of course, there are the various noises off stage. There are the pops and bangs and tinkles as corks are pulled and glasses are knocked over and broken, in addition to the sometimes hysterical giggling of commentators who have been reduced to such a state, mostly by Johnners. Little things always seem funnier because one is not

*Clutching some of the medicine, or fizz, Trevor says 'Good mooooooooorning' to Henry*

allowed to laugh, just as they do in church. Finally, there are those commentators with two left feet, principally me.

As usual, we would be on the air fifteen minutes before the start on the first day at Old Trafford and John Arlott was preparing to discuss the prospects with Fred who was in position beside him. Time was getting on when there came a rather more noisy clattering of feet up the stairs and a broadly smiling face came round the corner, followed by a loud and cheerful, 'Good Moooooooorning'. Trevor Bailey had completed the drive from Southend.

As well as the four microphones and all Bill Frindall's equipment, there was a pile of letters and packages on the main table. They were listeners' letters, and presents of sweets and cakes and other goodies which always seem to be sent to Brian Johnston. As one day's mail is opened it is replaced by yet another pile and at the end of the match there are still a great many letters which have not been opened and which Peter Baxter has eventually to answer.

The scene was therefore set and Peter Baxter, in studio B8 in Broadcasting House, London, handed over to John Arlott to begin the pre-match discussion. I was the third commentator on the rota that morning but, as I had not done any commentary since Tony Lewis and I shared commentary in the Jubilee Test match from Bombay in March, I stayed in the box until my turn arrived. Listening to John Arlott and Brian Johnston helped me to pick up the rhythm which is so important to cricket commentary.

England began disastrously, recovered through Rose and Gatting, before collapsing again after lunch. Cornhill Insurance, the sponsors, produced some delicious but extremely noisy lunch boxes with transparent perspex covers which creaked and crackled and must have sounded to listeners a bit like feeding time at the zoo, and enough Vin Rosé to have lasted until the start of the fourth Test.

But the first moment we all wait for came at approximately midday. Having handed over to Fred Trueman, Trevor Bailey navigated his way slowly out of the box on his way to his car to get 'some of the medicine'. He returned ten minutes later with four bottles of Laurent Perrier Champagne under his arm and a smile on his face and the popping of corks began. Trevor has a friend, Frank, who is sales director and always sends Trevor to a Test match with a good supply for the *TMS* team. The standard of commentary improves markedly after this particular drinks interval.

I gave John Arlott a lift back to Bucklow Hill that evening. It was an even earlier start to Manchester the next day for we had all of us been invited to a champagne breakfast in the restaurant at Old Trafford by Trevor Bailey on behalf of Wrigleys. They had decided to put some money into a scheme devised by Trevor to start soft-ball cricket at the primary school level in England, a level at which schools so often do not have any facilities to play cricket. Soft-ball cricket is very inexpensive and all that is needed is a flat bat, an old tennis ball (for a new one has too much bounce), some stumps and any open piece of ground. In the West Indies all children are introduced to cricket through soft-ball cricket and it is a game which teaches them the correct fundamentals. Trevor explained his plans and the reasoning behind them. It was an excellent breakfast, too.

For the second day we had a beautiful addition to the box in the form of a journalist called Pat Roberts from the *Sheffield Telegraph*. She sat in the back row making notes all day for a feature she was going to write about the programme. She was a great tactician too because before the start that morning she gave us each a delicious box of chocolates and her presence probably made us all behave just that much better.

Another amusing event was the arrival of a small parcel which produced a brand new pipe for Trevor. He had just taken up a pipe and the day before we pulled his leg about his inability to keep it alight. We had been listened to by the public relations officer at Dunhill in Duke Street in Piccadilly, one Sue Graham, who had sent Trevor a pipe. We pulled his leg all day, and although Fred filled it for him he was still unable to keep it alight.

In spite of some less than cheerful weather and the strong position of the West Indies, this was another day of much laughter. When Richards launched a vicious assault against Willis's bowling, C. M. J. said that he thought Willis was bowling him half-volleys on purpose. Fred Trueman said rapidly that, in which case, he ought to change his mind and fast. Johnners reduced me to speechlessness on three occasions. On the first, we were talking about C. K. Nayudu, who was the first man to captain India in a Test match. I said that his daughter, Chandra, was the only female cricket commentator in the world and that I had met her at Indore on an MCC tour. From the back of the box Johnners came back with, 'Indoors was a very good place to meet her, too.'

On another occasion I said that Derryck Murray had left alone a ball which had barely missed the off stump and that, like the experienced player he is, he knows the exact width of his stumps. I compared this to a good driver knowing the width of his car. A voice from behind me said, 'I always think it is much more important to know the width of the car coming towards you.' And finally, towards the end of the day, I said that so and so drove a bump ball back to the bowler but I only pronounced the first three letters, BUM. Back came a highly audible, 'What happened to the P?'

During the afternoon an old friend of ours, Mike Howell from Oldham, who is blind but is passionate about cricket, came into the box and talked to C. M. J. and Johnners about the problems of being a blind cricket 'watcher', and also about the cricket which blind people manage to play with a ball with a bell inside. Later Reg Simpson, the former Notts and England opening batsman, came up with Lance Murray from Trinidad, the father of Derryck Murray. And at the end of each day we all repaired to the Cornhill Tent at the Stretford End and talked the day over and laughed at our various blunders.

There was no play at all on the Saturday for it had rained all night and most of the morning. In the box we kept on all the morning and most of the afternoon talking of this and that and the other, mostly the other. The shape of Brian's nose and the well-being of Fred's dog were among the more unlikely topics, and some interesting people came and talked to us.

One was Johnny Woodcock, *The Times* cricket correspondent, who had recently been appointed to succeed Norman Preston as the editor of *Wisden*. Normally he shies away from being interviewed if Brian Johnston is there, for Brian invariably makes him laugh helplessly, but for an hour and a half he was extremely interesting about his future plans for *Wisden*. Later, at lunch time, Jack Fingleton came up and was in scintillating form. He discussed bouncers and slow over-rates and was very funny besides and we pulled each other's legs for a longish while.

Sunday was a day of rest for some but I had to drive over to Chesterfield for *The Guardian* to watch Derbyshire play Somerset in the John Player League, where I think I was the victim of a practical joke by Mike Carey and Gerald Mortimer in the Derbyshire press box. I had complained about the slow drive over from Bucklow Hill which although it was only 55 miles was very slow and winding. They persuaded me to go back by way of the M1 and then the M62 to Manchester and down to Bucklow Hill on the M6. I set off and found that, by the time I got back, I had driven 119 miles and I was almost too late for dinner.

The Monday got off to a bad start when C. M. J., who had gone home to Surrey for the weekend, rang John Arlott at the Swan, saying that he had knocked down a bicyclist in Slough. He was talking from the police station where he had been for more than an hour and he would be late. The bicyclist had gone to hospital. Tony Lewis stood in for C. M. J. before lunch when a rather ashen-faced BBC cricket correspondent arrived. It was a nasty shock for all concerned. He rang the hospital during the afternoon and learned that the man had been discharged.

Johnners did not reappear after the weekend because he was commentating on the Queen Mother's eightieth birthday service from St Paul's Cathedral, but the Test match now dissolved into a wet draw. England had to bat for a time in their second innings to make it safe but did so without too much trouble. We did our best to make it sound interesting – and Trevor strove frantically to keep his new pipe alight without much success.

In spite of the weather it had been a typical *TMS* Test match. There was masses of laughter, bags of fun, any amount of good conversation and chat, and, at the end of it, the feeling that one had had five splendid days with some great friends.

## ENGLAND 1ST INNINGS v WEST INDIES 3RD TEST at OLD TRAFFORD, MANCHESTER on JULY 10, 11, 12 (no play), 14, 15, 1980.   TOSS: WEST INDIES

| IN | OUT | MINS | No. | BATSMAN | HOW OUT | BOWLER | RUNS | WKT | TOTAL | 6s | 4s | BALLS | NOTES ON DISMISSAL |
|---|---|---|---|---|---|---|---|---|---|---|---|---|---|
| 11.30 | 11.48 | 18 | 1 | GOOCH | LBW | ROBERTS | 2 | 1 | 3 | · | · | 15 | Played 'half-cock' push across line. |
| 11.30 | 12.19 | 49 | 2 | BOYCOTT | C GARNER | ROBERTS | 5 | 2 | 18 | · | 1 | 36 | Bouncer - fended to gully via bat 'shoulder'. |
| 11.50 | 3.09 | 158 | 3 | ROSE | BOWLED | MARSHALL | 70 | 5 | 131 | · | 9 | 106 | Off-stump via pads - breakback. |
| 12.21 | 12.41 | 20 | 4 | LARKINS | LBW | GARNER | 11 | 3 | 35 | · | 1 | 16 | Played across full-length inswinger. |
| 12.43 | 2.58 | 94 | 5 | GATTING | C RICHARDS | MARSHALL | 33 | 4 | 126 | · | 6 | 62 | Edged drive to 3rd slip. |
| 3.00 | 3.34 | 34 | 6 | BOTHAM * | C MURRAY | GARNER | 8 | 8 | 142 | · | 1 | 18 | Edged to 'keeper - defensive push. |
| 3.11 | 3.12 | 1 | 7 | WILLEY | BOWLED | MARSHALL | 0 | 6 | 132 | · | · | 2 | Missed leg glance - bowled behind legs. |
| 3.14 | 3.32 | 18 | 8 | KNOTT † | RUN OUT (PARRY/GARNER) | | 2 | 7 | 142 | · | · | 11 | Hesitated over run to square leg. |
| 3.33 | 3.53 | 20 | 9 | EMBUREY | C MURRAY | ROBERTS | 3 | 10 | 150 | · | · | 14 | Edged offside push. |
| 3.35 | 3.36 | 1 | 10 | DILLEY | BOWLED | GARNER | 0 | 9 | 142 | · | · | 1 | Yorked off stump - 1st ball. |
| 3.38 | (3.53) | 15 | 11 | WILLIS | NOT OUT | | 5 | - | - | · | 1 | 14 | — |

* CAPTAIN   † WICKET-KEEPER   EXTRAS   b - lb 4   w 3   nb 4   11   0s 19s 295 balls (including 5 no balls)

TOTAL (OFF 48.2 OVERS IN 222 MINS)   150 all out at 3.53pm.

13 OVERS 0 BALLS/HOUR
3.10 RUNS/OVER
51 RUNS/100 BALLS

| BOWLER | O | M | R | W | nb/w | HRS | OVERS | RUNS |
|---|---|---|---|---|---|---|---|---|
| ROBERTS | 11.2 | 3 | 23 | 3 | - | 1 | 13 | 25 |
| HOLDING | 14 | 2 | 46 | 0 | 1/3 | 2 | 14 | 70 |
| GARNER | 11 | 2 | 34 | 3 | 2/- | 3 | 13 | 37 |
| MARSHALL | 12 | 5 | 36 | 3 | 3/- | | | |
| | | | 11 | | | | | |
| | 48.2 | 12 | 150 | 10 | | | | |

| | RUNS | MINS | OVERS | LAST 50 (in mins) |
|---|---|---|---|---|
| | 50 | 85 | 19 | 85 |
| | 100 | 129 | 29.1 | 44 |
| | 150 | 220 | 48 | 91 |

LUNCH: 95-3   ROSE 51s (67 balls, 100)   GATTING 18s (32 balls, 47)
OFF 27 OVERS IN 120 MINUTES

TEA TAKEN AT END OF INNINGS

| WKT | PARTNERSHIP | | RUNS | MINS |
|---|---|---|---|---|
| 1st | Gooch | Boycott | 3 | 18 |
| 2nd | Boycott | Rose | 15 | 29 |
| 3rd | Rose | Larkins | 17 | 20 |
| 4th | Rose | Gatting | 91 | 94 |
| 5th | Rose | Botham | 5 | 9 |
| 6th | Botham | Willey | 1 | 1 |
| 7th | Botham | Knott | 10 | 18 |
| 8th | Botham | Emburey | 0 | 1 |
| 9th | Emburey | Dilley | 0 | 1 |
| 10th | Emburey | Willis | 8 | 15 |
| | | | 150 | |

## WEST INDIES 1ST INNINGS   (IN REPLY TO ENGLAND'S 150 ALL OUT)

| IN | OUT | MINS | No. | BATSMAN | HOW OUT | BOWLER | RUNS | WKT | TOTAL | 6s | 4s | BALLS | NOTES ON DISMISSAL |
|---|---|---|---|---|---|---|---|---|---|---|---|---|---|
| 4.15 | 4.39 | 24 | 1 | GREENIDGE | C LARKINS | DILLEY | 0 | 2 | 25 | · | · | 18 | Middled 'pick-up' shot - square-leg dived forward (low cat.) |
| 4.15 | 4.26 | 11 | 2 | HAYNES | C KNOTT | WILLIS | 1 | 1 | 4 | · | · | 6 | Edged push/drive at outswinger. |
| 4.28 | 1.07 | 91 | 3 | RICHARDS | BOWLED | BOTHAM | 65 | 5 | 100 | · | 13 | 68 | Attempted mid-wicket stroke - bowled leg stump behind legs. |
| 4.41 | 4.41 | 1 | 4 | BACCHUS | C BOTHAM | DILLEY | 0 | 3 | 25 | · | · | 1 | First ball - edged lifting ball high to 2nd slip's right (R handed) |
| 4.43 | 12.35 | 44 | 5 | KALLICHARRAN | C KNOTT | BOTHAM | 13 | 4 | 67 | · | 3 | 29 | Top-edged cut at short offside ball. |
| 12.37 | 12.12 | 205 | 6 | LLOYD * | C GOOCH | EMBUREY | 101 | 8 | 250 | · | 11 | 159 | Edged drive at leg-break. |
| 1.09 | 6.04 | 45 | 7 | MURRAY † | BOWLED | BOTHAM | 17 | 6 | 154 | · | 2 | 35 | Played outside line of ball which removed off stump. |
| 6.06 | 7.03 | 57 | 8 | MARSHALL | C GOOCH | DILLEY | 18 | 7 | 209 | · | 3 | 45 | Edged off-drive to 1st slip. |
| 7.05 | 12.30 | 85 | 9 | ROBERTS | C KNOTT | EMBUREY | 11 | 10 | 260 | · | · | 72 | Under-edged cut. |
| 12.14 | 12.15 | 1 | 10 | GARNER | LBW | EMBUREY | 0 | 9 | 250 | · | · | 2 | Missed sweep at faster ball |
| 12.17 | (12.30) | 13 | 11 | HOLDING | NOT OUT | | 4 | - | - | · | · | 15 | — |

* CAPTAIN   † WICKET-KEEPER   EXTRAS   b 2   lb 13   w 3   nb 12   30   0s 32s 450 balls (including 15 no balls)

TOTAL (OFF 72.3 OVERS IN 297 MIN.)   260 all out (LEAD: 110)

14 OVERS 4 BALLS/HOUR
3.59 RUNS/OVER
58 RUNS/100 BALLS

| BOWLER | O | M | R | W | nb/w | HRS | OVERS | RUNS |
|---|---|---|---|---|---|---|---|---|
| WILLIS | 14 | 1 | 99 | 1 | 12/3 | 1 | 13 | 59 |
| DILLEY | 28 | 7 | 47 | 3 | 3/- | 2 | 13 | 54 |
| BOTHAM | 20 | 6 | 64 | 3 | - | 3 | 14 | 52 |
| EMBUREY | 10.3 | 1 | 20 | 3 | - | 4 | 17 | 54 |
| | | | 30 | | | | | |
| | 72.3 | 15 | 260 | 10 | | | | |

| | RUNS | MINS | OVERS | LAST 50 (in mins) |
|---|---|---|---|---|
| | 50 | 49 | 10.2 | 49 |
| | 100 | 101 | 22.3 | 52 |
| | 150 | 146 | 32.2 | 45 |
| | 200 | 202 | 46.2 | 56 |
| | 250 | 276 | 67.1 | 74 |

BLSP at 4.49pm (25 minutes lost) WI 31-3
BLSP at 5.24pm (66 minutes lost) 91 MIN. LOST TOTAL
STUMPS: 38-3 (1st DAY)   RICHARDS 32s in 31 min.   KALLICHARRAN 0s in 16 min.
OFF 9 OVERS IN 44 MINUTES

LUNCH: 125-5   LLOYD 25s (53 min)   MURRAY 5s (21 min)
OFF 28 OVERS IN 127 MINUTES

RAIN DELAYED RESTART UNTIL 5.40pm   210 min lost
STUMPS: 219-7 (2nd DAY 7.30pm)   LLOYD 79s (163 min)   ROBERTS 4s (25 min)
167 MIN (NETT) LOST   OFF 56 OVERS IN 237 MINUTES
3RD DAY — NO PLAY (RAIN)
WEST INDIES added 41 runs off 16.3 overs in 60 minutes for loss of last 3 wickets on 4th day.

| WKT | PARTNERSHIP | | RUNS | MINS |
|---|---|---|---|---|
| 1st | Greenidge | Haynes | 4 | 11 |
| 2nd | Greenidge | Richards | 21 | 11 |
| 3rd | Richards | Bacchus | 0 | 1 |
| 4th | Richards | Kallicharran | 42 | 44 |
| 5th | Richards | Lloyd | 33 | 30 |
| 6th | Lloyd | Murray | 54 | 45 |
| 7th | Lloyd | Marshall | 55 | 57 |
| 8th | Lloyd | Roberts | 41 | 67 |
| 9th | Roberts | Garner | 0 | 1 |
| 10th | Roberts | Holding | 10 | 13 |
| | | | 260 | |

ENGLAND  2ND INNINGS          (110 RUNS BEHIND ON FIRST INNINGS)

| IN. | OUT | MINS | No. | BATSMAN | HOW OUT | BOWLER | RUNS | WKT | TOTAL | 6s | 4s | BALLS | NOTES ON DISMISSAL |
|-----|-----|------|-----|---------|---------|--------|------|-----|-------|----|----|-------|--------------------|
| 12.43 | 1.14 | 31 | 1 | GOOCH | C⁺ MURRAY | MARSHALL | 26 | 1 | 32 | . | 3 | 28 | Edged ball that lifted and left him off pitch. |
| 12.43 | 11.37 | 325 | 2 | BOYCOTT | LBW | HOLDING | 86 | 4 | 217 | . | 8 | 273 | Beaten by breakback. |
| 1.16 | 3.00 | 64 | 3 | ROSE | C⁺ KALLICHARRAN | HOLDING | 32 | 2 | 86 | . | 3 | 44 | Edged firm-footed drive at half-volley to 1st slip. |
| 3.02 | 5.55 | 151 | 4 | LARKINS | C⁺ MURRAY | MARSHALL | 33 | 3 | 181 | . | 5 | 107 | Edged ball that moved away off pitch. |
| 5.57 | 1.58 | 164 | 5 | GATTING | C⁺ KALLICHARRAN | GARNER | 56 | 5 | 290 | . | 8 | 119 | Top edged cut at lifting ball to 1st slip (held at 3rd attempt) |
| 11.39 | 2.03 | 95 | 6 | BOTHAM * | LBW | HOLDING | 35 | 6 | 290 | . | 3 | 60 | Missed turn to leg - beaten by pace. |
| 2.00 | (5.30) | 144 | 7 | WILLEY | NOT OUT | | 62 | | | 1 | 9 | 123 | |
| 2.05 | 2.47 | 42 | 8 | KNOTT † | C⁺ AND BOWLED | GARNER | 6 | 7 | 309 | . | . | 37 | Mistimed turn to leg. |
| 2.49 | (5.30) | 95 | 9 | EMBUREY | NOT OUT | | 28 | | | . | 2 | 84 | |
| | | | 10 | DILLEY | ⎱ Did not bat | | | | | | | | |
| | | | 11 | WILLIS | ⎰ | | | | | | | | |

* CAPTAIN  † WICKET-KEEPER  |  EXTRAS  b 5  lb 8  w 1  nb 13  = 27  |  1⁶ 41⁴ 875 balls (including 17 no balls)

TOTAL  (OFF 143 OVERS IN 562 MIN.)  391-7

15 OVERS 1 BALLS/HOUR
2.73 RUNS/OVER
45 RUNS/100 BALLS

TOTAL TIME LOST : 11 HOURS 10 MINUTES.

| BOWLER | O | M | R | W | nb/w | HRS | OVERS | RUNS |
|--------|---|---|---|---|------|-----|-------|------|
| ROBERTS | 14 | 2 | 36 | 0 | - | 1 | 14 | 56 |
| HOLDING | 34 | 8 | 100 | 3 | - | 2 | 14 | 42 |
| MARSHALL | 35 | 5 | 116 | 2 | 9/1 | 3 | 17 | 34 |
| GARNER | 40 | 11 | 73 | 2 | 8/- | 4 | 16 | 45 |
| RICHARDS | 16 | 6 | 31 | 0 | - | 5 | 15 | 31 |
| LLOYD | 1 | 0 | 1 | 0 | - | 6 | 14 | 33 |
| BACCHUS | 1 | 0 | 3 | 0 | | 7 | 12 | 49 |
| HAYNES | 1 | 0 | 2 | 0 | | 8 | 15 | 26 |
| KALLICHARRAN | 1 | 0 | 2 | 0 | | 9 | 18 | 52 |
| | 143 | 32 | 391 | 7 | | | | |

2ND NEW BALL taken at 11.50 am 5th day.
- ENGLAND 228-4 after 85 overs.

| RUNS | MINS | OVERS | LAST 50 (in mins) |
|------|------|-------|-------------------|
| 50 | 53 | 12.1 | 53 |
| 100 | 124 | 29 | 71 |
| 150 | 199 | 50.4 | 75 |
| 200 | 285 | 71.1 | 86 |
| 250 | 368 | 92.1 | 83 |
| 300 | 456 | 111 | 88 |
| 350 | 525 | 129.5 | 69 |

MATCH DRAWN.  MAN OF THE MATCH: C.H.LLOYD

LUNCH: 43-1   BOYCOTT 11* (47 min.)  ROSE 4* (14 min.)
(67 BEHIND)   OFF 11 OVERS IN 47 MINUTES

TEA: 127-2   BOYCOTT 46* (167 min.)  LARKINS 15* (68 min.)
OFF 41 OVERS IN 167 MINUTES

STUMPS : 201-3   BOYCOTT 81* (288 min.)  GATTING 12* (36 min.)
(4TH DAY)   OFF 72 OVERS IN 288 MINUTES

B.LSP At 12.53pm (7 minutes lost)  GATTING 52* (148 min.)

LUNCH: 283-4   WILLEY 37* (101 min.)  BOTHAM 34* (74 min.)
173 AHEAD   OFF 98 OVERS IN 400 MINUTES

TEA: 345-7   WILLEY 37* (101 min.)  EMBUREY 10* (52 min.)
235 AHEAD   OFF 128 OVERS IN 519 MINUTES

| WKT | PARTNERSHIP | | RUNS | MINS |
|-----|-------------|---|------|------|
| 1st | Gooch | Boycott | 32 | 31 |
| 2nd | Boycott | Rose | 54 | 64 |
| 3rd | Boycott | Larkins | 95 | 151 |
| 4th | Boycott | Gatting | 36 | 72 |
| 5th | Gatting | Botham | 73 | 90 |
| 6th | Botham | Willey | 0 | 3 |
| 7th | Willey | Knott | 19 | 42 |
| 8th | Willey | Emburey | 82* | 95 |
| | | | 391 | |

# HOME THOUGHTS FROM ABROAD

## —— Henry Blofeld and Don Mosey ——

*Henry Blofeld*

Over the last few years *Test Match Special* has mounted its own operation from India (twice), Pakistan and Australia and each time I have been lucky enough to take part, sharing commentary at different times with Chris Martin-Jenkins, Don Mosey and Tony Lewis. Commentating from overseas always produces its own special problems and amusements, and frustrations and moments of drama too.

It has always given me a great kick to sit in a commentary box on an overseas Test ground and listen to Peter Baxter in Continuity in Broadcasting House in London hand over to us in, say, Hyderabad (Sind), Madras, Brisbane or Bombay at some unearthly hour on an English morning. At that same moment listeners are probably struggling with alarm clocks, freezing temperatures and trying not to spill early morning cups of tea, having only just succeeded with cold fingers in turning on their transistors which they have probably knocked off the bedside table at least twice. With blankets and eiderdowns pulled up to their chins, they wait eagerly for the latest score. On those occasions I cannot help feeling a tiny bit smug as one prattles on about cloudless blue skies, a temperature in the nineties, a shirt-sleeved crowd and the rigours of great humidity.

Although the commentary, thanks to modern technology, usually goes swiftly and smoothly across the world to listeners' bedrooms, it is often far from being incident-free at our end. To start with, the relief is profound when, twenty minutes or so before the start of the programme when one is

T.M.S. *goes overseas – C.M.J., Blowers and the Bearded Wonder on their rooftop perch at Brisbane in December 1979*

sitting in a converted something or other which has to make do as a commentary box in Hyderabad (Sind), Peter Baxter's cheerful voice suddenly comes floating across the ether. It seems nothing short of a miracle – and that he should be cheerful too after an early morning drive in the dark from arctic St Albans.

Then there is the almost inevitable agony when, with seven minutes to go, the line goes dead and all the engineers and technicians start to throw their hands in the air and gabble at you in Urdu, a language of which neither Don nor I acquired a working knowledge while in Pakistan. On these occasions voices are raised and tempers are frayed and one longs to be warmly in bed in England.

That particular Test match, the second against Pakistan in 1977-78, went off particularly smoothly apart from two unseemly incidents in the commentary box, both of which I was responsible for. At the far end of the ground was a Mosque which Don had been calling by some marvellously exotic name, without sensibly enough attempting the pronunciation. After three days of the match I thought I discovered that it was called something different and blithely described it as such to Don's dismay. I had of course got it wrong and was quite properly called to order by a producerly lecture. Just by the Mosque there was a tidy, new, shining factory about which Don had also done his homework. For no better reason than it looked like one, I referred to it as a toothpaste factory. It looked too ultrabright for words. This prompted a producerly sucking of teeth.

Perhaps my strongest memory of *Test Match Special* on that tour centres on the Gaddafi Stadium during the first Test in Lahore. Domestically, Pakistan was in something of a turmoil for General Zia was in charge, having put ex-President Bhutto in prison. Bhutto's wife and daughter and supporters of his Pakistan People's Party were doing all they could within the limits of martial law to stir it up. Public meetings with more than a score or so of people had been forbidden and so a crowd of thirty to forty thousand at a Test match was a heaven-sent opportunity for the unscrupulous. We had riots on successive days at the match although the first was nothing more than a rehearsal for the second and was not politically inspired. The spark which set it off was the frenzied excitement of watching Mudassar Nazar approach the slowest century in the history of Test cricket.

I was live on the air to London on the second day of the match when Mudassar ('Mud' to Bob Willis) turned a ball to long leg and ran a single. The crowd, who were perhaps not too aware of the finer intricacies of the game, imagined that it was a certain two and decided in unison that the only thing left for them to do was to come out and deliver their personal congratulations to their hero.

Undeterred by the fact that the figure 99 glared solemnly down from alongside his name on the scoreboard, Mudassar was submerged in a mass of humanity which would have kept at it if it had not been for the arrival of a considerable number of civil police whom the public despise and treat with scant respect. These police were dressed in khaki shirts and shorts and carried long wooden lathi sticks and in general looked like so many overgrown Boy Scouts and hardly inspired either respect or confidence. Their policy was not so much peacefully to coerce the multitude from the pitch as to give chase to anyone and everyone at the first possible opportunity. The result was that the ground was soon filled with a blur of 200-yard sprints which were inevitably won by the spectators. Those watching in the stands loved it and cheered their colleagues to the echo.

At this point it was all good-humoured enough until the inevitable happened. One athletic boy, who was leading a couple of police the most fearful dance, slipped as he tried yet another U-turn and fell down. His assailants were swiftly on to him and proceeded to flay him with their lathi sticks which was more than the crowd were prepared to tolerate. Not surprisingly, they, or most of them, immediately intervened on the boy's behalf. The ground was invaded from several directions and in moments the

civil police were put to flight. I remember saying over the air, 'This seems to be growing more serious,' as it suddenly occurred to me that all humour had disappeared. The police raced back across the ground to the members' area in front of the pavilion, where presumably they felt that the behaviour of the members could be relied upon rather better than at Lord's.

The police now regathered below us for we were sitting in the open on the pavilion roof. They tried a counter attack which the populace beat back without too much trouble and then the smarter, more lethally equipped, military police came into the arena from the pavilion area and at once the crowd drew back. With the help of some tear-gas canisters it was not long before the ground was cleared and then members of the crowd even volunteered to help clean up the debris which had been thrown on to the playing area.

When Mudassar did in fact reach his hundred, mercifully the celebrations were not in the same class as those which had greeted his arrival at 99. Anyway, I was able to say, in a way which I hoped would have made Brian Johnston positively green with envy, that 'it could truthfully be described as a riotous hundred'.

One problem from that day still remains with me. After describing the first twenty-five minutes of the riot, it became time to hand over to Don Mosey. I have never been sure of the words I should have used: 'And after a breath of tear gas it will be Don Mosey', or 'For the next public flogging it will be none other than Don Mosey', or maybe, 'Your narrator for the second half of cops and robbers will be Don Mosey'. And at this stage Don takes up the story himself. . . .


The following day was a very different matter. Friday is the Muslim Sabbath (if that does not offend Mohammedans too much) and Mudassar Nazar duly completed his century which had covered three days, thirteen hours and God alone knows how many minutes, to take its place in the *Guinness Book of Records, Wisden,* Bill Frindall's list of games-I-would rather-forget and the Wombwell Cricket Lovers' Society role of honour for that winter. H. C. Blofeld and I were happily contemplating a place in BBC Archives, as the commentators when this historic moment arrived – a reasonable amount of relief that it *had* arrived – when Madame Bhutto arrived, accompanied by a fair number of members of the Pakistan People's Party which at the time was proscribed in the republic. We knew that she was due in the stadium. Indeed, we had been told that the Pakistan Cricket Board of Control were not only expecting the lady but that she had been offered a seat in the VIP area. She had declined this.

There was a certain amount of trumpeting in various quarters as the PPP contingent hove into view but the first positive evidence we had in the commentary box of their arrival was when the Ladies' stand began to smoulder gently. The awnings in due course burst into flames, a pitched-battle began between rival factions on either side of the Ladies' stand, and gradually it overflowed on to the playing area. Police appeared, followed by Military Police in their American-Marines livery. The battle developed into a war and from there it escalated. I left the commentary box to ask the England team manager, Ken Barrington, if the tour could continue in these conditions and found the whole of the lower reaches of the pavilion in a state of siege.

It was totally impossible to get into the dressing-rooms to talk to either manager or players and, as I tried, a tear-gas bomb exploded at my feet. Other than certain English soccer-fans in Italy in June 1980, and assorted malefactors in various other categories, it is probable that most Radio 3 listeners have never been tear-gassed. In that case I advise them not to try it, especially if around ten or eleven recordings have to be put on tape in Broadcasting House, London, an hour or so later. With tears streaming down my face, and with vocal chords rather seriously constricted, I recorded all my pieces for the edification of Radio 2, 3 and 4 listeners at various stages of the day which was then in mid-afternoon with us, shortly after the rising of the lark with you at home in Britain. To complete my duties for the day I had to stay in the stadium and await the next stages of communication from London. By this time the Gaddafi stadium was deserted and the fires on the other side of the ground were quietly reaching the stage of Guy Fawkes night at 6 a.m. the following morning, but away in the distance I could see new and brighter fires springing up as the PPP followers wended their pyrotechnic way homewards. The only people left in the Gaddafi stadium were Jon Henderson, the Reuter's correspondent (although I had no means of knowing this), one Pakistan Post Office telex-operator and two Pakistan Radio engineers and myself. Henderson (again unknown to me) had flung himself in front of the last car to leave the area and found to his relief that it was driven by Wing-Commander Imtiaz Ahmed, chairman of the Pakistan selectors, who gave him a lift back to the Inter-Continental Hotel something more than three miles away. That left me, and my two engineering colleagues who, the minute the last broadcast was out of the way, left for *their* homes with all possible speed.

So there I was in the fast-gathering gloom of suburban Lahore, the fires of the Bhutto faction burning brightly in the distance – but a distance which separated me from my hotel. Now on the way into Pakistan from England the doyen of the press corps had impressed upon me: 'No one must be left behind in any ground, old son. I've been on 28 tours and it can be bloody nasty, I can tell you. So before we get out of any ground we've all got to make sure that none of us is left behind.' Great. Nice to think that we all look after each other. I've got no problems here in the darkness of the deserted stadium, with the fires of the rioters blazing away between me and the hotel – all I've got to do is to wait.

So I waited. And I waited. And I waited. No bus returned to take back the remnants of the media party. The words of the doyen rang in my ears: 'No one must be left behind . . . it can be bloody nasty.' There was no telephone to ring for a taxi. No taxi-driver, no rickshaw-wallah saw any point in turning down the lane to the long-deserted stadium. And the doyen and all-but-one of his colleagues were safely ensconced in the Inter-Continental Hotel.

There was only one thing for it and that was to walk back to the hotel. In the first half-mile I passed the Bhutto fans gaily dancing round the burned-out coachwork of a bus they had overturned on the main road. I passed through them in a silence which (to coin a phrase) could be felt. I had never fully understood the significance of the term until that moment. I got back to the pub and the first person I saw as I walked through the door was the doyen of the press corps.

'Hello, old son,' he said. 'They're not bloody fit to stage Test matches in this country, are they?' My reply was written on a piece of asbestos and will be sent to Freddie Trueman as a birthday card.

From Pakistan we progressed, rather happily, to New Zealand via Colombo (Sri Lanka) and Singapore. It was a largely uneventful journey except that, as we were about to leave Colombo, Henry – dear Henry – discovered that the manuscript of his magnum opus on 'The Packer Affair' had been left on his seat whilst we disembarked for a leg-stretching break and had now been removed by the aircraft cleaners. There was a pandemonium which echoed across Asia while Henry – dear Henry – ravaged through the Sri Lankan dustbins and Ken Barrington muttered darkly that, if we missed our connection in Singapore, Henry – dear Henry – would not be in the top ten at Lord's, or with the tour party. We made the connection with minutes to spare, thanks to the super-efficiency of the ground staff in Singapore who appeared to be all women, and singularly beautiful women too. We reached Auckland the following afternoon and found that the hotel had been damaged by a fire during the night, and that our accommodation, in consequence, had been changed.

Back in Britain, of course, the watchword was: 'So who's surprised? Mosey is there.' I swear I had nothing to do with that fire. It occurred when I was in distinguished company – I was playing Scrabble with Geoff Miller, I promise you – at 35,000 feet over Australia. I could not have had anything to do with the fire. But who, within or without the BBC, believes me? No one. No one at all. Chris Martin-Jenkins had sent me a letter to await my arrival at the Mon Desir Motel and I took delivery of it a year later. And I don't think he believes that I didn't burn the place myself!

New Zealand is quite incredibly beautiful and populated by the nicest people I have ever met anywhere in the world. The seven-weeks tour there was marvellous for everyone, with the possible exception of Geoff Boycott who had to skipper an English side to its first-ever defeat in New Zealand. He shouldn't worry. He did his stuff as batsman and captain, but he couldn't do everything for everyone else in Wellington in February 1978. But New Zealand rejoiced, and rightly so. They had beaten the last remaining first-class country on their list, and beaten them emphatically. It was a wonderful tour and we loved New Zealand. So at the end of it we returned to Auckland for the final Test and one of the great moments of my life occurred when, on the next-to-last-day of the tour, I received a message that Wilson

Whineray, that great All-Black rugby captain who is known quite simply throughout New Zealand as 'God', would like to have a drink with me in the Barbarians Club (which, handily, is just outside Eden Park, Auckland). After a couple of hours in the company of the great man – and his hospitable colleagues of the New Zealand Baa-Baas – I was driven back to my hotel. Police blocked our way down Queen Street; three fire engines prevented our entering Custom House Street. So I completed the last 400 yards on foot to find that the South Pacific Hotel, too, had been infested by my personal gremlins and had caught fire.

Now Henry Blofeld, for reasons best known to himself (maybe it's the Old Etonian philosophy), had found fault with hotels throughout New Zealand. I could never understand this but then I am more accustomed to eating at Harry Ramsden's Fish and Chip Emporium than at Boodle's Club. Nevertheless, whenever I came downstairs in a New Zealand hotel, there would be Henry with the manager of the hotel standing with his (the manager's) heels smartly together as H.C.B. pronounced:

'I. . . I. . . I. . . I. . . really can't have this sort of thing at all. I mean I'm not going to stand for it, old man. I mean. . . really. . . it's not good enough.'

Usually it was a problem of a quite cataclysmic nature, such as Henry's bed not being seventeen feet wide, or facing Mecca, or his breakfast being delivered to his room for one person only instead of for the thirty-two for whom he had forgotten to order. It was all very serious, and generations of hotel managers throughout North and South Islands had been given the Old Etonian hard word about it.

So I feared the worst as I threaded my way between fire engines into the South Pacific Hotel, Auckland, on our penultimate night of the tour. The first person I encountered in the foyer was the doyen of the press corps who – we were now again on speaking terms after the Lahore incident – addressed me in the well remembered bleat of protest: 'I don't know, old son. I was sitting writing my piece when three firemen smashed down the bloody door with axes and told me to get out. I've been on 28 bloody tours and this is the worst I've ever known. . . .' I offered my sympathy, went to the reception desk and asked about the fire. 'It was a television set which exploded on the eighth floor,' said the receptionist. 'It hasn't caused a *lot* of damage but the dining-room is not in operation tonight because of the smoke.'

'On the eighth floor, was it?' I asked. 'Not, by any chance, in Mr Blofeld's room?'

New Zealanders are the nicest and most reasonable people I have met anywhere in the world but they clearly have their breaking point. 'Unfortunately not,' replied the receptionist.

Well, *I* didn't start the fire and *I* didn't take Henry to New Zealand. But they both happened to me, just the same. Anyone feel like joining me for a round-the-world cruise?

And finally back to Henry. . . .

In February 1980, India played England in a Test match in Bombay to celebrate the fiftieth Jubilee of the founding of the Indian Board of Control. *Test Match Special* mounted its own operation from the Wankhede stadium and I shared the commentary with Tony Lewis.

The England party arrived in Bombay after an exhausting series in Australia and by then it was a relief for all concerned to come to another country. The chaos at Bombay Airport, which is undergoing an overdue facelift, the interminable drive to the Taj Mahal Hotel, the early morning smells and the hopelessly crowded streets provided a welcome contrast.

We had a week off before the start of the Test match and obviously I spent a certain amount of time in touch with All India Radio to make sure that everything was organised. *TMS* were mounting their own commentary and not sharing the All India Radio studio. There was much that might have gone wrong.

After three days lying beside the swimming pool, I summoned a taxi outside the hotel, or rather an impressively dressed Sikh in a turban and uniform did so for me. I asked him to tell the driver that I wanted to go to All India Radio. I knew the building was not far away and full of enthusiasm the driver set off at a colossal rate. After ten minutes or so he was still going like a bat out of hell and I was certain that the studios were not much more than round the corner from the Taj. Of course, the driver had no idea whether to turn right or left or go straight on. He chose the latter, hoping that something would turn up. I suggested he was going the wrong way; he shrugged his shoulders and replied to me in Hindi. I raised my voice; he smiled and shrugged his shoulders and continued to talk in Hindi. A marvellous scene was developing. Eventually, in order to make him stop the car, I was forced to tap him on the shoulder by which time we were, as far as I could make out, well on the way to Madras.

Tempers all round were somewhat frayed by now and I am afraid that it was with the minimum of good grace that I paid off the driver and hailed another cab. This time the driver spoke English and I shortly discovered that we had passed the AIR building some twenty minutes before.

But after this unhappy start, everything went perfectly. AIR, thanks to Jasdev Singh who runs their Outside Broadcasts, could not have been more efficient and helpful. At the ground we had our own box which was next door to All India Radio's; it had plenty of room and was in an excellent position. Also we had two charming ladies who took it in turns to sit with us each day and twiddle the knobs. I also had to make a great many telephoned reports each day to the various news and sports bulletins. Getting through on a collect call from somewhere like India can be much more wearying than doing the actual broadcast. But these two ladies were superb for they put the calls through and whenever they were delayed or the operator was unhelpful they gave him the most tremendous stick, with wonderful results.

During the four days of the match (five were scheduled but it ended in four) Tony and I found various celebrities to come up to the box and help us with comments. Everyone who had ever been anything in Indian cricket was in Bombay, although sadly and surprisingly the match did not make too much of an impression on the public who had already seen two Tests in Bombay during the season and apparently felt this particular one was going to be a festival match. Consequently, the ground was never more than about a third full.

This was in great contrast to the impressive firework display held the night before the Test began at the Brabourne Stadium, the old Test ground just a few hundred yards down the road from Wankhede. The ground was packed with all of 30,000 people inside. It is a tragedy that domestic politics and personality clashes had forced the Wankhede stadium to be built a few years ago at vast expense about a quarter of a mile from the Brabourne stadium, which is still a marvellous arena although rather sad these days without cricket. The Brabourne has an infinitely better atmosphere.

On the first day of the match I persuaded Pearson Sureta, who is well known to *TMS* listeners having been India's guest commentator on various Indian tours of England, to join us. On another day the former Nawab of Pataudi (Tiger), who edits a flourishing cricket magazine, helped us out. Another Oxford Blue and Test player, Abbas Ali Baig, did likewise the next day, as on one occasion did a charming lady, Chandra Nayudu, whose father C. K. Nayudu was India's first Test captain. I had first met Chandra three years earlier when Tony Greig's side had played at Indore where she lives. She was then one of the All India Radio commentators. Now, and rather shyly at first, she answered all sorts of questions about herself and her father and was always interesting. I only wish listeners could have seen her for she is extremely pretty and always wore the most lovely sarees.

Perhaps the most bizarre aspect of the match occurred on the rest day which came, curiously enough, on the second day. The reason for this was that during that afternoon there was a total eclipse of the sun in Bombay. The sun is a Hindu God and the population had been told to stay indoors – in any case, watching a total eclipse with the naked eye can cause blindness.

During the afternoon it grew dark as if the city was in heavy shadow. It was during the afternoon that I got a taxi in order to lodge a telex at the cable office and it was almost eerie driving through the completely deserted streets which normally seem to hold about six million people. I did not see one car or person on the five minute journey. I had chosen the best time this century to go to the cable office.

THE OVAL

# A HUNDRED YEARS ON
## Trevor Bailey

There are few Test grounds in the world with a less attractive exterior and approach than The Oval. It is like so many Victorian hostelries to be found in the London suburbs, where the surrounding streets have declined from middle-class, terraced respectability to dingy flatlets and bedsitters. Although nothing can disguise the ugliness of the pubs' much painted exteriors, some of the bars within have been tastefully renovated and retain much of their original character. The changes and the repairs undertaken over the years give the buildings that worn charm to be found on the wrinkled face of an aged, yet active grandmother, with the result that they become much loved focal points for the community.

In the same way, the visitor, once he is inside The Oval, quickly forgets the gloom of an underground journey, or the delights of driving through places like the Lambeth Walk, the Elephant and Castle, Balham, or Brixton. He is immediately transported to a ground which has seen countless epic battles, and was the home of so many of the game's immortals, including Tom Richardson, Tom Hayward, Sir Jack Hobbs, and the great Surrey eleven of the fifties. If he has any imagination he will relish the Cockney humour, the ingrained charm and the atmosphere.

The Oval has become the accustomed venue for the final Test of a five match series, but for the 1980 summer it was used for the fourth against the West Indies. The Centenary Test was, largely for financial reasons, allocated to Lord's, even though the first Anglo-Australian Test did, in fact, take place on the Surrey ground.

The commentary box at The Oval is perched on the battlements of the

*The commentary box at The Oval, 'perched on the battlements of the ancient pavilion'*

ancient pavilion. It provides an excellent view of the action, but the accommodation is rather cramped, especially on a hot day, although normally there is plenty of space outside. However, for the West Indies match, in addition to the *Test Match Special* team, there were the usual BBC television cameras, commentators and an army of attendants, plus another set of cameras and producers with their plethora of lackeys, a posse of happy policemen, and, finally, a never ending stream of people who were doing something on, or about, the retirement of John Arlott, so that it was difficult to move.

Apart from a brief spell in mid afternoon by Gooch and Rose, the first day was largely passive as England amassed 241 for three. The West Indian fast bowlers were anything but quick when it came to the time they spent actually bowling. At stumps their grand total was 76 overs.

Spectators do not worry about funereal over rates when wickets are tumbling, or runs flowing, but when neither occurs it is hard on the watcher and a problem for commentators. The chief sufferer on this occasion was Don Mosey, who, in twenty minutes, which included running repairs to Boycott after he had been struck by a bouncer, described two overs producing one magical extra, which much amused Brian Johnston and brought forth some remarks from the Alderman.

This was not Don's favourite match as his spells at the mike invariably seemed to coincide with the excitement of a drinks session, lengthy maiden overs, and various external interruptions. He described them all with the expertise and an enthusiasm they did not really deserve, but this is, of course, the skill of the class commentator. I have always considered that John Arlott's most brilliant and inspired twenty minute stint was at Lord's when he devoted the entire session to describing the putting on of the covers. It was a genuine tour de force which was so good that it left the rest of the box, for once, speechless in sheer admiration.

After the departure of Gooch and Rose the chief excitement in the box was provided by our human computer, Bill Frindall, who revealed that the scoreboard had failed to include a no ball, an indication of the entertainment provided in six easily forgotten hours.

If the day was largely uneventful, the evening provided a sharp contrast. This was when the active members of the *Test Match Special* team paid their own tribute to our senior player, John Arlott, who was hanging up his boots and retiring to·Alderney at the end of the season.

Arranging a function of this nature is not as simple as it might appear. First, it was necessary to select a date to suit twelve busy, raving extraverts. Second, one had to avoid clashing with a never ending stream of farewell Arlott dinners, which seemed to be scheduled for every other night throughout the summer. Third, a suitable venue and a rough programme were essential.

I suggested the Wig and Pen in Fleet Street, because it was convenient, the food good, the cellar extensive, the atmosphere different and a private room available. It proved ideal. John chose the menu in advance: Scotch salmon, roast lamb, raspberries, and cheese, enriched by a succulent dry Bordeaux and a truly imperial claret. In entrusting me with the organisation, my colleagues showed a touching faith, as the odds on my booking the wrong time and date were high. Because the twelve who assembled for that last supper had all attended, spoken at, and suffered from numerous cricket dinners, we avoided any similarity. It was not so much a dinner as an informal occasion.

I left the ground with John Arlott and Tony Cozier with Peter Baxter at the wheel. John, who knows the 'back-doubles' to and from the cricket grounds of England rather better than most, navigated an interesting and unusual route via the Lambeth Walk, while Tony managed to leave his copy behind causing a moment of panic and some delay, but we did eventually arrive.

A few days earlier, Dick Brennan, the proprietor of the Wig and Pen, phoned me, almost apologetically, to ask if we minded him making a small presentation to John for his services to cricket on behalf of his members, and did I think John would like some vintage port? Having drunk a goodly quota of port over the years with John, I accepted on his behalf with alacrity and gratitude. The result was that while we were having a few pre-dinner drinks, mine host presented John with a case of Warre 1963, suitably inscribed with the outstanding feats on the cricket field during that vintage

*The family dinner for Arlott at the Wig and Pen Club*

year – a splendid opening for a memorable night.

John took his rightful place at the head of the table with the window of the fifteenth-century room behind him, because he is allergic to heat, which is unusual for a cricket commentator, and why he has not covered matches abroad as often as his many admirers would have liked.

What followed was an evening which melted away in a wealth of humour, anecdotes and nostalgia, a classic case of good food, good wine and good fellowship. There were no formal speeches, but plenty of chat. Johnston said a few appropriate words, presented John with an inscribed microphone on our behalf and then asked Christopher Martin-Jenkins to play recorded messages from three of John's absent friends, or, to be accurate, from a trio for whom John had little time and no respect. Although not generally known, Christopher is an excellent mimic and his taped impersonations were brilliant (even deceiving John at the outset) and the contents wickedly funny. I particularly enjoyed the two way conversation between Peter Baxter and a well known South African now resident in Australia.

After the celebrations of the previous evening, the team arrived remarkably fit at the ground, though it was as well that they did not have to take part in the pre-start limbering-up exercises which the players do these days, and have become part of the Test match ritual.

Initially, the chief talking point concerned the missing run which Bill

*John Arlott enjoying a glass with Bailey, Baxter and Johnston*

Frindall had spotted on the previous day, but had not been included on the scoreboard. In due course the run was added to the England total, much to Bill's delight, and it was agreed in the box that if England won by one run Bill would qualify for the man of the match award, while I described him, not without some difficulty, as 'an ecstatic statistician'. Apart from this it proved a quiet second day, until the last session. Don Mosey was given further opportunities to describe eloquently the taking on and off of the drinks by the respective twelfth men and England squandered the opportunity of putting together a really substantial total by some rather insipid batting and were all out for 370.

Throughout the summer the lunchtimes of the commentary team were made the more enjoyable by Laurent Perrier Champagne, provided by Frank Arnold, a director of the firm, and ferried by myself, which John Arlott described as 'the ideal medicine' for hard working commentators. Frank came to see us at work, which gave us the chance to toast him in his own champagne. After the Arlott dinner, it was even more welcome, and life giving, than usual.

As so often happens, the long stint in the field under hot sun had its effect on the West Indian players. Their batsmen began uncertainly against fresh bowlers with a new ball, which produced an exciting last session. The pitch no longer looked quite so sluggish and the tourists lost two wickets, while

Vivian Richards, the *bête noir* of the England attack, would also have departed if a difficult, but far from impossible, catch had been accepted. However, with two back in the hutch and Lloyd, who had badly torn a muscle while fielding, unlikely to bat, that 370 total looked a possible match winner.

On Saturday morning the weather was so hot and sunny at my home in Westcliff-on-Sea that it seemed the ideal occasion for me to sport that standard West Indian rig, a shirt-jacket suit. It proved a fatal error, as shortly after arriving at The Oval the sky darkened and the heavens opened. The storm was so intense that it was necessary to switch on the lights in the box to read the letters and within an hour the ground resembled a lake. Much to the disappointment of a rain-soaked capacity crowd, play had to be abandoned shortly after lunch. Naturally this did not apply to our lunchtime session which was enlivened by our guest, the author of the *Doctor in the House* series, Richard Gordon. He bubbled with enthusiasm and fun and really raised the gloom of a rainy day with his humour. After Ben Travers at Lord's he became the second *TMS* guest to defy B.J. to get a word in edgeways.

When it rains, cricketers retire to the boredom of their dressing-room and relax, but the *Test Match Special* team works overtime. On this occasion we kept going for some three hours of unrehearsed cricket chit-chat in an effort to entertain cricket lovers, which brought forth the following comments from Gillian Reynolds in *The Daily Telegraph*:

'On Saturday morning, when rain wiped out play at The Oval, the Radio 3 *Test Match Special* team remained undampened. There had been a bit of a squelch the evening before when Brian Johnston invited Fred Trueman to comment on the duties of the Twelfth Man and Fred snapped back that it was something he didn't know much about.

'But on Saturday, as John Arlott commented on the inches of rain on the corners of the ground and Bill Frindall said he was just looking out of the window and not at anything special, the team got down to the listeners' letters. It was, as usual, one of those interludes which quite made the heart rejoice even in a thunderstorm. Perhaps the central question of when the bail needs to fall for the batsman to be out will prove to be a *Test Match Special* long-runner.'

And of the Arlott voice:

'It's one which has deepened over the years and was, at first, thought by the BBC to be "a very vulgar voice". Valentine Dyall, to his eternal credit, told Mr Arlott early on, however, that he would personally cut his tongue if he ever strayed from Hampshire to BBC English Poetry. Powers of observation, and a certain degree of passion underline the Arlott prose style and all of them, along with the voice, will indeed be sorely missed.'

Speaking at our annual end of summer dinner given by the BBC, John Arlott once said, with much truth, that *Test Match Special* was no longer a strictly sporting programme, but we had really become a folk show, which was rather borne out by several letters from people who said that they preferred us when it rains!

Following my Saturday experiences, I decided against taking any chances with the weather and set forth on Monday suited and carrying a mac. The outcome predictably proved to be a fine, hot and sticky day.

We had all noted how chatty Fred had recently become about his exploits on the golf course and, knowing that he had been playing on Sunday and failing to receive an unsolicited in-depth account, I enquired what had happened from his partner, the luckless Alderman. It was an hilarious, if not a pretty tale, which Don unfolded with Yorkshire relish. The little white ball had failed to behave as Fred wanted, which immediately brought back to me memories of Fred, as a golfer, on various courses throughout the world. These were in the days when, like my own, his only handicap was his golf. Although he did sometimes hit the ball vast distances and usually had the happy knack of landing on a fairway, it was not always the correct one, while he was liable to explode, literally, in a bunker. These recollections put me into a happy mood for the rest of the day, or at least until the final session when the West Indies delivered four knock down punches which sent England staggering uncertainly towards – what, at the start of play, had appeared unthinkable – a possible defeat.

Thanks largely to the efforts of Bacchus and Marshall the tourists saved the follow-on and then their tail was permitted to reduce their first innings deficit by more than they should have done, because the England bowling, with the exception of Dilley and Emburey, was lacking in bite and the unfortunate Willis was suffering from an acute attack of 'Noballitis', which destroyed his rhythm, confidence and effectiveness.

Although, sadly, we in the commentary box had become all too accustomed to batting failures by England, and the Tourists had rather been let off the hook, the collapse which occurred in the last period took everybody by surprise. From a position of command, which justified Ladbrokes offering 100 to 1 against a West Indian victory, England suddenly found themselves in danger of defeat, as Holding and Croft in a few very fast overs ripped out four wickets. This sudden transformation from riches to rags provided a beautiful example of how the greatest excitement in cricket is derived from the situation. When the West Indies began, their fields were defensive and the main purpose was to stop the runs coming too quickly; but by stumps the crowd was roaring, the batsmen were surrounded by close fielders, and nobody was moaning about a slow over rate, because it was completely forgotten in the tension and the noise.

All too often the last day of a Test match proves to be little more than a formality with the outcome, a commentator's nightmare, the foregone conclusion – like 70 required on an easy pitch with 10 wickets in hand, or, worse still, the complete stalemate with both teams simply going through the motions. In contrast, the start of the Tuesday of the Oval Test was the commentator's dream, with plenty of atmosphere in the ground and in our

ENGLAND 1st INNINGS v. WEST INDIES 4TH TEST at KENNINGTON OVAL, LONDON on 24, 25, 26/ (no play) 28, 29 JULY, 1980. TOSS: ENGLAND

| IN | OUT | MINS | No. | BATSMAN | HOW OUT | BOWLER | RUNS | WKT | TOTAL | 6s | 4s | BALLS | NOTES ON DISMISSAL |
|---|---|---|---|---|---|---|---|---|---|---|---|---|---|
| 11.30 | 3.45 | 217 | 1 | GOOCH | LBW | HOLDING | 83 | 1 | 155 | · | 11 | 128 | Missed on drive. |
| 11.30 / 3.48 | 12.01 / 12.23 | 226 | 2 | BOYCOTT | RUN OUT (GREENIDGE) | | 53 | 4 | 269 | · | 4 | 146 | Attempted single to mid-on's left. |
| 12.03 | 3.54 | 192 | 3 | ROSE | BOWLED | CROFT | 50 | 2 | 157 | · | 6 | 135 | Missed firm-footed off-drive - off stump out |
| 3.56 | 5.08 | 54 | 4 | LARKINS | LBW | GARNER | 7 | 3 | 182 | · | 1 | 38 | Beaten by breakback - pushed half-forward |
| 5.10 | 1.27 | 197 | 5 | GATTING | BOWLED | CROFT | 48 | 5 | 303 | · | 5 | 129 | Missed hook - ball kept low. |
| 12.25 | 3.36 | 151 | 6 | WILLEY | C LLOYD | HOLDING | 34 | 8 | 343 | · | 2 | 98 | Cut half-volley hard to gully's left (brilliant left-handed catch) |
| 1.29 | 2.32 | 23 | 7 | KNOTT † | C LLOYD | MARSHALL | 3 | 6 | 312 | · | · | 19 | Failed to avoid bouncer that hit glove and flew low to gully. |
| 2.34 | 3.07 | 33 | 8 | BOTHAM * | LBW | CROFT | 9 | 7 | 336 | · | 1 | 16 | Misjudged line - ball delivered wide of crease kept low. |
| 3.09 | 4.45 | 77 | 9 | EMBUREY | C HOLDING | MARSHALL | 24 | 10 | 370 | · | 3 | 63 | Mistimed off-drive - skier to mid-off's left. |
| 3.38 | 4.40 | 43 | 10 | DILLEY | BOWLED | GARNER | 1 | 9 | 368 | · | · | 22 | Late on yorker - middle stump out. |
| 4.42 | (4.45) | 3 | 11 | WILLIS | NOT OUT | | 1 | · | · | · | · | 1 | |
| | | | | EXTRAS | b 7 lb 21 w 10 nb 19 | | 57 | | | | | | 0s 33  795 balls (inc. 24 no balls) |

* CAPTAIN   † WICKET-KEEPER

TOTAL (OFF 128·3 OVERS IN 618 MINUTES) 370 all out at 4.45pm on 2nd DAY.

12 OVERS 3 BALLS/HOUR
2.88 RUNS/OVER
47 RUNS/100 BALLS

| BOWLER | O | M | R | W | nb/w | HRS | OVERS | RUNS |
|---|---|---|---|---|---|---|---|---|
| HOLDING | 28 | 5 | 67 | 2 | -/6 | 1 | 11 | 26 |
| CROFT | 35 | 9 | 97 | 3 | 7/3 | 2 | 12 | 41 |
| MARSHALL | 29.3 | 6 | 77 | 2 | 12/1 | 3 | 13 | 48 |
| GARNER | 33 | 8 | 67 | 2 | -/4 | 4 | 11 | 43 |
| RICHARDS | 3 | 1 | 5 | 0 | -/5 | 5 | 14 | 48 |
| | | | | | 57/or 18 | 6 | 13 | 30 |
| | | | | | | 7 | 14 | 35 |
| | 128.3 | 29 | 370 | 10 | | 8 | 12 | 32 |
| | | | | | | 9 | 12 | 33 |
| | | | | | | 10 | 12 | 27 |

2ND NEW BALL taken at 12.26pm on 2nd DAY
- ENGLAND 263-4 after 87 overs.

| RUNS | MINS | OVERS | LAST 50 (in mins) |
|---|---|---|---|
| 50 | 101 | 18.2 | 101 |
| 100 | 163 | 32.2 | 62 |
| 150 | 215 | 42.5 | 52 |
| 200 | 297 | 60 | 82 |
| 250 | 382 | 78.5 | 85 |
| 300 | 466 | 97 | 84 |
| 350 | 590 | 121.3 | 124 |

LUNCH: 67-0  GOOCH 28* (121 min.)  ROSE 25* (88 min.)
OFF 23 OVERS IN 121 MINUTES

TEA: 167-2  BOYCOTT 7* (55 min.)  LARKINS 3* (16 min.)
OFF 48 OVERS IN 243 MINUTES

STUMPS: 236-3  BOYCOTT 39* (173 min.)  GATTING 18* (80 min.)
(1ST DAY)  OFF 74 OVERS IN 362 MINUTES

LUNCH: 303-5  WILLEY 13* (65 min.)  KNOTT 0* (1 min)
OFF 100 OVERS IN 482 MINUTES

TEA: 364-8  EMBUREY 20* (64 min.)  DILLEY 0* (35 min.)
OFF 125 OVERS IN 605 MINUTES

| WKT | PARTNERSHIP | | RUNS | MINS |
|---|---|---|---|---|
| 1st | Gooch | Boycott / Rose | 9* / 146 | 31 / 186 |
| 2nd | Rose | Boycott | 2 | 6 |
| 3rd | Boycott | Larkins | 25 | 54 |
| 4th | Boycott | Gatting | 87 | 131 |
| 5th | Gatting | Willey | 34 | 62 |
| 6th | Willey | Knott | 9 | 23 |
| 7th | Willey | Botham | 24 | 33 |
| 8th | Willey | Emburey | 7 | 27 |
| 9th | Emburey | Dilley | 25 | 43 |
| 10th | Emburey | Willis | 2 | 3 |

WEST INDIES 1ST INNINGS     (In reply to ENGLAND'S 370 all out)

| IN | OUT | MINS | No. | BATSMAN | HOW OUT | BOWLER | RUNS | WKT | TOTAL | 6s | 4s | BALLS | NOTES ON DISMISSAL |
|---|---|---|---|---|---|---|---|---|---|---|---|---|---|
| 4.57 | 5.21 | 24 | 1 | GREENIDGE | LBW | WILLIS | 6 | 1 | 15 | · | · | 27 | Missed hook. |
| 4.57 | 5.53 | 56 | 2 | HAYNES | C GOOCH | DILLEY | 7 | 2 | 34 | · | · | 32 | Followed short off side ball - edged to 1st slip. |
| 5.23 | 11.51 | 90 | 3 | RICHARDS | C WILLEY | BOTHAM | 26 | 3 | 72 | · | 3 | 66 | Cut hard to gully (held at 2nd attempt). BOTHAM'S 150th TEST WKT |
| 5.55 | 3.04 | 211 | 4 | BACCHUS | C KNOTT | EMBUREY | 61 | 6 | 187 | · | 8 | 159 | Gloved sweep towards leg-slip. |
| 11.53 | 12.43 | 50 | 5 | KALLICHARRAN | C ROSE | DILLEY | 11 | 4 | 99 | · | 1 | 42 | Swept to backward short leg - held at 2nd attempt. |
| 12.45 | 12.50 | 5 | 6 | MURRAY † | HIT WICKET | DILLEY | 0 | 5 | 105 | · | · | 1 | Played back too far and kicked off stump. |
| 12.52 | 3.30 | 118 | 7 | MARSHALL | C ROSE | EMBUREY | 45 | 7 | 197 | · | 6 | 115 | Clipped off break hard and low to leg slip. |
| 3.06 | 5.01 | 94 | 8 | GARNER | C GATTING | BOTHAM | 46 | 9 | 265 | 1 | 6 | 99 | Mistimed off-drive - skier to mid-off. |
| 3.32 | 4.57 | 64 | 9 | HOLDING | LBW | DILLEY | 22 | 8 | 261 | 1 | 3 | 60 | Hit across full-toss. |
| 4.59 | (5.01) | 2 | 10 | CROFT | NOT OUT | | 0 | · | · | · | · | 1 | |
| - | - | · | 11 | LLOYD * | ABSENT HURT | | - | · | · | · | · | · | Pulled hamstring fielding on 2nd day. |
| | | | | EXTRAS | b - lb 12 w 1 nb 28 | | 41 | | | | | | 2b 27* 602 balls (including 30 no balls) |

* CAPTAIN   † WICKET-KEEPER

TOTAL (OFF 95·2 OVERS IN 365 MINUTES) 265

15 OVERS 4 BALLS/HOUR
2.78 RUNS/OVER
44 RUNS/100 BALLS

| BOWLER | O | M | R | W | nb/w | HRS | OVERS | RUNS |
|---|---|---|---|---|---|---|---|---|
| WILLIS | 19 | 5 | 58 | 1 | 20/1 | 1 | 13 | 35 |
| DILLEY | 23 | 6 | 57 | 4 | 9/- | 2 | 15 | 37 |
| BOTHAM | 18.2 | 8 | 47 | 2 | 1/1 | 3 | 13 | 39 |
| EMBUREY | 23 | 12 | 38 | 2 | -/- | 4 | 14 | 45 |
| GOOCH | 1 | 0 | 2 | 0 | -/- | 5 | 19 | 41 |
| WILLEY | 11 | 5 | 22 | 0 | -/- | 6 | 20 | 60 |
| | | | | | 41 | | | |
| | 95.2 | 36 | 265 | 9 | | | | |

2ND NEW BALL taken at 4.40pm on 4th DAY
- WEST INDIES 237-7 after 91 overs.

| RUNS | MINS | OVERS | LAST 50 (in mins) |
|---|---|---|---|
| 50 | 103 | 24.1 | 103 |
| 100 | 171 | 39.2 | 68 |
| 150 | 225 | 53.4 | 54 |
| 200 | 307 | 76.1 | 82 |
| 250 | 354 | 93.1 | 47 |

STUMPS: 45-2  RICHARDS 14* (69 min)  BACCHUS 5* (37 min)
(2ND DAY)  OFF 22 OVERS IN 95 MINUTES

NO PLAY POSSIBLE 3RD DAY - Abandoned at 3.00 pm

LUNCH: 145-5  BACCHUS 49* (157 min)  MARSHALL 20* (38 min)
OFF 51 OVERS IN 215 MINUTES

TEA: 221-7  GARNER 19* (64 min)  HOLDING 8* (38 min)
OFF 88 OVERS IN 335 MINUTES

| WKT | PARTNERSHIP | | RUNS | MINS |
|---|---|---|---|---|
| 1st | Greenidge | Haynes | 15 | 24 |
| 2nd | Haynes | Richards | 19 | 30 |
| 3rd | Richards | Bacchus | 38 | 58 |
| 4th | Bacchus | Kallicharran | 27 | 50 |
| 5th | Bacchus | Murray | 6 | 5 |
| 6th | Bacchus | Marshall | 82 | 92 |
| 7th | Marshall | Garner | 10 | 24 |
| 8th | Garner | Holding | 64 | 64 |
| 9th | Garner | Croft | 4 | 2 |
| | | | 265 | |

ENGLAND 2ND INNINGS        105 RUNS AHEAD ON FIRST INNINGS

| IN | OUT | MINS | No. | BATSMAN | HOW OUT | BOWLER | RUNS | WKT | TOTAL | 6s | 4s | BALLS | NOTES ON DISMISSAL |
|---|---|---|---|---|---|---|---|---|---|---|---|---|---|
| 5.13 | 5.24 | 11 | 1 | GOOCH | LBW | HOLDING | 0 | 1 | 2 | . | . | 10 | Pushed across line - beaten by pace |
| 5.13 | 5.56 | 43 | 2 | BOYCOTT | C⁑ MURRAY | CROFT | 5 | 2 | 10 | . | . | 24 | Edged push at widish off side ball - 'walked'. |
| 5.26 | 12.23 | 147 | 3 | ROSE | LBW | GARNER | 41 | 6 | 67 | . | 1 | 112 | Hit across full-toss. |
| 5.58 | 6.02 | 4 | 4 | LARKINS | BOWLED | HOLDING | 0 | 3 | 13 | . | . | 2 | Late on stroke - off stump out. |
| 6.04 | 6.08 | 4 | 5 | EMBUREY | C⁑ BACCHUS | CROFT | 2 | 4 | 18 | . | . | 2 | Pushed full-toss to forward short-leg. |
| 6.10 | 12.12 | 92 | 6 | GATTING | C⁑ MURRAY | GARNER | 15 | 5 | 63 | . | . | 50 | Edged off-drive at widish ball. |
| 12.14 | 12.40 | 26 | 7 | BOTHAM * | C⁑ GREENIDGE | GARNER | 4 | 7 | 73 | . | . | 17 | Edged away - seamer low to 2nd slip's left. |
| 12.25 | (5.21) | 236 | 8 | WILLEY | NOT OUT | | 100 | | . | 17 | | 203 | Maiden hundred in Test matches. |
| 12.42 | 1.45 | 24 | 9 | KNOTT † | LBW | HOLDING | 3 | 8 | 84 | . | . | 25 | Beaten by fast breakback - no stroke. |
| 1.47 | 2.07 | 20 | 10 | DILLEY | C⁑ SUB (CL.KING) | HOLDING | 1 | 9 | 92 | . | . | 15 | Diving catch at backward square-leg. |
| 2.09 | (5.21) | 171 | 11 | WILLIS | NOT OUT | | 24 | | . | 3 | | 114 | - |

* CAPTAIN   † WICKET-KEEPER    EXTRAS    b -   lb 6    w 1   nb 7    14      - 21⁴ 574 balls (including 10 no balls)

TOTAL    (OFF 94 OVERS IN 398 MIN.)   209-9 DECLARED at 5.21 pm

14 OVERS 1 BALLS/HOUR
2.22 RUNS/OVER
36 RUNS/100 BALLS

| BOWLER | O | M | R | W | nb w | | HRS | OVERS | RUNS |
|---|---|---|---|---|---|---|---|---|---|
| HOLDING | 29 | 7 | 79 | 4 | - | | 1 | 12 | 18 |
| CROFT | 10 | 6 | 8 | 2 | - | | 2 | 14 | 25 |
| MARSHALL | 23 | 7 | 47 | 0 | 7/1 | | 3 | 12 | 30 |
| GARNER | 17 | 5 | 24 | 3 | 3/ | | 4 | 14 | 26 |
| RICHARDS | 9 | 3 | 15 | 0 | - | | 5 | 14 | 42 |
| KALLICHARRAN | 6 | 1 | 22 | 0 | - | | 6 | 19 | 38 |
| | | | | | 14 | | | | |
| | 94 | 29 | 209 | 9 | | | | | |

2ND NEW BALL taken at 4.44 pm 5th Day
- ENGLAND 180-9 after 86 overs.

| RUNS | MINS | OVERS | LAST 50 (in mins) |
|---|---|---|---|
| 50 | 126 | 28 | 126 |
| 100 | 245 | 53 | 119 |
| 150 | 308 | 68.5 | 63 |
| 200 | 384 | 91 | 76 |

STUMPS: 20-4   ROSE 11* (64 min)
(4TH DAY)    GATTING 1* (20 min)
OFF 17 OVERS IN 77 MINUTES

LUNCH: 83-7   WILLEY 5* (36 min)
      KNOTT 3* (19 min)
OFF 42 OVERS IN 198 MINUTES

TEA: 175-9   WILLEY 80* (186 min)
     WILLIS 15* (121 min)
OFF 82 OVERS IN 348 MINUTES

MATCH DRAWN

MAN OF THE MATCH: PETER WILLEY

TOTAL TIME LOST: 6 HOURS 0 MINUTES

| WKT | PARTNERSHIP | | RUNS | MINS |
|---|---|---|---|---|
| 1st | Gooch | Boycott | 2 | 11 |
| 2nd | Boycott | Rose | 8 | 30 |
| 3rd | Rose | Larkins | 3 | 4 |
| 4th | Rose | Emburey | 5 | 4 |
| 5th | Rose | Gatting | 45 | 92 |
| 6th | Rose | Botham | 4 | 9 |
| 7th | Botham | Willey | 6 | 15 |
| 8th | Willey | Knott | 11 | 24 |
| 9th | Willey | Dilley | 8 | 20 |
| 10th | Willey | Willis | 117* | 171 |
| | | | 209 | |

box. England were 20 for four, 125 ahead with six hours to play, and there was a heavy, misty sky with the promise of sunshine later. All four results were feasible, the ideal situation. Everybody wanted to broadcast and there was no shortage of material.

Although I expected and predicted a draw, I did not think England, once they had safely negotiated the first hour and the West Indies were reduced to three bowlers, would bat so indifferently; at the same time nobody, including the two heroes themselves, could have considered an undefeated last-wicket partnership of 117 between Willey and Willis as anything less than a major miracle due to direct divine intervention.

The Willey-Willis stand effectively killed the game as a spectacle. Before the middle of the afternoon all hopes of anything but a draw departed, as there was insufficient time for the West Indies to make the runs, or England to bowl them out. Richards and Kallicharran sent down a few perfunctory overs and the only point of interest in the final session, until Botham put everybody out of their misery by declaring at 5.20, was Willey reaching an admirable first century in Test cricket.

Another ball by ball was over and the team departed.

# THE CRITICS
## ——— Trevor Bailey ———

As a former player, who over the years received a considerable amount of criticism, I can claim to appreciate better than most that cricket is far, far easier to play from the press or commentary box than out in the middle. The media representatives do not have to cope with a hard ball being propelled towards them at eighty miles per hour; bowl at Vivian Richards after the two previous immaculate deliveries have been casually dismissed to the boundary; or go to the wicket knowing that failure almost certainly means non-selection for a coming enjoyable, and highly lucrative, tour. They are not personally involved and can talk blithely about the result not being really important; whereas it does, and should matter enormously to the players. If it did not, the match would become an exhibition rather than a hard fought contest.

In *Test Match Special* we try to provide an accurate and interesting description of what is happening and explain why. This can be difficult, as there are odd occasions when the tactics are utterly incomprehensible to all but those actually participating.

A classic example occurred on the first morning of the fifth Test against the West Indies at The Oval in 1976. After only two overs from Bob Willis, in which he had removed Gordon Greenidge for a duck, he was taken off by Tony Greig and replaced by Derek Underwood, because the England captain thought the pitch would prove receptive to spin. The West Indies went on to plunder 687 for eight declared. What was hard to understand was not that Tony should have misread that docile pitch, but that he should have wasted a new ball and a Bob Willis with his tail up. It did not make sense at the time and still does not.

When Essex were set a target to chase, our captain, Tom Pearce, would smile benignly round our dressing-room and issue the following instructions: 'Play your shots, but don't get out.' Easy orders to obey within the confines of the commentary box, but rather more demanding for the batsmen who actually had to score those runs.

There are times when we have to be critical in order to give the listener a true account; but we try not to be over critical and we attempt to explain the actions of the players, even if sometimes disagreeing with them. Take the case, which I know so well from personal experience, of the batsman who stages a recovery by watchful crease occupation and achieves his objective. Some three hours later there could well be a need for acceleration, but the ordinary, as distinct from the great player may well find that he is unable to switch gear. Again, with no pressure and time to analyse the need for another slip, a short leg, or a positional change in the field to block a particular stroke may be obvious in the box, but not to a harassed skipper in the middle. However, despite our intentions, undoubtedly there are times when we become too critical – but we do expect the highest standards at Test match level.

We are, of course, far more likely to be intolerant on the air than in print because we have to make an instant assessment, rather than a carefully considered opinion, of an event in which we may be emotionally, though not actually, involved. At the end of an over which contained a wide, full toss and a couple of long hops, Brian Johnston might say: 'What do you think of that over, Trevor?' My off-the-cuff reply would be more pungent than if I was writing. Again, describing the fall of a wicket, when the striker has been brilliantly caught at mid-wicket off a slow ball which had pitched outside the off stump, half way down the pitch, I might describe it thus: 'Bad ball, poor shot; beautifully taken, shoulder-high, one-handed catch by David Gower moving quickly to his left – a perfect illustration of a rank long-hop taking a wicket and changing the course of a match, and the stupidity of lifting the head and trying to hit the ball too hard.'

I like to think that I have remained very much on the side of the players and seek to find reasons or excuses for errors and mistakes. What I cannot tolerate, and never could in my playing days, is bad behaviour, or bad cricket. What do I consider bad behaviour? The verbal or physical abuse of umpires; swearing at the opposition; throwing bricks into the crowd; deliberate cheating and meanness of spirit are examples. Nobody expects too many prisoners to be taken in an Anglo-Australian Test series, while gamesmanship (sometimes ethically doubtful, often very funny) has always abounded; but to bowl 'grubs', though within the laws, simply kills cricket as a spectacle. No spectacle means no crowd, no television, no sponsor and no money – a self-defeating exercise.

What do I mean by bad cricket? The nightwatchman who is stumped trying to hit a six; the seam bowler who fails to maintain a reasonable line and length; slovenly fielding; or the very late call which leaves the other unfortunate batsman stranded, are all unpardonable offences. I would never blame anyone for losing his wicket trying to punish a loose ball, but have no sympathy for the player who is bowled round his legs by a straight one, unless it occurred when runs were needed quickly and he was improvising, because he has offended against a fundamental of batsmanship.

There are also times when cricketers entirely misread a situation, as instanced by the Centenary Test at Lord's, when England failed to realise that this was intended to be a great cricketing occasion, a one-off affair, not part of a series to decide the Ashes.

Players, even international, are human and, like commentators, will make mistakes. This is perfectly illustrated by the following incident, involving of all people Geoff Boycott – which, of course, is why I remember it so clearly. It was so utterly uncharacteristic. Geoff is one of the most professional, dependable, and dedicated batsmen England have produced, and one who makes fewer unforced errors than anyone in the game. Keith Boyce was bowling the last over of the day in the Lord's Test of 1973 to Geoff and, fairly predictably, sent down a bouncer. Rather surprisingly, Geoff was unable to resist the challenge and mishooked in the square-leg region, but it did not matter as it was a no ball. The West Indies captain, Rohan Kanhai, immediately reinforced the on-side boundary and I was for once left speechless in the box, for Keith let fly another and Geoff holed out to the newly stationed fielder. I could not believe that Geoff had fallen into that obvious trap in that situation; or, indeed, that Keith should have used the bouncer rather than a yorker. Perhaps it was an intentional double bluff, but I have my doubts.

# RAIN IN THE STUDIO
## —————— Peter Baxter ——————

A beautiful day in London – the sort of day that makes me wish I was in the rugby stand at Headingley instead of making my way to the bowels of Broadcasting House. Surely the forecast of continuing rain in the North can't be right? Into the sanctuary of the security controlled studio and almost immediately comes the news down the line from Leeds: 'No play today, Backers. They've just called it off and they're not too happy about tomorrow, either.'

Decisions to be made. It would obviously not be right to abandon the programme outright, but to deprive the music lovers of their normal Radio 3 programmes to no good end seems harsh. Knowing that there will be no play on this first day makes the commentators understandably reluctant to embark on one of their discussion sessions, but they are persuaded to start with at least twenty minutes of speculative chat. Scanning the *Radio Times* indicates that there is a programme junction at a quarter past twelve and that becomes my target. However, there is the question of our lunchtime feature, 'The Great Match', which is billed in the *Radio Times*. This is the vital factor in deciding that it must go on, although, perhaps unworthily, the thought uppermost in my mind is the amount of work that Christopher Martin-Jenkins and I have put in on it. It is a look back at the 1976 Headingley Test which is etched in my memory for personal reasons.

On the last morning of that match, with the game still very much in the balance, our line from Leeds suddenly went dead. As one does on these occasions, I started to read the scorecard. This usually gives enough time for the sound to be restored, but on this occasion nothing happened and so, as Wayne Daniel started to pound in to bowl, I started commentary off my television monitor. I ended up doing ten minutes of commentary, always imagining that each ball would be my last, and during that time England lost the vital wicket of Alan Knott. The most unnerving aspect was the total silence in the studio, with no crowd noise to back the description of the action, and I was enormously relieved when a voice said in my headphones that we were in contact again.

Anyway, that story forms no part of the Great Match programme which Radio 3 agree they will be able to put out on time. Just before *Test Match Special* opens up all our plans have been laid.

On Friday morning there is an early call from John Helm producing the Test match at Headingley to tell me that prospects are much brighter for a start after lunch. We go on the air as scheduled with the commentators in good voice, discussing such contentious issues as Sunday play for nearly an hour and a half. When they finally run out of steam I am able to keep the cricket talk going by putting on the tape of one of our old Great Match features, this time on the great Australian victory at Leeds in 1948.

Meanwhile the calls are flowing in to a neighbouring studio for our lunchtime phone-in, 'Call the Commentators', and David Gordon, the sports producer looking after it, has been in a couple of times to go through some of the suggested questions for Christopher Martin-Jenkins, Fred Trueman and Tony Cozier. By the time the 1.35 news is being read the first callers are being raised and plugged through. Because there is still no play at Headingley, we take an extended 'Call the Commentators' but happily, as we start the second half of the programme, the announcement comes that play will start at 2.45 and at last the fifth Test is under way.

# A GREAT
# YORKSHIRE OCCASION
## ——— Fred Trueman ———

Yorkshire County Cricket Club was formed at a meeting in Sheffield on 5 January 1863, although the first county match to be played in Yorkshire dates back, as far as I can trace, to 1833 against Norfolk at Sheffield Hyde Park ground. Headingley itself was opened as a cricket ground in 1889 and Yorkshire played their first game there about 1890. Not until 1893, when the Sheffield domination of thirteen committee members (all club officers) against nine others was finally broken, did Headingley become Yorkshire's premier ground. In the same year, Yorkshire won their first county championship under Lord Hawke, who, I suspect, had a lot to do with Yorkshire staging its first Test match, England against Australia, in 1899.

Yorkshire moved its offices and records to Headingley, from the famous old buildings of Park Row in Leeds city centre, for the start of the 1964 season. Today, of course, the ground is the hub of all Yorkshire cricketing business, which becomes more demanding every day with the advent of modern-day cricket and its complications of one-day fixtures. But although Headingley is Yorkshire's cricket headquarters, the ground itself does, in fact, belong to the Leeds Cricket, Football and Athletic Co Ltd whose main interest lies in the rugby league ground. Yorkshire CCC thus has a lease and has to pay rent to play county matches there.

The ground has gone through a steady change over the years, the most famous one being the building of the new stand which provides viewing for both cricket and rugby league. I say famous because the old stand was burned down on Good Friday in 1932 and Yorkshire CCC advanced the L.C.F. & A. Co Ltd the sum of five thousand pounds, free of interest, towards

*Up and under the rugby league stand at Headingley, the lights are on in the box*

the cost of rebuilding. Gone also is the old pavilion where both sides used to change, with its three dressing-rooms and four baths. One of the smaller rooms was for the amateurs and the pros used the others.

Headingley's history is littered with happenings and records, some to be beaten, some, possibly, never to be beaten. Let's look back at 1900, when the all-conquering Yorkshire side was playing against Somerset. Somerset arrived, the side not a very good one, and it was expected that Yorkshire would beat them quite easily. But what a shock was in store for the cocky Yorkshiremen. Somerset had batted first and, as was expected, were all out for 87. Yorkshire then batted and made 325. On the second day, the Somerset players made arrangements for travelling that evening in order to save the hotel bill. It was fully expected that Yorkshire would finish the match that day. But what a shock, as I say – by the evening, Phillips had made a century; Braund had made a century; Palairet was still batting, and he made a century; and Somerset amassed in their second innings 630, one of the highest scores ever against Yorkshire in its history. They say the wicket broke up in the second innings and Yorkshire were all out for 113 – very soundly and truly thrashed.

It was at Headingley that Hedley Verity returned those magnificent bowling figures against Nottinghamshire of ten wickets for ten runs. But I think one of the most amazing records at Headingley must concern that run-machine, Donald Bradman, later Sir Donald Bradman. He must have thought Headingley was the greatest ground in the world to play cricket on.

He came to this country on his first tour in 1930, and then again in 1934, 1938 and 1948 – four tours in all. On his first visit to the Headingley wicket, in 1930, he made 334: 100 before lunch, 100 between lunch and tea, and 100 between tea and the close of play. Will the likes of that ever be seen again? I don't think so. In 1934, he returned to Headingley and made 304. In 1938, which could possibly be put down as a failure, he made only 103, and in the second innings he made 16. In 1948 he returned, once again, with that all-conquering triumphant side, which is possibly the greatest side that has ever played in Test cricket anywhere in the world. In the first innings he made 33. Had Bradman gone? No. In the second innings he came out to bat and made 173 not out. What startling performances! In the six innings he had at Headingley, one of which was not out, he amassed 967 runs at a staggering average of 192.6. What a remarkable piece of cricket history!

I have seen a lot of changes in my 33 years association with Headingley but I must admit I have some very happy memories and I still laugh at times when they come flooding back.

I first went to Headingley in 1948. When I saw the size of the ground I was as nervous as a kitten. It was a bit different to Roche-Abbey at the bottom of the Maltby Craggs when you had to use a shovel to move the cow pats before you started playing. If you were hit by the ball when fielding, the rule was that it should be rolled back to the keeper and not thrown. Another rule was that the home side, if fielding first, would leave the field fifteen minutes early in order to wash their hands before helping to serve tea to the visiting team and their ladies.

It was always a great thrill to walk down the steps through the crowd on to the field and listen to some of the comments from the members who used to get to the ground early to command the best seats nearest to the dressing-rooms. Against Lancashire, if Yorkshire batted first you would have heard such things directed to Len Hutton as 'Don't lift gate before lunch, Len. We don't want to give this away.' It was that fabulous gentleman and humorist Maurice Leyland who, when he had dropped a catch in front of them, heard a voice say, 'I could have caught that in my mouth.' 'If mine was as big as thine he would a dun,' he replied.

I remember in the nets one day in April Maurice Leyland was coaching. We had a young left-arm fast bowler by the name of James who was trying to impress, and quite rightly so. He kept pitching the ball short, causing the batsman to duck and weave. Maurice went up to him and said that the essence of using the new ball is to pitch it up which should help to swing the ball and move it off the seam. He took all the advice and said he would try to put it into practice. That he most certainly did. It was one of the sights I shall not forget in a hurry.

In those days our president, Tom Taylor, used to sit on his shooting stick behind the nets watching young and old alike with his chauffeur in close attendance dressed in peak cap and grey livery. James came tearing up and let the ball go. It was still going up when it passed over the top of the net. Our president whipped round to watch the ball's progress. It hit just under

*'I don't know what's going off out there, sunshine, but it's sending me to sleep'*

the roof of the old winter shed, about twenty-five feet high, and rebounded back towards him. His manservant had also observed the path of the now lethal object and made to protect his employer. In so doing, he hit the two tie-ropes with his feet, pulling both pegs clean out of the ground, and fell on top of the president. Both men fell to the ground with the net firmly wrapped round them. Maurice Leyland was on the floor with his tummy shaking like a freshly made jelly, with the batsman asking if he could please leave the net. Practice was held up for about fifteen minutes while order was restored and the president rescued from his temporary imprisonment. There is a happy ending to the story: after all those traumas, James went on to play quite a few games for Yorkshire's first team.

There are many stories of happenings at Headingley, but one of my favourites concerns the legendary Bright Heyhirst, the Yorkshire Rubber – the same position today has the sophisticated title of 'physiotherapist'. It was the practice in those bygone days for the home county to provide their rubber to look after the England side when the Test match was at Headingley. It was taken as a feather in one's cap to be entrusted with the health and well-being of the finest players of the day, and, what is more, the rubber would also have the task of looking after the touring side if they did not have their own man with them, thus giving the job even more importance.

In 1950 the West Indies were touring England and Bright Heyhirst had the job of looking after both sides for the five days, an encounter which he looked forward to with great pride and happiness. All that was to change by the end of the match. It was always the done thing by the manager of the touring side to give the rubber anything between five and ten pounds for his work. On this occasion they had not given Bright a brass penny. On the Wednesday morning after the Test, Yorkshire were playing at Headingley in a county match. Bright was observed to be sitting in the corner of the dressing-room, quietly smoking his pipe, when one of the Yorkshire team said, 'What's the matter, Bright. You're looking a bit miserable this morning.' He took his pipe out of his mouth, looked for a few seconds and said, 'So would you be if had happened to you what has to me after five days with yon West Indies. They never gave me nowt and I've rubbed till Alleyne shone like ebony.'

Of course, there are stories of the modern-day players as well. One of these stories which comes to light straightaway involves that mighty man, the captain of Yorkshire, Denis Brian Close. Now Brian Close was possibly, or is possibly, the worst driver that was ever granted a driving licence: he doesn't steer, he aims. And that I think would be a pretty true reflection. On the way back one Saturday evening from the game at Trent Bridge, Dougie Padgett was my passenger. We came towards Bawtry, trying to get back over the Yorkshire border before they caught us, and saw a green car halfway up a tree. Dougie Padgett said to me, 'Oh, don't worry, it'll only be Closey', and we drove on, laughing. The next morning when we read the paper, it was! That will just give you some idea of what his driving was like.

It was never his fault; that tree had possibly jumped out of the middle of a forest and savaged him on the way up.

Brian Close, once he had become captain, turned up at the Headingley nets when he felt like it, never at the same time as the players, and of course business commitments would find him in London when he ought to have been practising for the day. On one particular day we were standing at the nets, with all the boys running around and practising, when suddenly Brian Close drove on to the cricket ground. He had to drive by the nets in a brand new car which had been loaned to him for the year by a big manufacturer in this country. As the car went by it was noticed there was a deep scratch, and several other scratches, running from the front wing right through to the back, just missing the door handle. He came down the steps after changing and made his entrance to the nets, whereupon Ray Illingworth remarked, 'I see that the manufacturer's getting to know you, Closey.' He said, 'Why is that?' 'Well, they're giving you new cars, already damaged!' About ten minutes later Ray Illingworth came back, Closey having failed to catch him, and Arthur Mitchell, the Yorkshire coach, was heard to remark, 'I have never seen Closey train so hard.'

Of course I've talked about the many things that have happened at Headingley without mentioning some of the things that have happened there to me. It was on that ground that I met that cricketing immortal, George Hirst, one of my first coaches in 1948, who made that remarkable season of 200 wickets and 2000 runs. I also met that gallant prince of spin bowlers, Wilfred Rhodes, the man who went in number eleven for England and finished up opening the batting for England with the legendary John Berry Hobbs.

It was at Headingley that I made my Test debut in 1952, against India, and one of the greatest memories I shall ever carry in cricket is of looking at the scoreboard at the beginning of India's second innings, when I had opened the bowling with Alec Bedser. It read four wickets for no runs – India were in desperate trouble. Anybody watching that day couldn't have dreamed that I would be the first man in history to take 300 Test wickets, a figure they said could not be reached. Of course, today they play that many Test matches, in such a short time, that it's a figure that can be reached – and has been reached, by Lance Gibbs – and I suspect that some England bowlers and some Australian bowlers will pass it as well.

It was in 1961, against Australia at Headingley, on a wearing wicket that was turning slowly, that I realised that my fast-bowling days of sheer speed were numbered and I practised bowling off-cutters and leg-cutters at a medium pace. Then I put them into action and Australia lost five wickets in the next half hour, and went on to defeat. I finished up in the match with eleven wickets. In fact, it was the only Test match England won against Australia that year.

It was also on that ground that I took my thousandth wicket for Yorkshire, and I was met by the president (Sir William Worsley, one of the greatest men that I have ever met in cricket, and admired so much) who stood at the bottom of the steps, in front of the crowd, to congratulate me as I came off the field at lunchtime. I count that wicket as a treasured one – it was that of Roy Marshall, the West Indian opening batsman who did such valiant work for Hampshire, the county of John Arlott.

Headingley was host to another historic occasion when Geoffrey Boycott, a young man who had come into the Yorkshire side in my time, made his hundredth first-class century to become the first man ever to make it in a Test match. Who knows, he might well go on to join the legendary Herbert Sutcliffe who still remains the only Yorkshireman to make a hundred centuries for his county.

Yorkshire has paid tribute to Herbert Sutcliffe by naming the wrought-iron gates at the entrance to the ground after him. These gates have memories for me as well. It's amazing how things happen to me in my cricketing life, for I turned up at these gates to do a Test match for my newspaper and was refused permission to enter the ground!

This was one of the times that I really lost my temper. I got out of the car and said to the gentleman on the gates: 'I believe you know who I am.' He said, 'Yes. I know who you are, but you still can't come in.' Seething, I said, 'Right! If I can't come in, nobody else will get through this gate today because this is where I am going to park my car.' And I got out, shut the door and went to lock it, right in the middle of the Herbert Sutcliffe Gates.

A policeman rescued me. He came along and asked, 'What's the matter, Fred?' I replied, 'This so-and-so will not let me in after twenty years of service given to this county.' The policeman turned to the gateman and said, 'You know who it is', and the gentleman said, 'I know who it is' – some gentleman – and then I repeated that my car would be staying there for the day. With that, the policeman turned to me and said, 'Don't worry. Get into your car and drive into the ground.' I've been escorted from a ground, that's for certain, when incidents have happened over bouncers and things; but this was the first time that I had ever been escorted into one!

Yes, Headingley has lasting memories for me. It was even the ground where I was brought into the *Test Match Special* side – and I say side because we are in the commentary box – to do my first full Test match broadcast. I never dreamed, of course, that I would go on from there to become a full and regular member, and I hope a permanent one, of such a happy family.

I sat at Headingley, during the 1980 Test match between England and West Indies, and I watched that great man, John Arlott, start to climb the steps for the last time. John is not the greatest climber of steps and will say so whenever he has to do it, one of the reasons he didn't like Lord's pavilion. When he reached the broadcasting position he put down that battered old briefcase, which has carried so many immortal words, got his breath and sat and looked towards the wicket. I watched the great man and wondered what was going through his mind. He knew that this was his last Test match at Headingley. Was he reminiscing in his silent thoughts on the great matches that had taken place there on which he had broadcast and written? Was he thinking about how long it would take to get home that night? Was the match going to finish early? Whatever went through his mind, I don't know. But all I know is one thing – I was watching, at Headingley that day, the end of an era; possibly more, I was watching the end of    broadcasting legend.

John Arlott is, in my mind, and I suspect in many others, the greatest cricket broadcaster of all time. His technique was based on thinking that he was talking to blind people. No one has ever been able to paint a picture so vividly in people's minds with the use of words.

There are not many stories about John Arlott. He is a man of thought, a man that always conducted himself correctly wherever he was. But one story I did find about him, to do with his cricketing life, became very dear to him when he got close to making the Hampshire side, his beloved county. He was twelfth man for Hampshire against Worcester at Worcester. He was called on to the field when somebody had to leave because of an injury, and he was out to impress. He was fielding down towards the boundary, at either fine leg or third man, when somebody hit the ball towards the pavilion. he set off, haring round the boundary for the ball – seeing John today, could anyone visualise him 'haring' round the ground? But he did. On the way to this ball his whole character changed. He suddenly imagined himself as Learie Constantine, who he thought was the greatest fielder he ever saw. Constantine could run at full belt, get to the ball, flip it up with his foot and, all in one flowing movement, throw the ball back over the top of the stumps into the wicket-keeper's gloves. This flashed through John's mind as he raced towards the ball and the pavilion. It looked as though the ball might beat him, but he got there and went through the Constantine act. Flipping up the ball with his foot, he went head over heels on to his back with the ball following him. He looked round, and there was the ball. He picked it up and, with an attempt to throw it to the wicket-keeper, he raised his eyes as his arm went back, only to see the Worcester members parting like the Red Sea right in front of him, thinking that the ball was going to travel their way. He turned around and threw the ball eventually to the wicket-keeper, but vowed he would never again try to emulate the great Learie Constantine.

As well as sharing in John Arlott's last Headingley commentary, I was very much aware of the presence on the field of a young man who will, certainly, write his name in the cricketing history books. I might have been seeing the end of one legend, but I was also, possibly, seeing the start of a new one. I am, of course, talking about that brilliant prince of modern-day batsmen, Viv Richards of the West Indies. What a superb player this young man is. Due to injury to his captain, Clive Lloyd, he had taken over the captaincy of the West Indies. He was leading his country for the very first time, and I suspect it will not be for the last. I feel sure that he will, in the future, be West Indies' regular captain. Once again, Headingley had thrown up that little piece of history – Viv Richards leading his country for the very first time.

## ENGLAND 1ST INNINGS v WEST INDIES 5TH TEST at HEADINGLEY, LEEDS, on 7 (no play), 8, 9, 11½, 12 AUGUST 1980. TOSS: W. INDIES

| IN | OUT | MINS | No. | BATSMAN | HOW OUT | BOWLER | RUNS | WKT | TOTAL | 6s | 4s | BALLS | NOTES ON DISMISSAL |
|----|-----|------|-----|---------|---------|--------|------|-----|-------|----|----|-------|--------------------|
| 2.45 | 3.30 | 45 | 1 | GOOCH | C MARSHALL | GARNER | 14 | 2 | 27 | · | 1 | 37 | Mistimed leg glance - backward square leg catch. |
| 2.45 | 3.04 | 19 | 2 | BOYCOTT | C KALLICHARRAN | HOLDING | 4 | 1 | 9 | · | · | 12 | Edged push drive to 1st slip - Holding round wicket. |
| 3.06 | 3.38 | 32 | 3 | ROSE | BOWLED | CROFT | 7 | 3 | 28 | · | · | 20 | Middle stump out - bowled through gate. Late on stroke |
| 3.32 | 4.06 | 34 | 4 | LARKINS | C KALLICHARRAN | GARNER | 9 | 5 | 52 | · | · | 30 | Edged push at offside ball to 1st slip |
| 3.40 | 3.51 | 11 | 5 | GATTING | C MARSHALL | CROFT | 1 | 4 | 34 | · | · | 5 | Turned short ball to backward square leg. |
| 3.53 | 5.09 | 57 | 6 | BOTHAM * | C RICHARDS | HOLDING | 37 | 7 | 89 | 1 | 6 | 37 | Mistimed lofted drive to deep mid-off. |
| 4.08 | 4.16 | 8 | 7 | WILLEY | C MURRAY | CROFT | 1 | 6 | 59 | · | · | 6 | Chased wide offside ball. |
| 4.18 | 6.09 | 92 | 8 | BAIRSTOW † | LBW | MARSHALL | 40 | 8 | 131 | · | 7 | 73 | Played across breakback that kept low. |
| 5.11 | (6.27) | 76 | 9 | EMBUREY | NOT OUT | | 13 | · | · | · | 2 | 48 | - |
| 6.11 | 6.20 | 9 | 10 | OLD | C GARNER | MARSHALL | 6 | 9 | 140 | · | 1 | 11 | Glanced to backward square leg. |
| 6.21 | 6.27 | 6 | 11 | DILLEY | BOWLED | GARNER | 0 | 10 | 143 | · | · | 9 | Yorked leg stump. |

* CAPTAIN   † WICKET-KEEPER   EXTRAS   b 3  lb 3  w 1  nb 4   **11**     1s 17s  288 balls (inc. 6 no balls)

**TOTAL** OFF 47 OVERS IN 203 MINUTES   **143** all out at 6.27pm 2nd DAY.

ENGLAND'S LOWEST TOTAL v WEST INDIES at LEEDS

13 OVERS 5 BALLS/HOUR
3.04 RUNS/OVER
50 RUNS/100 BALLS

| BOWLER | O | M | R | W | nb/w | HRS | OVERS | RUNS |
|--------|---|---|---|---|------|-----|-------|------|
| HOLDING | 10 | 4 | 34 | 2 | | 1 | 14 | 31 |
| CROFT | 12 | 3 | 35 | 3 | 1/1 | 2 | 14 | 56 |
| GARNER | 14 | 4 | 41 | 3 | 1/- | 3 | 14 | 40 |
| MARSHALL | 11 | 3 | 22 | 2 | 4/- | | | |
| | | | 11 | | | | | |
| | 47 | 14 | 143 | 10 | | | | |

| | RUNS | MINS | OVERS | LAST 50 (in mins) |
|--|------|------|-------|---------|
| | 50 | 79 | 18 | 79 |
| | 100 | 154 | 35.4 | 75 |

NO PLAY 1ST DAY (Abandoned at 11 a.m.) 360 MIN. LOST
2ND DAY - START DELAYED until 2.45 pm
TEA: 85-6   BOTHAM 35* (31 balls, 48 min)   BAIRSTOW 8* (23 min)
OFF 27 OVERS IN 116 MINUTES

| WKT | PARTNERSHIP | | RUNS | MINS |
|-----|-------------|--|------|------|
| 1st | Gooch | Boycott | 9 | 19 |
| 2nd | Gooch | Rose | 18 | 24 |
| 3rd | Rose | Larkins | 1 | 6 |
| 4th | Larkins | Gatting | 6 | 11 |
| 5th | Larkins | Botham | 18 | 13 |
| 6th | Botham | Willey | 7 | 8 |
| 7th | Botham | Bairstow | 30 | 32 |
| 8th | Bairstow | Emburey | 42 | 58 |
| 9th | Emburey | Old | 9 | 9 |
| 10th | Emburey | Dilley | 3 | 6 |
| | | | 143 | |

## WEST INDIES 1ST INNINGS          (In reply to ENGLAND's 143 all out)

| IN | OUT | MINS | No. | BATSMAN | HOW OUT | BOWLER | RUNS | WKT | TOTAL | 6s | 4s | BALLS | NOTES ON DISMISSAL |
|----|-----|------|-----|---------|---------|--------|------|-----|-------|----|----|-------|--------------------|
| 6.39 | 2.24 | 163 | 1 | GREENIDGE | LBW | BOTHAM | 34 | 2 | 105 | · | 3 | 133 | Played across line. Ball held its own. |
| 6.39 | 1.17 | 135 | 2 | HAYNES | BOWLED | EMBUREY | 42 | 1 | 83 | · | 4 | 108 | Played on via inside edge. |
| 1.19 | 3.03 | 65 | 3 | RICHARDS * | BOWLED | OLD | 31 | 3 | 133 | 1 | 2 | 38 | Edged offside force - leg stump down. |
| 2.26 | 3.18 | 52 | 4 | BACCHUS | C AND BOWLED | DILLEY | 11 | 4 | 142 | · | 1 | 40 | Mistimed force to mid-wicket - edged return catch. |
| 3.05 | 5.05 | 100 | 5 | KALLICHARRAN | C LARKINS | DILLEY | 37 | 9 | 207 | · | 6 | 75 | Mistimed off-drive - skier to wide mid-off. |
| 3.20 | 3.58 | 38 | 6 | KING | C BAIRSTOW | GOOCH | 12 | 5 | 170 | · | · | 31 | Edged drive at outswinger. |
| 4.00 | 4.41 | 21 | 7 | MURRAY † | C EMBUREY | DILLEY | 14 | 6 | 198 | · | 2 | 15 | Edged lifting ball to 2nd slip. |
| 4.43 | 4.49 | 6 | 8 | MARSHALL | C BAIRSTOW | DILLEY | 0 | 7 | 198 | · | · | 4 | Edged off-drive low to 'keeper. |
| 4.50 | 5.04 | 13 | 9 | GARNER | C EMBUREY | GOOCH | 0 | 8 | 207 | · | · | 11 | Edged outswinger to 1st slip. |
| 5.05 | 5.58 | 53 | 10 | HOLDING | BOWLED | OLD | 35 | 10 | 245 | · | 4 | 44 | Missed vast heave. |
| 5.07 | (5.58) | 51 | 11 | CROFT | NOT OUT | | 1 | · | · | · | · | 26 | |

* CAPTAIN   † WICKET-KEEPER   EXTRAS   b 2  lb 9  w 3  nb 14   **28**     1s 22s  525 balls (inc. 16 no balls)

**TOTAL** (OFF 84.5 OVERS IN 357 MIN)   **245** all out at 5.58pm 3RD DAY.

14 OVERS 1 BALLS/HOUR
2.89 RUNS/OVER
47 RUNS/100 BALLS

| BOWLER | O | M | R | W | nb/w | HRS | OVERS | RUNS |
|--------|---|---|---|---|------|-----|-------|------|
| DILLEY | 23 | 6 | 79 | 4 | 4/2 | 1 | 14 | 33 |
| OLD | 28.5 | 9 | 64 | 2 | 10/1 | 2 | 15 | 40 |
| BOTHAM | 19 | 8 | 31 | 1 | -/1 | 3 | 16 | 42 |
| EMBUREY | 6 | 0 | 25 | 1 | | 4 | 13 | 43 |
| GOOCH | 8 | 3 | 18 | 2 | | 5 | 14 | 49 |
| | | | 28 | | | | | |
| | 84.5 | 26 | 245 | 10 | | | | |

| | RUNS | MINS | OVERS | LAST 50 (in mins) |
|--|------|------|-------|---------|
| | 50 | 85 | 20.2 | 85 |
| | 100 | 160 | 40.3 | 75 |
| | 150 | 227 | 55.3 | 67 |
| | 200 | 294 | 70.5 | 67 |

BAD LIGHT STOPPED PLAY at 7.07pm   GREENIDGE 6*
STUMPS (2ND DAY): 20-0   HAYNES 13*
OFF 7 OVERS IN 28 MINUTES

LUNCH: 95-1   GREENIDGE 33* (149 min)   RICHARDS 4* (12 min)
OFF 37 OVERS IN 149 MINUTES

TEA: 179-5   KALLICHARRAN 18* (65 min)   MURRAY 6* (10 min)
OFF 65 OVERS IN 269 MINUTES

WEST INDIES LEAD: 102

| WKT | PARTNERSHIP | | RUNS | MINS |
|-----|-------------|--|------|------|
| 1st | Greenidge | Haynes | 83 | 135 |
| 2nd | Greenidge | Richards | 22 | 26 |
| 3rd | Richards | Bacchus | 28 | 37 |
| 4th | Bacchus | Kallicharran | 9 | 13 |
| 5th | Kallicharran | King | 28 | 38 |
| 6th | Kallicharran | Murray | 28 | 21 |
| 7th | Kallicharran | Marshall | 0 | 6 |
| 8th | Kallicharran | Garner | 9 | 13 |
| 9th | Kallicharran | Holding | 0 | - |
| 10th | Holding | Croft | 38 | 51 |
| | | | 245 | |

**ENGLAND  2ND INNINGS**                 **102 RUNS BEHIND ON FIRST INNINGS**

| IN | OUT | MINS | No. | BATSMAN | HOW OUT | BOWLER | RUNS | WKT | TOTAL | 6s | 4s | BALLS | NOTES ON DISMISSAL |
|----|-----|------|-----|---------|---------|--------|------|-----|-------|-----|-----|-------|--------------------|
| 6.10 | 12.34 | 116 | 1 | GOOCH | LBW | MARSHALL | 55 | 1 | 95 | · | 7 | 88 | Missed backfoot push to mid-wicket (5 lbw's in 10 inns) |
| 6.10 | 2.12 | 176 | 2 | BOYCOTT | c̓ KALLICHARRAN | CROFT | 47 | 2 | 126 | · | 4 | 127 | Gloved bouncer (bowled from round the wicket) to 1st slip. |
| 12.36 | 3.12 | 118 | 3 | LARKINS | LBW | MARSHALL | 30 | 4 | 162 | 1 | 1 | 70 | Missed backfoot force across break-back. |
| 2.13 | 2.23 | 10 | 4 | GATTING | LBW | HOLDING | 1 | 3 | 129 | · | · | 6 | Beaten by break-back. |
| 2.25 | (5.22) | 145 | 5 | ROSE | NOT OUT | | 43 | | | · | 7 | 93 | [Batted with Gooch as runner] |
| 3.14 | 3.32 | 18 | 6 | BOTHAM * | LBW | MARSHALL | 7 | 5 | 174 | · | · | 13 | Played across line. |
| 3.34 | 4.47 | 41 | 7 | WILLEY | c̓ MURRAY | HOLDING | 10 | 6 | 203 | · | 2 | 35 | Edged inswinging away-seamer. |
| 4.49 | (5.22) | 33 | 8 | BAIRSTOW † | NOT OUT | | 9 | | | · | 2 | 26 | |
| | | | 9 | EMBUREY | } | | | | | | | | |
| | | | 10 | OLD | } DID NOT BAT | | | | | | | | |
| | | | 11 | DILLEY | } | | | | | | | | |
| * CAPTAIN   † WICKET-KEEPER | | | | EXTRAS | b 5   lb 11   w 2   nb 7 | | 25 | | | 1⁶ 23⁴ 458 balls (inc 8 no balls) | | | |

TOTAL  (OFF 75 OVERS IN 334 MINUTES)  **227-6 DECLARED**

13 OVERS 3 BALLS/HOUR
3.03 RUNS/OVER
50 RUNS/100 BALLS

| BOWLER | O | M | R | W | Nb/w | HRS | OVERS | RUNS |
|--------|---|---|---|---|------|-----|-------|------|
| HOLDING | 23 | 2 | 62 | 2 | -/1 | 1 | 13 | 56 |
| CROFT | 19 | 2 | 65 | 1 | 1/1 | 2 | 15 | 40 |
| MARSHALL | 19 | 5 | 42 | 3 | 7/- | 3 | 14 | 31 |
| GARNER | 1 | 0 | 1 | 0 | - | 4 | 12 | 40 |
| KING | 12 | 3 | 32 | 0 | - | 5 | 13 | 36 |
| RICHARDS | 1 | 1 | 0 | 0 | - | | | |
| | | | 25 | | | | | |
| | 75 | 13 | 227 | 6 | | | | |

| RUNS | MINS | OVERS | LAST 50 (in mins) |
|------|------|-------|-------------------|
| 50 | 52 | 11·1 | 52 |
| 100 | 128 | 29·3 | 76 |
| 150 | 213 | 48·4 | 85 |
| 200 | 295 | 66 | 82 |

STUMPS: 22-0    GOOCH 12*
3RD DAY          BOYCOTT 9*
                 OFF 5 OVERS IN 22 MINUTES
4TH DAY – NO PLAY (RAIN)

LUNCH: 109–1   BOYCOTT 37* (144')
                LARKINS 6* (26')
                OFF 34 OVERS IN 144 MINUTES

TEA: 189–5    ROSE 25* (75')
               WILLEY 1* (6')
               OFF 59 OVERS IN 264 MINUTES

BLSP 4.26/4.35 pm – 9 min lost.
TOTAL TIME LOST : 14 HOURS 7 MINUTES

MATCH DRAWN

MAN OF THE MATCH: D.L. HAYNES.   MAN OF SERIES: J. GARNER

| WKT | PARTNERSHIP | | RUNS | MINS |
|-----|-------------|------|------|------|
| 1st | Gooch | Boycott | 95 | 116 |
| 2nd | Boycott | Larkins | 31 | 58 |
| 3rd | Larkins | Gatting | 3 | 10 |
| 4th | Larkins | Rose | 33 | 47 |
| 5th | Rose | Botham | 12 | 18 |
| 6th | Rose | Willey | 29 | 41 |
| 7th | Rose | Bairstow | 24* | 33 |
| | | | 227 | |

# WITH LOVE FROM OUR FRIENDS OUT THERE

## —————— Peter Baxter ——————

From all over the world letters and gifts pour in, in a tide which grows throughout the season until, by the final Test, it has become a deluge. 1980 was no exception, with over 2,000 listeners' letters passing through the commentary box.

The overall impression one gets is how very nice our listeners are. Not that we don't get our critics, but very few of them are critical of more than one of the commentators. This is only healthy, for the commentators' strength lies in their individuality and it would be most odd if everyone liked all the team.

I am always most gratified by the letters from people who have never had any connection with the game, but who have been brought into the fold, as it were, by the programme. Many of these ask questions on some point which has been baffling them about the basics of the game and they make very good subjects for discussion in our Monday lunchtime letters session. It is also apparent that the programme is company for a lot of people who feel they are part of the friendly, informal atmosphere. One lady wrote to say that as each commentator says 'Good morning' on his first appearance at the microphone during the day, she replies out loud to her radio 'Good morning, Brian' or Trevor or whoever.

Our listeners in India are among the most devoted. Long effusive missives arrive in the box couched in splendid language and always touchingly polite and full of praise. From this direction in particular flooded in the valedictory eulogies for John Arlott.

The majority of the mail is traditionally addressed to B.J. but during the Centenary Test – quite rightly – Arlott beat him by several lengths and on

*Without them we couldn't go on the air – the engineers at Headingley and Lord's*

the last morning I piled up the telegrams, good luck cards and parcels to greet him when he entered the box. He could not fail to have been moved by it all.

John feels his greatest triumph came during the Lord's Test a couple of years ago when, following a spell in which Brian had been thanking a list of people for sweets, cakes, biscuits and the like, he enquired, in flippant vein, why B.J. didn't ask for something useful – like champagne! Before he had finished that commentary stint a bottle had arrived in front of him – ready chilled – delivered by a friend in the Victoria Sporting Club who had been organising a champagne sponsorship for the England team. As a result of Trevor's friendly connections with Laurent Perrier, champagne has become almost a tradition. One year a tea manufacturer felt that our frequent references to 'a cuppa' should not go unrewarded and our wives were delighted to be presented with gift boxes of the sacred leaf. Another year it was wine-gums (non-alcoholic).

At the end of the season comes the time when I have to deal with the backlog of mail. I try to answer it all but it is a mammoth task at a time when a winter tour is usually in its final planning stage – so if you are one of those still waiting, please be patient!

One correspondent pointed out that cricket nowadays is no more danger- ous than it used to be, when he sent us a photostat of his club accounts from the twenties, marking an item: '6*s*. 6*d*. for a protector for second team umpire'. But my 1980 award for devotion goes to a gentleman in the west of Ireland who wrote that the only place he could get good reception of *TMS* was in his car – so to find out the score he had to go for a drive!

# LETTER FROM DOWN UNDER

## Alan McGilvray

It was in the mid-1930s . . . I was captain of the NSW Sheffield Shield team in Brisbane, Queensland. Prior to the game a representative of the Australian Broadcasting Commission came to my room in my hotel and suggested I might consider doing a radio summary of the game at the end of each four days' play.

After a brief outline about what was required I went to the studios in Brisbane and was placed in a room with the instructions that when the green light went on I must start talking, and when a red light showed on my desk I should terminate the broadcast within one minute. It seemed endless waiting for that red light to show, and I later found out I had talked for a full ten minutes. I thought my talk was dreadful but apparently the ABC were satisfied and I continued on the following three nights. Radio of course was in its infancy in that period. I continued along these lines as our team travelled through the States. In 1936 Gubby Allen's MCC played a Test series in Australia and as I was taking an active part in Sheffield Shield cricket I did not broadcast during that season.

In 1934 during the Australian tour of the United Kingdom, the general manager of the ABC, Charles Moses, now Sir Charles, introduced what was then termed 'Synthetic Broadcasts'. Profiting from the initial broadcasts the general manager provided a similar coverage in 1938 but this time on a larger scale. I was invited to join the panel of broadcasters which included two former Australian captains, M. A. (Monty) Noble and Victor Richardson. Monty played in eight series against England, four in each country, and was captain in three of them. Vic Richardson played in four series, one in

*Alan McGilvray and his old friend Lindsay Hassett in the commentary box at Lord's during the Centenary Test match*

England. The other member of the ball-by-ball panel was Halford Hooker, who, with the late Alan Kippax, had established a world record partnership of 307 runs for the tenth wicket playing for NSW against Victoria in 1928-29. Halford and myself were lacking in experience and knowledge of the Test grounds in England, but were assisted by having large photographs of each ground placed in front of the microphone, whilst Monty and Vic gave us considerable information about their various features.

Our representative in England, namely Eric Sholl, would send cables before the start of each day's play providing information about weather conditions, the state of the pitch and other general information. The next cable to arrive would be the field placings of every player, followed later by a cable about the placings for the second over. These were most important for Moses insisted that the correct fielders be named. Accuracy was the keynote in this regard, and any change in field placings required a further cable.

The broadcasters were housed in a small studio, approximately fifteen feet by twelve feet, which contained a scoreboard, a table and chairs. In addition to the broadcasters there was a sound-effects operator who would provide such things as applause at various levels. He also received a copy of the cable used by the broadcaster so that he could co-ordinate the sound effects. The commentator himself made the sound of the bat meeting the ball, and of a ball striking the pad, by tapping a wooden cup with a pencil or the heavy rubber band around it which produced a dull thud.

Initially cables were sent at the end of each over, later increased to at least two an over. The following cable, from the 1938 series, is typical of the hundreds which would be sent during a Test match:

BRIGHTENING FLEETWOOD HAMMOND FIRSTLY FULL 2 HASSETT SECONDLY
FULL 4 STRAIGHT UNCHANCE BOWLER THIRDLY NOBALL FULL 2 OFFDRIVEN
RUNAPPEAL HUTTON FOURTHLY 4 SWEPT BOWLER KEEPER OFFPUSHED

This would be built up and reconstructed with the aid of the fielding charts
and then be passed on to the commentator. This particular cable was
decoded as follows and would form the basis of the commentator's impro-
vised rendering of the over:

| | Message | Over | | Bowler | |
| | 46 | 34 | | Fleetwood-Smith | |
| Ball | Batsman | Where hit/fielded | Score | Comments |
|---|---|---|---|---|
| 1 | Hammond | Full toss – off drive – Hassett | 2 | Chasing, fields brilliantly |
| 2 | Hammond | Full toss – uppish straight drive | 4 | Almost a catch to bowler |
| 3 | Hammond | Full toss – no ball – off drive – Hassett | 2 | Appeal for run out against Hutton at bowler's wicket |
| 4 | Hammond | Swept past Barnes on fence | 4 | At deep square leg |
| 5 | Hammond | Back to bowler | — | |
| 6 | Hammond | Keeper | — | |
| 7 | Hammond | Played slowly to cover – McCabe | — | |

Remarks: Weather brightening

We see that the weather was brightening and that Fleetwood-Smith was
bowling to Hammond. Adding further information: when a fieldsman's
name was mentioned it meant he fielded well; unchance . . . almost a chance.
We knew that Hassett was at mid-off so he was mentioned in the run-out
appeal against Hutton. After early problems were resolved, our broadcasts
were only 90 seconds behind the actual play. One of these problems was that
upon the receipt of a cable the broadcaster would rush it through in some
two minutes, overlooking the fact that it took approximately four minutes to
bowl an over. This meant we had a lot of 'padding' to do to allow time to
catch up with us.

These were early days in radio in Australia and many mistakes were
made, but as the season progressed we profited and became more proficient,
so much so that listeners accused the ABC of deceit in broadcasting. This
caused the general manager to set up a studio to provide the newsreels and
various picture theatres with the opportunity of showing just how it was
done. The newsreels were played throughout Australia and apparently
convinced the doubtful.

It was common for thousands of people, who evidently did not have radios
or crystal sets, to stand outside the many stores which supplied radio
equipment whilst the stores provided a description of the ABC's broadcasts.

On several occasions, whilst Halford was at work Vic and myself would wander into the streets in Sydney and mix with the crowds. With Vic's great sense of humour he provided much amusement amongst those people. It was also good for us to get a little fresh air.

The synthetic broadcasts were a great challenge to all of us. We were spearheaded by the general manager, who motivated (if that term was then known) all of us by calling us to the studio early to run through our previous night's broadcasts and suggest improvements. Our broadcasts started at 8.30 p.m. and ended at 3.30 a.m. and during that period he had us all 'motivated' to thinking it was by day, and the various meals and refreshments were provided accordingly.

As my memory turns back to 1938, there are countless happenings to recall. My great blunder came when we received a cable that McC was out. As there were two McCs batting at the time – McCabe and McCormick – we were in a quandary who to give out. I recall turning to Vic, who was sitting nearby, and whispering 'Who will I give'. He replied 'Give Napper' (a nickname for Stan McCabe). Stan had played a great innings of 232 and Vic and I thought it just had to be him. So off went Stan in my broadcast accompanied by thunderous applause following a great innings (provided by the sound effects operator). Then came the shattering cable . . . McCormick bowled by Wright. It could have been the other way round, I cannot quite recall, but whatever it was, it called for an apology. At least it reminded listeners that it was a synthentic broadcast.

This was certainly a blunder in broadcasting and I was not allowed to forget it for some time afterwards, but perhaps it was not as bad as when Vic and Monty were summarising during an interval. When Monty said, 'Vic, the wind is so strong it has blown Fleetwood-Smith's balls off,' Vic replied, 'His what, Monty?' Monty's reply that the umpires were having difficulties in keeping the bails on in the windy conditions, did, I fear, leave a lot to be desired. Brian Johnston would have undoubtedly put Monty in the same predicament as he has often done to me when I dare attempt to eat a slice of cake . . . I never did like a mouthful of chocolate cake in my hands!

And so to one of the great moments in my cricket life: to be associated with two great broadcasters, Vic Richardson and Arthur Gilligan, on the MCC tour of Australia in 1946. I had first seen Arthur Gilligan in 1924, when my father had given me two shillings to go to the Sydney Cricket Ground to watch the first Test between England and Australia. I sat with my head jammed between the pickets as I watched with utmost joy Arthur Gilligan lead his team out, with such men as Hobbs, Sutcliffe, Woolley, Hendren, Chapman and the great Maurice Tate, who took six wickets in the innings – which I saw, for I persuaded my father to let me go on the following day. He didn't mind for no one gave me greater help in my cricket life. I was too young then to appreciate the extent to which Herbie Collins had nursed Bill Ponsford through to his century in his first Test. That was to come later as I began to meet most of the players in that Test.

In all I covered 25 England-Australia Test matches with Arthur and at no time did he do other than give me the greatest assistance. The 1946 season was a joyful season for close friendships were made amongst the three of us and our wives as we toured Australia together. Australians were hungry for cricket after the war and Vic and Arthur became household names, and are still remembered by the catch-phrase 'What do you think, Arthur?' Vic died in 1969 at the age of 75, and Arthur in 1976 aged 82. What service they gave to cricket is not possible to assess, but my memories of these two wonderful men will never fade.

Although I played against Vic on several occasions I had never met him before the 1938 synthetic series. How could a young hopeful meet such a great cricketer. He was a dignified and true cricketer on the field and I was grateful to be out there with him, even though I did not appreciate the first words he spoke to me when he said, 'What are you doing standing there, lad. Nick off . . . you might get hurt.' My captain, Alan Kippax, had placed me at very short leg to an average medium-paced bowler. I stood my ground and the first ball smashed past my head and hit the boundary fence on the full. Vic turned to Kippax and said, 'Kip, don't you think you should do something about the fellow' – meaning me. I looked at my captain and was pleased to hear him say, 'You better drop back a little, Al. This fellow can hook pretty well when he is in the mood.' I was more than pleased to do so for Vic was later to reveal, as his innings progressed, that he was 'in the mood'.

It was during this innings that I gained a further appreciation of Vic's sense of humour. As he played a ball past mid-off, where Kippax was fielding, he called, 'You had better slip into second gear, Kip, for I will run three if you don't.' Kippax always reminded us that he had two speeds on the field, 'dead slow' and 'stop', attributed to him by Vic. They were the closest of friends.

From that simple but challenging beginning came a sequence of events which took me on nine visits to England, and to the West Indies, South Africa and New Zealand to broadcast on an approaching total of some 200 Test matches played by Australia.

My first, which of course must be the most memorable, as 'firsts' tend to be, was to accompany the 1948 Australian team to England, there to meet and work with John Arlott, Rex Alston, Arthur Gilligan and Jim Swanton. Recently I happened to listen to one of John Arlott's broadcasts during that tour. Even then he was brilliant in coining a phrase, although it was one of his early commentaries.

Our styles of presentation were entirely different. The Australian commentator was trained by people like Charles Moses who demanded more of the speed and racy style, whereas in England at that time they gave the listener a slower but more colourful approach. For a time I was reproached regularly by listeners, but was instructed by Moses to maintain my type of descriptions for I was also broadcasting to my own people in Australia. Hence, I maintained my calling of the loss of wickets as, for example, six for 180 instead of 180 for six. I was severely criticised in England for using this method and hundreds of letters of complaint came to me. Happily as the tour went on the complaints decreased and recent tours have revealed almost an absence of correspondence over this method. I will admit that I have tried to blend it now, using both methods in an endeavour to satisfy both sides. In fairness I think it should be known that when I used the English method I received letters from listeners in my own country, complaining that I was becoming a 'Pommy broadcaster'. (I dislike that expression as much as I dislike an Australian being called an 'Aussie'.)

The coverage of Test matches has taken me into the company of some splendid fellows, all of whom have consistently worked as a unified team. From South Africa, with the great Charles Fortune, to West Indies and New Zealand I have worked in complete unison with my colleagues, even if under difficult conditions. Most commentary boxes are too small and provide little opportunity for preparing oneself and keeping notes. I have been advised that our broadcasts, when broadcasting in Australia, reach some 40 million listeners – surely a sufficient audience to justify providing adequate conditions. Rest areas for contemplation of a session just completed by a commentator, and for writing notes, are necessary, but neglected: for example, Brisbane, Adelaide, Melbourne and Perth all provide most inadequate facilities and very small boxes.

That great cricket ground, Melbourne, must win the Oscar for providing the worst situation in the world of cricket. Here one almost has to get on one's knees to enter the box, and then work shoulder to shoulder with statistician and summariser. Actually when summariser Lindsay Hassett has to change places with another commentator he has to climb over the backs of the statistician and ball-by-ball commentator, as does the person who changes places. Perth is little better and not fit for broadcasting. One has to work in the open amongst spectators and journalists whose necessary typewriters provide interference in reception – although I believe work is in progress on a new box. The Sydney Cricket Ground box is spacious and excellent and fully answering all requirements.

Although one would expect the home of cricket to provide all that should be required, conditions for radio commentaries in England are little better than in Australia. When a broadcaster completes his session, it is necessary, as I said before, to have somewhere to go to prepare and watch the game. At The Oval, Lord's, Old Trafford and Headingley this is not possible unless sitting amongst the public. The boxes at Trent Bridge and Edgbaston also leave little to be desired. My remarks on these grounds are, of course, based on radio positions.

One of my great thrills in broadcasting comes at the start of play after the tea adjournment, roughly 5.00 a.m. to 6 a.m. in England, during a Test match between Australia and England. The custom is to commence calling in the BBC two minutes before the scheduled start: 'Calling the BBC. This is the ABC here. Are you with me, for we will be commencing our broadcast in two minutes from now?' The reply, in recent years usually from Peter Baxter or Brian Johnston, will hopefully be, 'Yes, McGillers, we are with you.' Then I might say, 'I am afraid you are in a bit of trouble, old chap.' This will bring out the usual 'Oh dear' from Brian, followed by 'Oh good' when I say, 'Sadly you have us right in the can.' By this time there would be about 90 seconds left and I would then give the score – that England were, perhaps, 120 for eight. At that the usual reply would be unprintable. I would then enquire after the weather, to be told that conditions were Arctic – still maintaining the count down in seconds – and finally the announcement would come to me of '. . . and now we cross to Alan McGilvray at the Sydney Cricket Ground'. I would probably start my broadcast with, 'On this beautiful warm day in Sydney . . . some 85 degrees . . .' and would then hear a click in my earphones with the comment, 'You blighter'.

Yes, great fun and a tremendous thrill to be able to communicate thus with my friends over so many thousands of miles. The compliment is, of course, returned when I am in England broadcasting to an Australian winter.

I can say with certainty that I would not change my life if I was given the opportunity. It has been a wonderful experience to work amongst so many great people. Cricket provides the world with great people and, for the most part, cricketers are good people – cricket over the years has had the habit of ridding itself of those it does not want. I will ever be grateful for what cricket has done for my country, and the splendid closeness, associations and friendships it has created amongst the peoples who are interested in it. I know it has been of great benefit to Australia, and I am reminded that it was greatly helped in the beginning by two Surrey players.

In my experience this mutual feeling of goodwill culminated in the two Centenary Tests, which I was privileged to broadcast. Both were magnificent occasions which have left wonderful memories. Most of those players I met and with whom I talked came in the area of my commentary, and how often I heard or said 'do you remember?' To those administrators of both countries who promoted these matches, particularly to the late Hans Ebeling, who under extreme difficulties finally got the Melbourne Centenary off the ground, and to the players, past and present, who contributed, I offer my most sincere gratitude. I doubt if fitting is the right word, but that it should combine with the retirement of John Arlott was of moment. The acknowledgement by the spectators and players when this announcement was made was a marvellous tribute to one who served the game so well.

# A SOGGY CENTENARY AND TEARFUL FAREWELLS

## Peter Baxter and
## —— Christopher Martin-Jenkins ——

The days leading up to the Centenary Test match at Lord's were that much more hectic than for a normal Test. We had dragooned Keith Miller and Lindsay Hassett, both old friends of *Test Match Special*, into our team as summarisers and Alan McGilvray had just arrived from Australia to join the commentators. There seemed to be more letters arriving than ever and the fact that this match not only marked a hundred years of Test cricket in England but also the end of an era, with John Arlott's retirement, just intensified the pressure. Television and newspaper reporters were on the telephone constantly, making arrangements to cover the final commentary by the great man. Questions like, 'When did Stork Hendry play his last Test?' or 'How long has Harold Larwood been living in Australia?' were thrown in from all directions as I tried to plan commentary rotas and make sure that all the celebration breakfasts, lunches, teas and dinners would leave us with some commentators in the box. There was also a great deal of anxious scanning of weather forecasts, which did not bode too well, but we all said our prayers for a respite in the summer rain for the great occasion.

To be at Lord's on that first morning of the match was to turn back the pages of a cricket history book. The 'double takes' as one suddenly thought 'Wasn't that Bill O'Reilly?' or Tony Lock or Bill Ponsford, were quite theatrical. One almost got to the stage of believing that round the next corner would be Trumper or Hobbs.

My feeling that this was to be no ordinary Test match was reinforced as I arrived at the commentary box. Across our gangway at the top of the pavilion the Australian Broadcasting Commission were setting up a camera

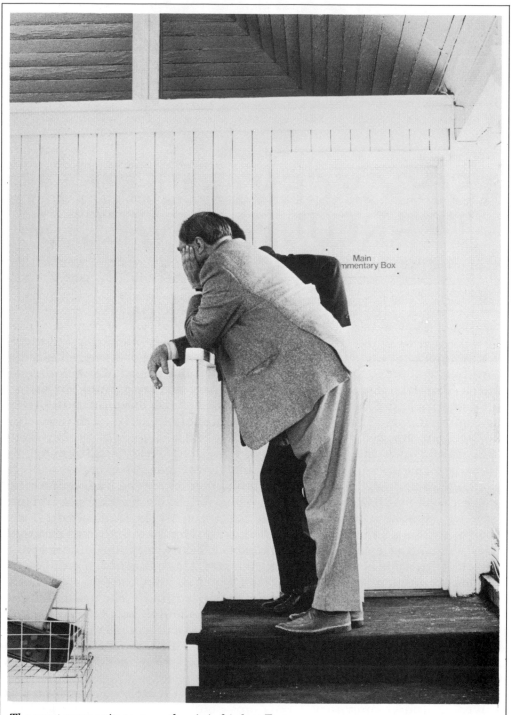

*The great man waits to go on the air in his last Test*

and lights for interviews – 'Nah, mate, we won't get in your way'. Very reassuring, although I was not convinced. However, there was a festival atmosphere which communicated charitable feelings. As the commentary team assembled, my next fear looked like being realised. Even the comparative roominess of the Lord's box would not be enough for the extra large commentary team and all our itinerant visitors. To meet Lindsay Hassett, with whom I had so often talked over a pre-dawn satellite circuit during winter tours, was a real delight and he was one of the first to appear in the box. Keith Miller – always in demand – was to prove more elusive with so many commitments to newspapers and television but he breezed in and out of the commentary box, taking it over completely on each visit. Brian Johnston bubbled with all the old friends he kept meeting, as did Fred and Trevor. The latter was to show us a great new talent as an interviewer with two fascinating lunchtime sessions with some of his former players. (One or two, to be fair, may have been before his time!)

John Arlott arrived in the box happy in the knowledge that his climbs up the pavilion stairs were now numbered. The coffee was served and I tried to call the crowded box to quiet as Dick Maddock in the studio handed over to Christopher Martin-Jenkins . . .

Looking back, I suppose the game was ill-starred from the start. After a week of good weather, the eagerly awaited Thursday was dank and drizzly. Play did not begin until 12.15. Greg Chappell won the toss and chose to bat first on one of Jim Fairbrother's most benign pitches. Thereafter, after playing dreadfully below par (why is below-par above average in golf and below it in everything else?) during their short tour, and having twice been thrashed by England in the limited-over internationals, the Australians rose characteristically to the big occasion.

The first day was a more or less constant story of frustration for England's bowlers. Australia owed their happy position at the close of play – 227 for two – mainly to the little left-handed West Australian Graeme Wood who batted throughout with intense concentration, admirable patience and great skill. It took him five and a quarter hours to reach his third Test hundred and, having been obliged to rebuild a promising career since losing his place in both his national and his state side after the return of the Packer men, he described his innings as the most important in his life.

A crowd which filled Lord's almost to bursting point watched it all with quiet appreciation. Old bowled outstandingly well, Hendrick with great accuracy though rather too short, and Emburey very steadily on his home wicket, with nice variations, though there was precious little turn in the turf. Gooch also bowled well, as he had whenever he had been called on this season, but Botham was simply not the true Botham. Still bothered by his back trouble, he was hit for 89 runs from 22 overs.

Each of the Australian batsmen played an innings of substance. Wood and Laird put on 64 in 83 minutes but, soon after lunch, Laird flashed half-heartedly outside the off-stump against the terrier-persistent Old and was caught behind for 24. A stand of 86 between Wood and Chappell followed, Chappell hitting nine fours but never taking complete control against some mean bowling: Hendrick, especially, kept him on a tight leash. Eventually it was Old who ensnared the Australian captain, caught at square-leg.

The arrival of Hughes, brimming with stylish strokes, brought an increased scoring-rate and he hit one especially memorable leg-side six with a flick of the wrists off Botham. England's captain took the new ball fifteen minutes from the close and his team were to rue the fact that Hughes survived two confident lbw shouts from Old.

The second day established a truer pattern for this occasion: one long and joyful party off the field; one spluttering, sodden and at times thoroughly miserable cricket match on it. Play on the second day lasted only until 12.45. Wood was stumped for 112 off Emburey at 260; Yallop leg before to Hendrick for two. The stumper was Bairstow and neither of his immediate predecessors, Knott and Taylor, both more renowned as wicket-keepers, could have done it better. Hughes made 35 of the 51 runs scored in an hour and a quarter and, apart from the bubbly in the box, he was about the only thing that sparkled. How one relished him dancing down the pitch to Emburey and pouncing on the ball like a cat on its prey!

Play stopped at 12.45. At first they came off only because of bad light, which irritated some people because no fast bowler was operating. But this time the umpires had got it right: before long it was pouring down. Up in the box we talked and talked, trying not to repeat the things we had said before in this rotten spoilsport of a summer.

The last note in my diary of the day was: 'an anxious and busy night lies ahead of the ground staff because there is still water on the outfield'. I then departed to a cricket-writers' party for the visiting press, calling in *en route* at a launching party for Frank Tyson's book. Rather to my surprise I briefly met Lord Longford there.

Most of the night was fine but listening to Tony Adamson on Tony Lewis's *Sport on Four* programme at 8.15 on Saturday morning as I breakfasted at home, I was dismayed to hear that it was raining again. This was the start of the most disastrous day for cricket. Officials at Lord's have worked tirelessly in recent years to eradicate the public misapprehension that the first-class game in England is managed by a doddering oligarchy. Alas, much of the good work was undone as a huge crowd milled about the circumference of the ground, some inside, some in long queues outside, many from overseas and many having waited all night for the privilege of being there on the great day.

When I arrived at 10.15 the sun was shining brightly. The Nursery ground near where I parked the car was still very wet but there was a breeze as well as sun and hope was very much in the air. A start around lunchtime perhaps? No one has or ever will persuade me that this is not what should have happened. Instead, for reasons which have since been well aired, play did not begin until ten to four. It did not do so in the first instance because the square had not been completely covered, two strips on the Tavern side therefore being much wetter than anywhere else. Despite the misfortune of the weather, and this very serious oversight, the umpires and players were at least as culpable as those who failed to cover the pitch. David Constant and Harold Bird refused in the face of mounting anger from the crowd of 20,000, and steadily more earnest requests on the part of MCC officials, to countenance play until they were absolutely satisfied that conditions were safe. The captains, who could have agreed to start, put no pressure on the umpires. Ian Botham's opinion is that Test cricket is not the real thing if conditions are poor. But club cricketers and first-class cricketers have very different views of when a ground is playable. In club cricket a little sawdust and a bit of extra caution on the part of the fielding side is taken for granted. *They play if they possibly can because that is what they have come to do.* The attitude of professional players and umpires should be exactly the same. Indeed for the sake of the public who pay their wages they should be *even more* determined to play whenever possible. If conditions favour one side or the other, that is merely the luck of the game. After all, luck has always played a part in cricket – from the moment that the coin is tossed.

Whether one holds this view that the show should go on whenever it is humanly possible, or agrees with Botham that a Test 'should take place in conditions enabling players to use their full skills' (*The Cricketer,* November 1980), the essential point on this occasion was that this was no ordinary Test match. The players and umpires totally failed to realise the deep implications for the whole image of cricket in their reluctance to take risks after all the publicity and effort which had surrounded this special festival match. It was a celebration, not a war. The marvellous spirit of the Melbourne Centenary Test was, on this Saturday at least, forgotten.

Up in the box we were all agreed that it was wrong that play did not begin much earlier than it did. There were varying degrees of apoplexy. I had a temperature and a heavy cold which perhaps made my attitude even more impatient than normal. Brian Johnston and I happened to be talking to the harassed and ailing president of MCC, Billy Griffith, when David Constant arrived back from his final inspection of the pitch. He had just been involved in a scuffle on the pavilion steps which perhaps accounted for the way that this normally equable umpire pushed his way past the startled president and refused at first to answer his anxious question about when they had decided to start play.

When at last the cricket did begin, Kim Hughes hastened to his fourth Test hundred with a superb pulled six off Old and a classic straight driven four off Emburey. He hit Old for another six and also hit two more fours before Athey ended his charming innings with a catch at extra cover. Border, stocky and pugnacious, took up the assault with some savage pulling (14 off one over from Hendrick) and he was 56 not out when Chappell declared at tea. Sadly bad light stopped England's reply after only two balls and soon after rain ended a day which by mutual agreement had in theory been extended until eight o'clock. We had some hilarious scenes to describe, however, before we went off the air, because, after the rain, and when most of a disillusioned crowd had gone home, the ground staff optimistically rushed out to get the covers off, aided by the MCC secretary Jack Bailey, looking very like Inspector Clouseau in his long white mackintosh, and his staunch and cheerful assistant John Stephenson. Alas it was all much to late.

That was the nadir. Things improved, first with the official TCCB dinner at the Russell Hotel on Saturday night (a marvellous gathering of the clans), then with a happy Lord's Taverners' match between Old Australia and (mainly) Old England at Arundel on Sunday – a glorious day of course – and finally with two good authentic days of Test cricket on the Monday and Tuesday.

Seven hours were played on each of the last two days. But it was not to prove quite enough time to salvage the match. Lillee and Pascoe bowled England out for 205, a characteristic collapse following some good batting by Boycott and the happily reinstated Gower. There was some more dazzlingly brilliant batting by Hughes and, more briefly, Border, and the fall of early England wickets followed by a stout recovery maintained considerable interest until tea on the last day after which the immaculate Boycott and the worthy Gatting obeyed their captain's unimaginative orders to play safe. England, 169 for three at tea, would have needed to score at about five an over. This was not very likely, and perhaps we were expecting too much, but it would have been less of a disappointment if England had at least given an impression of urgency. Again, one thought back to Melbourne 1977, when England could easily have played for a draw, but Greig had ordered a chase for runs in the true spirit of the occasion. Even if England *had* lost by following a similar policy this time, which is unlikely, they would have gained in good will the £2,250 which they would have lost as their share of the prize money. Instead, all ended in anti-climax, but that final day was nevertheless momentous in one particular, as Peter Baxter recalls . . .

After four days of mixed fortunes – nostalgia, controversy, some brilliant cricket, some not so brilliant and, of course, that rain – we came to the day which, for us in the commentary box at any rate, concentrated our minds on one event. For the last time John Arlott, in the voice recognised instantly from Bournemouth to Bombay and from Adelaide to Antigua, would describe the action of a day's Test cricket.

It had, as I had felt beforehand that it would be, been an unusual match. The box always seemed crowded. My colleagues continually greeted me with 'you look harassed'. Most of us had a touch of that same flu-type bug which had troubled Christopher. Rain always makes our job harder, but against that we had had the great pleasure of meeting so many of the great names of the past. The occasion also seemed to have brought out a number of other personalities including an assortment of actors. One tea interval found Nicol Williamson, Michael Jayston and Robin Bailey all together in the commentary box. But now the stage belonged to one man.

Two television news crews greeted me at the top of the pavilion stairs with requests to site cameras, lights and recording machines in the box. While I was negotiating with them, four different newspapers' representatives interrupted me with telephone calls for interviews. One reporter said that he would like to interview John as he climbed the stairs. 'You're mad,' I advised him.

It was a strange feeling that the departure of our friend and colleague should have become such public property and I was glad to be able to reflect on our own farewell dinner for him in the pleasantly secluded environment of the Wig and Pen a month before. The usual chores of a Test match morning were submerged in a plethora of arrangements with the cameramen, reporters and even some of our colleagues from other radio programmes.

At last the great man entered, rather flustered, muttering, 'I don't know what's going on; some bloody fool just tried to interview me on the last flight of stairs.' The black coffee has rarely been more rapidly and sympathetically applied.

John was determined that his last day should be treated absolutely normally. I am not quite sure if he regarded as normal the fact that his first twenty-minute spell at the microphone was spent under the glare of a television light, with one cameraman filming him from a precarious position on a ledge looking into the front window of the box and another taking

*Ian Botham is appointed captain for the West Indies tour and his first assignment is a grilling in the box by Bailey, Johnston and Trueman*

pictures, it seemed, of his left ear. Anyway, he was at his best. He did not want any dramatic gestures like being given the last commentary session in his last Test match and when he came to the end of his final commentary we simply stood and applauded him. The crowd and the players were to pay their tribute later with affectionate – and thunderous – applause to make the day anything but normal, but at that moment John simply ended with the time honoured *Test Match Special* formula: 'And after Trevor Bailey, it will be Christopher Martin-Jenkins . . .'

Follow that as they say! I did not and will not try, for John Arlott is unique. When one thinks of him one thinks first of a voice. But that voice would never have become famous had not its owner possessed a rare depth of humanity and a rare breadth of knowledge about cricket and much else besides. Computers don't have hearts, but John has a mind which can store facts and anecdotes as efficiently as any computer, allied to a heart as warm as a summer day.

It was his intellect, combined with a rare capacity for compassion and a wonderfully observant eye, which made him a cricket commentator of unrivalled range. With his sharp memory for cricket history he could relate anything going on on the field in front of him to anything which had happened before, placing it judiciously in context. What is more he could describe it with an effortless recourse to wide vocabulary and a poet's sense of drama and colour. Add to these qualities a sense of humour and a mellow voice with a gentle Hampshire accent that engaged many and offended no one and it is easy to understand John Arlott's fame as a cricket commentator. He cannot be directly replaced nor precisely emulated. Like all true originals he is inimitable; yet perhaps only a handful of high-ranking politicians have been more frequently imitated by a host of amateur impressionists – myself included!

Since the advent of television, 'stars' have been two a penny. Most, however, are ephemeral stars. Radio helped John Arlott achieve a lasting fame, the size and substance of which none of us can have appreciated until his retirement in 1980. Every last appearance at a cricket ground was marked by a wave of public affection towards him. Off the field poor John, the great connoisseur of food and wine, was overwhelmed by hospitality. Everyone wanted to give him a good send off. The pity about his fame was that, although he was as ambitious and acquisitive as the next man, he never really sought fame. He wanted to mix with friends, not celebrities. He was happiest with a small company drinking wine at his own dinner table in Hampshire.

No doubt it will be just as convivial at the Arlott table in Alderney. In the box we'll miss his knowledge, the shaggy dog stories he told off-mike with such relish, his ability to induce gifts of vintage wine and his peerless quality as a professional who took as much trouble over the small tasks as he did with the big ones.

'I'm going while people are still asking me *why* I'm going rather than thinking why doesn't he go.' This was John's explanation of his decision to retire. His public and his colleagues regret it, though I hope he has the deserved reward of a happy retirement.

I personally decided at about the same time that in the interest of my family life I could no longer justify going away on long overseas tours each winter. But I am happy to say that I shall continue as a regular member of the *Test Match Special* team. All of us associated with the programme feel both loyal and affectionate towards it and although the senior pro has hung up his boots we shall carry on under our incomparable amateur captain Johnston, doing our best to inform and entertain. We shall enjoy it; we hope you will too.

*Arlott and the Australians – flanked by Hassett and McGilvray behind the box at Lord's*

## AUSTRALIA 1ST INNINGS v. ENGLAND CENTENARY TEST MATCH at LORD'S, LONDON on AUGUST 28, 29, 30, SEPT. 1, 2, 1980.

TOSS: AUSTRALIA

| IN | OUT | MINS | No. | BATSMAN | HOW OUT | BOWLER | RUNS | WKT | TOTAL | 6s | 4s | BALLS | NOTES ON DISMISSAL |
|----|-----|------|-----|---------|---------|--------|------|-----|-------|----|----|-------|--------------------|
| 12.20 | 12.21 | 363 | 1 | WOOD | St BAIRSTOW | EMBUREY | 112 | 3 | 260 | · | 10 | 295 | Missed drive - splendid stumping (off side). |
| 12.20 | 2.21 | 83 | 2 | LAIRD | Ct BAIRSTOW | OLD | 24 | 1 | 64 | · | 3 | 64 | Edged half-hearted square-cut to 'keeper. |
| 2.23 | 4.56 | 138 | 3 | CHAPPELL * | Ct GATTING | OLD | 47 | 2 | 150 | · | 9 | 115 | Square-leg catch - turned ball on hip - firm stroke. |
| 4.59 | 4.25 | 205 | 4 | HUGHES | Ct ATHEY | OLD | 117 | 5 | 320 | 3 | 14 | 209 | Drove half-volley to extra-cover. |
| 12.23 | 12.34 | 11 | 5 | YALLOP | LBW | HENDRICK | 2 | 4 | 267 | · | · | 11 | Played outside line - ball kept low. |
| 12.36 | (5.15) | 96 | 6 | BORDER | NOT OUT | | 56 | | | 1 | 7 | 80 | - |
| 4.27 | (5.15) | 48 | 7 | MARSH † | NOT OUT | | 16 | | | · | 3 | 32 | - |
| | | | 8 | LILLEE | | | | | | | | | |
| | | | 9 | MALLETT | DID NOT BAT | | | | | | | | |
| | | | 10 | BRIGHT | | | | | | | | | |
| | | | 11 | PASCOE | | | | | | | | | |

* CAPTAIN  † WICKET-KEEPER  EXTRAS  b 1  lb 8  w -  nb 2  = 11

4b 46s 806 balls (inc 2 no balls)

TOTAL (OFF 134 OVERS IN 475 MIN.)  385-5 declared at 5.15pm (TEA) on 3rd day.

16 OVERS 5 BALLS/HOUR
2.87 RUNS/OVER
48 RUNS/100 BALLS

| BOWLER | O | M | R | W | nb | | HRS | OVERS | RUNS | | RUNS | MINS | OVERS | LAST 50 (in mins) |
|--------|---|---|---|---|----|----|-----|-------|------|----|------|------|-------|------|
| OLD | 35 | 9 | 91 | 3 | · | | 1 | 16 | 47 | | 50 | 66 | 18 | 66 |
| HENDRICK | 30 | 6 | 67 | 1 | · | | 2 | 16 | 51 | | 100 | 125 | 34 | 59 |
| BOTHAM | 22 | 2 | 89 | 0 | · | | 3 | 17 | 39 | | 150 | 216 | 60.4 | 91 |
| EMBUREY | 38 | 9 | 104 | 1 | 2 | | 4 | 18 | 36 | | 200 | 265 | 73.4 | 49 |
| GOOCH | 8 | 3 | 16 | 0 | | | 5 | 19 | 51 | | 250 | 344 | 97.2 | 79 |
| WILLEY | 1 | 0 | 7 | 0 | | | 6 | 16 | 36 | | 300 | 410 | 115.3 | 66 |
| | | | 11 | - | | | 7 | 16 | 48 | | 350 | 452 | 127.4 | 42 |
| | 134 | 29 | 385 | 5 | 2 | | | | | | | | | |

2ND NEW BALL taken at 6.16pm 1st day
- AUSTRALIA 223-2 after 85 overs.

START DELAYED BY LIGHT RAIN - 50 MIN. LOST

LUNCH: 57-0   WOOD 34*  LAIRD 21*
OFF 20 OVERS IN 72 MINUTES

TEA: 141-1   WOOD 65* (192 min)  CHAPPELL 44* (107 min)
OFF 53 OVERS IN 192 MINUTES

STUMPS: 227-2   WOOD 100* (313 min)  HUGHES 47* (92 min)
(1ST DAY)   OFF 89 OVERS IN 313 MINUTES

BAD LIGHT STOPPED PLAY at 12.45 - RAIN - LUNCH
LUNCH (STUMPS): 278-4   HUGHES 82* (167 min)  BORDER 2* (9 min.)
2ND DAY   OFF 109 OVERS IN 388 MINUTES
3RD DAY - START DELAYED UNTIL 3.41pm

TEA: 385-5   OFF 134 OVERS IN 475 MINUTES   BORDER 56*  MARSH 16*

| WKT | PARTNERSHIP | | RUNS | MINS |
|-----|-------------|---|------|------|
| 1st | Wood | Laird | 64 | 83 |
| 2nd | Wood | Chappell | 86 | 138 |
| 3rd | Wood | Hughes | 110 | 143 |
| 4th | Hughes | Yallop | 7 | 11 |
| 5th | Hughes | Border | 53 | 46 |
| 6th | Border | Marsh | 65* | 48 |
| | | | 385 | |

## ENGLAND 1ST INNINGS   IN REPLY TO AUSTRALIA'S 385 FOR 5 DECLARED

| IN | OUT | MINS | No. | BATSMAN | HOW OUT | BOWLER | RUNS | WKT | TOTAL | 6s | 4s | BALLS | NOTES ON DISMISSAL |
|----|-----|------|-----|---------|---------|--------|------|-----|-------|----|----|-------|--------------------|
| 5.37 | 11.13 | 14 | 1 | GOOCH | Ct BRIGHT | LILLEE | 8 | 1 | 10 | · | 1 | 13 | Mistimed hook - ball 'stopped' - falling catch in front of sq. leg. |
| 5.37 | 2.50 | 193 | 2 | BOYCOTT | Ct MARSH | LILLEE | 62 | 4 | 151 | · | 5 | 146 | Edged off-drive to 'keeper. |
| 11.15 | 11.49 | 34 | 3 | ATHEY | BOWLED | LILLEE | 9 | 2 | 41 | · | 1 | 22 | Break back took inside edge - back foot cover force. |
| 11.51 | 2.29 | 120 | 4 | GOWER | BOWLED | LILLEE | 45 | 3 | 137 | 1 | 7 | 100 | Edged pull into stumps. |
| 2.31 | 3.24 | 53 | 5 | GATTING | LBW | PASCOE | 12 | 7 | 164 | · | 2 | 37 | Beaten by breakback. |
| 2.52 | 3.07 | 15 | 6 | BOTHAM * | Ct WOOD | PASCOE | 0 | 5 | 158 | · | · | 14 | Skied hook to mid-wicket - mid-on ran 20 yds - held at 2nd attempt. |
| 3.09 | 3.15 | 6 | 7 | WILLEY | LBW | PASCOE | 5 | 6 | 163 | · | 1 | 11 | Played back and across to overpitched ball. |
| 3.19 | 3.40 | 21 | 8 | BAIRSTOW † | LBW | PASCOE | 6 | 8 | 173 | · | 1 | 15 | Hit across full toss. |
| 3.26 | 3.55 | 29 | 9 | EMBUREY | LBW | PASCOE | 3 | 9 | 200 | · | · | 18 | Beaten by breakback. |
| 3.42 | (4.01) | 19 | 10 | OLD | NOT OUT | | 24 | · | · | 2 | 2 | 15 | Saved follow-on with a six off Bright. |
| 3.57 | 4.01 | 4 | 11 | HENDRICK | Ct BORDER | MALLETT | 5 | 10 | 205 | · | · | 6 | Edged via pad to silly point. |

* CAPTAIN  † WICKET-KEEPER  EXTRAS  b 6  lb 8  w -  nb 12  = 26

2 6s 19 4s 397 balls (inc. 17 no balls)

TOTAL (OFF 63.2 OVERS IN 264 MIN.)  205 all out at 4.01pm 4th day.

14 OVERS 2 BALLS/HOUR
3.23 RUNS/OVER
52 RUNS/100 BALLS

| BOWLER | O | M | R | W | nb | | HRS | OVERS | RUNS | | RUNS | MINS | OVERS | LAST 50 (in mins) |
|--------|---|---|---|---|----|----|-----|-------|------|----|------|------|-------|------|
| LILLEE | 15 | 4 | 43 | 4 | 5 | | 1 | 12 | 50 | | 50 | 57 | 11.2 | 57 |
| PASCOE | 18 | 5 | 59 | 5 | 8 | | 2 | 17 | 46 | | 100 | 133 | 31.4 | 76 |
| CHAPPELL | 2 | 0 | 2 | 0 | · | | 3 | 15 | 43 | | 150 | 191 | 46.2 | 58 |
| BRIGHT | 21 | 6 | 50 | 0 | 1 | | 4 | 14 | 30 | | 200 | 257 | 61.5 | 66 |
| MALLETT | 7.2 | 3 | 25 | 1 | 3 | | | | | | | | | |
| | | | 26 | | | | | | | | | | | |
| | 63.2 | 18 | 205 | 10 | 17 | | | | | | | | | |

BLSP at 5.39pm   STUMPS (3RD DAY): 1-0   2 mins 0.1 overs

LUNCH: 117-2   BOYCOTT 48* (144 min)  GOWER 35* (92 min)
OFF 35 OVERS IN 144 MINUTES

AUSTRALIA'S LEAD: 180

PASCOE took 5 for 10 in 32 balls and achieved his best analysis in Test cricket.

| WKT | PARTNERSHIP | | RUNS | MINS |
|-----|-------------|---|------|------|
| 1st | Gooch | Boycott | 10 | 14 |
| 2nd | Boycott | Athey | 31 | 34 |
| 3rd | Boycott | Gower | 96 | 120 |
| 4th | Boycott | Gatting | 14 | 19 |
| 5th | Gatting | Botham | 7 | 15 |
| 6th | Gatting | Willey | 5 | 6 |
| 7th | Gatting | Bairstow | 1 | 5 |
| 8th | Bairstow | Emburey | 9 | 14 |
| 9th | Emburey | Old | 27 | 13 |
| 10th | Old | Hendrick | 5 | 4 |

## AUSTRALIA 2ND INNINGS — 180 RUNS AHEAD ON FIRST INNINGS

| IN | OUT | MINS | No. | BATSMAN | HOW OUT | BOWLER | RUNS | WKT | TOTAL | 6s | 4s | BALLS | NOTES ON DISMISSAL |
|----|-----|------|-----|---------|---------|--------|------|-----|-------|----|----|-------|--------------------|
| 4.27 | 5.36 | 69 | 1 | LAIRD | C BAIRSTOW | OLD | 6 | 2 | 28 | · | 1 | 45 | Misjudged bounce - attempted offside glance. |
| 4.27 | 5.07 | 40 | 2 | WOOD | LBW | OLD | 8 | 1 | 15 | · | · | 35 | Beaten by inswinging breakback. |
| 5.09 | 11.22 | 134 | 3 | CHAPPELL * | BOWLED | OLD | 59 | 3 | 139 | · | 7 | 115 | Edged cut into leg stump - ball kept low. |
| 5.38 | 11.58 | 141 | 4 | HUGHES | LBW | BOTHAM | 84 | 4 | 189 | 2 | 11 | 99 | Missed turn to leg. |
| 11.24 | (11.58) | 34 | 5 | BORDER | NOT OUT | | 21 | · | · | 1 | 1 | 29 | . |
| | | | 6 | YALLOP | | | | | | | | | |
| | | | 7 | MARSH † | | | | | | | | | |
| | | | 8 | LILLEE | DID NOT BAT | | | | | | | | |
| | | | 9 | MALLETT | | | | | | | | | |
| | | | 10 | BRIGHT | | | | | | | | | |
| | | | 11 | PASCOE | | | | | | | | | |

* CAPTAIN  † WICKET-KEEPER   EXTRAS  b 1  lb 8  w -  nb 2   11   3 6s  20 4s  323 balls (inc. 3 no balls)

TOTAL (OFF 53.2 OVERS IN 212 MIN.)  189-4 DECLARED AT 11.58 am 5TH DAY.

15 OVERS 0 BALLS/HOUR
3.54 RUNS/OVER
59 RUNS/100 BALLS

| BOWLER | O | M | R | W | nb | HRS | OVERS | RUNS | | RUNS | MINS | OVERS | LAST 50 (in mins) |
|--------|---|---|---|---|----|-----|-------|------|--|------|------|-------|------|
| OLD | 20 | 6 | 47 | 3 | - | 1 | 15 | 28 | | 50 | 108 | 25.5 | 108 |
| HENDRICK | 15 | 4 | 53 | 0 | - | 2 | 15 | 43 | | 100 | 141 | 35.3 | 33 |
| EMBUREY | 9 | 2 | 35 | 0 | 2 | 3 | 15 | 68 | | 150 | 187 | 47 | 46 |
| BOTHAM | 9.2 | 1 | 43 | 1 | 1 | | | | | | | | |
| | | | | | | | 11 | | | | | | |
| | 53.2 | 13 | 189 | 4 | 3 | | | | | | | | |

STUMPS (4TH DAY): 106-2 286 AHEAD
CHAPPELL 47* (112')  HUGHES 38* (83')
OFF 39 OVERS IN 154 MIN.

AUSTRALIA SET ENGLAND 370 TO WIN IN 292 MINUTES PLUS 20 OVERS

AUSTRALIA added 83 runs off 14.2 overs in 58 minutes for loss of 2 wickets on final morning

K.J HUGHES emulated M.L. JAISIMHA and G.BOYCOTT by batting on all five days of a Test Match.

| WKT | PARTNERSHIP | | RUNS | MINS |
|-----|-------------|--|------|------|
| 1st | Laird | Wood | 15 | 40 |
| 2nd | Laird | Chappell | 13 | 27 |
| 3rd | Chappell | Hughes | 111 | 105 |
| 4th | Hughes | Border | 50 | 34 |
| | | | 189 | |

## ENGLAND 2ND INNINGS — SET 370 RUNS TO WIN IN A MINIMUM OF 350 MINUTES

| IN | OUT | MINS | No. | BATSMAN | HOW OUT | BOWLER | RUNS | WKT | TOTAL | 6s | 4s | BALLS | NOTES ON DISMISSAL |
|----|-----|------|-----|---------|---------|--------|------|-----|-------|----|----|-------|--------------------|
| 12.10 | 12.31 | 21 | 1 | GOOCH | LBW | LILLEE | 16 | 1 | 19 | · | 2 | 15 | Played across line - beaten by faster ball. |
| 12.10 | (6.30) | 316 | 2 | BOYCOTT | NOT OUT | | 128 | · | · | 12 | 252 | (19th in TESTS; 6th v AUSTRALIA); 7000 RUNS IN TESTS; 57th FIFTY. |
| 12.33 | 1.09 | 36 | 3 | ATHEY | C LAIRD | PASCOE | 1 | 2 | 43 | · | · | 21 | Edged via pad to forward short leg. |
| 1.11 | 3.27 | 95 | 4 | GOWER | BOWLED | MALLETT | 35 | 3 | 124 | · | 4 | 63 | Missed cut - quicker 'arm' ball - off stump. |
| 3.29 | (6.30) | 158 | 5 | GATTING | NOT OUT | | 51 | · | 7 | 153 | | | |
| | | | 6 | BOTHAM * | | | | | | | | | |
| | | | 7 | WILLEY | | | | | | | | | |
| | | | 8 | BAIRSTOW † | DID NOT BAT | | | | | | | | |
| | | | 9 | EMBUREY | | | | | | | | | |
| | | | 10 | OLD | | | | | | | | | |
| | | | 11 | HENDRICK | | | | | | | | | |

* CAPTAIN  † WICKET-KEEPER   EXTRAS  b 3  lb 2  w -  nb 8   13   0 6s  25 4s  504 balls (including 12 no balls)

TOTAL (OFF 82 OVERS IN 316 MINUTES)  244-3

15 OVERS 3 BALLS/HOUR
2.97 RUNS/OVER
48 RUNS/100 BALLS

| BOWLER | O | M | R | W | nb | HRS | OVERS | RUNS | | RUNS | MINS | OVERS | LAST 50 (in mins) |
|--------|---|---|---|---|----|-----|-------|------|--|------|------|-------|------|
| LILLEE | 19 | 5 | 53 | 1 | 2 | 1 | 13 | 46 | | 50 | 72 | 15.5 | 72 |
| PASCOE | 17 | 1 | 73 | 1 | 4 | 2 | 15 | 55 | | 100 | 120 | 28 | 48 |
| BRIGHT | 25 | 9 | 44 | 0 | - | 3 | 15 | 46 | | 150 | 185 | 44.1 | 65 |
| MALLETT | 21 | 2 | 61 | 1 | 6 | 4 | 17 | 46 | | 200 | 256 | 64.1 | 71 |
| | | | | | | 5 | 18 | 38 | | | | | |
| | | | 13 | | | | | | | | | | |
| | 82 | 17 | 244 | 3 | 12 | | | | | | | | |

LUNCH: 49-2  BOYCOTT 20* (70')  GOWER 3* (9')
OFF 15 OVERS IN 70 MINUTES
NEEDING 321 RUNS IN MINIMUM OF 280 MIN.

TEA: 169-3  BOYCOTT 93* (210')  GATTING 12* (52')
OFF 51 OVERS IN 210 MINUTES
NEEDING 201 RUNS IN MINIMUM OF 140 MINUTES
LAST HALF HOUR NOT PLAYED
MATCH DRAWN at 6.30 p.m.

MAN OF THE MATCH: K.J.HUGHES

TOTAL TIME LOST: 604 MINUTES (484 NET)
(120 MINUTES EXTRA PLAY ON LAST 2 DAYS)

| WKT | PARTNERSHIP | | RUNS | MINS |
|-----|-------------|--|------|------|
| 1st | Gooch | Boycott | 19 | 21 |
| 2nd | Boycott | Athey | 24 | 36 |
| 3rd | Boycott | Gower | 81 | 95 |
| 4th | Boycott | Gatting | 120* | 158 |
| | | | 244 | |